Organization Development
in Public Administration

PUBLIC ADMINISTRATION AND PUBLIC POLICY

A Comprehensive Publication Program

Executive Editor

NICHOLAS HENRY

Center for Public Affairs
Arizona State University
Tempe, Arizona

Publications in Public Administration and Public Policy

1. Public Administration as a Developing Discipline (in two parts)
   by Robert T. Golembiewski

2. Comparative National Policies on Health Care
   by Milton I. Roemer, M.D.

3. Exclusionary Injustice: The Problem of Illegally Obtained Evidence
   by Steven R. Schlesinger

4. Personnel Management in Government: Politics and Process
   by Jay M. Shafritz, Walter L. Balk, Albert C. Hyde, and David H. Rosenbloom

5. Organization Development in Public Administration (in two parts)
   edited by Robert T. Golembiewski and William B. Eddy

Other volumes in preparation

Developmental Editors

Organization Development in Public Administration

(IN TWO PARTS)

Part 2

PUBLIC SECTOR APPLICATIONS
OF ORGANIZATION DEVELOPMENT TECHNOLOGY

EDITED BY

Robert T. Golembiewski
The University of Georgia
Athens, Georgia

William B. Eddy
The University of Missouri
Kansas City, Missouri

MARCEL DEKKER, INC.   New York and Basel

83391

Library of Congress Cataloging in Publication Data
Main entry under title:
Organization development in public administration.

(Public administration and public policy; v. 5)
Includes index.
CONTENTS: Pt. 1. Organization development properties and
public sector features. —Pt. 2. Public sector applications
of OD technology.
1. Public administration—Addresses, essays, lectures.
2. Organizational change—Addresses, essays, lectures.
I. Golembiewski, Robert T. II. Eddy, William B., [DATE]
III. Series.
JF1411.0725   350   77-27574
ISBN 0-8247-6668-7

MARCEL DEKKER, INC.
270 Madison Avenue, New York, New York 10016

Current Printing (last digit):
10 9 8 7 6 5 4 3 2 1

PRINTED IN THE UNITED STATES OF AMERICA

PREFACE

This set of two volumes represents an effort whose time certainly has come. Indeed, if anything, these two books are long overdue. The editors plead guilty to neglect, but it is only because they were busy contributing to the growth of Organization Development and its associated technology that this necessary project kept being postponed to attend to more basic research and applied issues.

Despite the intense concern with organization development, that is, no volume has yet been targeted specifically to the public sector audience. The oversight of the public administration audience is not trifling. For the latest statistics tell us that as many as two employees out of every 11 work for a public agency or governmental unit. Moreover, there are some 20,000 first-year students in our nation's several programs awarding the Master of Public Administration degree. And numerous other public employees are involved every year in in-service seminars, and the like, which focus on organizational change and development. Similarly, OD has become a major topic at professional meetings of public administrationists, having been first emphasized at a convention of the International City Management Association six or eight years ago and now having attained the status of a common topic at meetings of the PA clan at local, regional, national, and international levels.

For the first time, then, such variegated users will have book-length resources in organization development tailored to their own needs and environments, with much of its content drawn from public sector experience. Reasonable coverage requires two volumes on the common theme Organization Development in Public Administration:

I. Organization Development Properties and Public Sector Features

II. Public Sector Applications of Organization Development Technology

Specifically the first part contains two major sections which provide generic perspective on OD as well as direct attention to issues particular to public sector usage. The first three chapters are basically generic, and the fourth emphasizes motivators and constraints more or less specific to the public sector. These major chapters deal with:

Descriptions and definitions of OD

Normative or value concerns about OD

Basic empirical processes or dynamics in OD

Some specific factors relevant to the choice of whether or not to use OD in a public agency

Specifically, also, the second part has a dual focus. Thus numerous OD designs are described, and their consequences are detailed. Moreover, applications of these designs in public agencies are illustrated in some detail. The second part, then, emphasizes both the what and the where of OD applications.

As usual, such efforts are clearly dependent on the wit and will of many contributors. Such debts in this volume are especially great, in fact, because many of the selections below reflect the commitment of many employees and managers trying to make a better worksite for themselves, and a better quality of public service for their clients. Special thanks go to Sandra Daniel, who again provided indispensable service at several stages of this volume's progress toward publication.

Robert T. Golembiewski
William B. Eddy

CONTENTS

CONTENTS OF PART 1

Organization Development
in Public Administration

SECTION I

Chapter 1

SOME EXAMPLES OF ORGANIZATION DEVELOPMENT
Illustrating the Reach and Range of Available Designs

Readings

William B. Eddy and Bernard Lubin, "Laboratory Training and Encounter Groups" 49

Neely Gardner, "Action Training and Research: Something Old and Something New" 63

Donald C. King and John J. Sherwood, "Monitoring the Process and Evaluating the Results of Organization Development" 205

W. J. Reddin, "My Errors in OD" 277

Robert T. Golembiewski and Frances Rauschenberg, "Third-Party Consultation: Principles and A Case Study of Their Violation" 118

Robert T. Golembiewski, Stokes B. Carrigan, Walter R. Mead, Robert Munzenrider, and Arthur Blumberg, "Toward Building New Work Relationships: An Action Design for A Critical Intervention" 106

Roger Harrison, "Role Negotiation: A Tough Minded Approach to Team Development" 178

William J. Crockett, "Team Building: One Approach to Organization Development" 36

Robert T. Golembiewski, Samuel Yeager, and Rick Hilles, "One Avenue for Expressing Central OD Values: Some Attitudinal and Behavioral Consequences of A Flexi-Time Installation" 129

William E. Reif and Robert M. Monczka, "Job Redesign: A Contingency Approach to Implementation" 287

Organization Development (OD) has a history that goes back only about two decades or so, but OD perspectives already have generated a substantial technology for inducing desired effects. The purpose here is to illustrate the reach and range of available designs in this growing OD technology, which seeks to induce relatively specific learning, change, or choice.

The emphasis below will be both generic and specific, as it were. That is to say, the discussion immediately below will introduce four selections that deal with certain overall features of the OD technology. These selections have a *generic* focus, in that the issues raised and the data provided apply to OD as broadly conceived. Later, eight additional selections will be introduced, each of which deals with a different kind of OD design and its probable consequences. This second group of selections provides *specific* counterpoint to the broader foci of the first four.

Generic Perspectives on OD Technology

To begin, the reader can gain overall perspective on the reach and grasp of the OD technology from "Strategies of Consultation," by Robert R. Blake and Jane Srygley Mouton, which is reprinted in the first volume of this book. Basically, their helpful focus is on both diagnosis and development, as they usefully systematize the broad range of possible OD interventions. That central focus is often overlooked, against which oversight Blake and Mouton persuasively develop their position. Each possible OD intervention, in short, must be related to a specific diagnosed situation; and each intervention also entails a model of the development which the intervention will help induce and which will help meet the diagnosed needs of several levels of individual and social organization. Using numerous illustrations, more specifically, Blake and Mouton introduce five different classes of interventions as they can be made in five kinds of settings, ranging from the level of individuals to that of society. Blake and Mouton focus on this central question: Which diagnosed situations are responsive to which kind of intervention? To say much the same thing, they emphasize the kind of development that each intervention might be expected to induce.

To turn now to introducing the four selections in this volume which provide overall perspective on the reach and range of available OD technology, William B. Eddy and Bernard Lubin introduce the reader to the class of learning designs that powerfully contributed to the development of OD, a class that includes the learning units variously called T-Groups, sensitivity training groups, or basic interaction groups. Eddy and Lubin's "Laboratory Training and Encounter Groups" makes some useful distinctions between varieties of this basic class of learning designs and it also recounts some major historical features in the development of what many see as a critical social intervention. Indeed, such a prominent observer as Carl Rogers sees the technology of encounter as perhaps *the* most critical social invention of the second half of the 20th century. As Eddy and Lubin show, laboratory training deals with powerful social forces and with essential human dynamics. The significance of "process," of *how* people relate to one another, is perhaps the most striking of the many kinds of learning that can be gained in T-Groups. "Process" contrasts with "substance", whose importance has long been appreciated. Interest in such learning vehicles is traced to two sources: the extraordinary rootlessness of our times, which apparently encourages people to seek even temporary experiences with community, and the fact that so much modern work is done in small task units of hopefully cooperating individuals.

Basically, OD designs seek to induce powerful forces and dynamics like those so strikingly unleashed in such small temporary learning units as T-Groups, but to do so in large, permanent organizations. The OD basic goal focuses on improving the quality of life in organizations, by simultaneously meeting individual and collective needs at work. Sometimes this linkage is attempted in OD by the direct use of laboratory training with small work units and their members. More often than not, OD specialists seek to induce analogs in organizations of laboratory training forces and processes, without direct resort to laboratory training.

However OD specialists seek to link such forces and processes to the simultaneous satisfaction of individual and organizational needs, the basic emphasis is on both study and application. Hence OD work often can be called "action-research." Neely Gardner directs attention to this central OD feature in his "Action Training and Research: Something Old and Something New." Of special value, Gardner traces what may be called a full OD sequence, from orientation or entry all the way to the evaluation of results. Striving for such data/action linkages is the central OD preoccupation.

Gardner's basic message is clear and insistent. OD can make use of a variety to techniques or designs to gather data, such as survey research or interviews by a skilled analyst. In this sense, OD is often "something old." Insistently, however, OD seeks to use such data to motivate effective plans and action for doing something about what the data show. This thrust toward action training and research is "something new" in organizational analysis, a something that is at once obvious and yet profound. In short, OD seeks to get it all together.

Given the primacy placed on action as well as analysis, OD ideally needs real-time feedback that will permit sensitive midcourse corrections of both analysis and action. This is the basic thrust of the selection by Donald C. King and John J. Sherwood, "Monitoring the Process and Evaluating the Results of Organization Development."

King and Sherwood undertake a significant but often neglected task. They first direct attention to five alternative approaches to evaluation, and carefully outline the advantages and disadvantages of each approach. Next, King and Sherwood detail why evaluation is so difficult in many organizations: the obstacles to doing what always should be done are several and stubborn. The authors conclude by discussing two central issues: the role of evaluation in OD efforts, and the target audience to whom the evaluation is addressed. These are ticklish issues, indeed. Much so-called "evaluation," perhaps most of it, is not primarily truth-seeking, and especially because a "bad" evaluation may jeopardize jobs and resources. So evaluation implies major political as well as technical issues.

Even heroic attention to monitoring and evaluating OD efforts, of course, does not produce a condition of "zero defects." An OD application can only by dumb luck be better than its underlying diagnosis, and diagnosis is now and no doubt will essentially remain a high art form. Mistakes in diagnosis will occur, and persons skilled in diagnosis no doubt always will be in short supply. There is no easy way out. The best that can be hoped for is that OD will stay aggressively busy learning from its own history. We need to know increasingly more about what designs are likely to work under which conditions, for example, so that we can become better and better at inducing desired effects appropriate for a diagnosed condition.

W. J. Reddin reflects one consultant's learning process about getting better and better about inducing desired outcomes. His "My Errors in OD" is one of a still-rare breed. For OD specialists, like almost everyone else, are more prone to emphasize their successes than their failures. There is much to be learned from failure, however. It may even be the case that nothing much is ever learned from success. Be that as it may, fellow OD specialists hold Reddin's effort in high esteem. His paper was chosen the 1976 prizewinner by the OD Division of the Academy of Management, which implies that OD specialists are willing to put their money where their mouth is in the critical area of learning from their own errors, as well as of communicating that learning to others.

Specific OD Designs for Learning, Choice, and Change

Let us shift our focus from the generic to the specific—to individual designs in the growing OD arsenal for achieving reasonable precise and bounded effects. The focus below is on eight separate OD designs, as well as their probable consequences. The designs focus on:

Interaction

Policies or procedures

Job and organization structure

For convenience only, in order, the individual designs first deal mostly with individuals, then small groups, and finally large organizations.

First, Robert T. Golembiewski and Frances Rauschenberg introduce a basic OD application relevant to conflictual pairs in "Third-Party Consultation: Principles and a Case Study of Their Violation." The design is one spin-off from an OD program in the U.S. Department of State, which placed initial emphasis on training in "cousin" T-Groups composed of State Department members who may have known one another but who were not members of the same immediate work unit. The name of Richard Walton is associated most closely with the design and theory of third-party consultation.

"Third-Party Consultation" provides multiple contrasts. Thus, it sketches some general guidelines on which third parties might usefully rely to help resolve or ameliorate conflict between pairs, and the selection describes a case study that highlights the disregard of these guidelines. The intended overall effect is that of a package: problem, theoretical insight, and also technology for acting on the theory to resolve or ameliorate the problem. A growing body of research and experience permits substantial confidence in that package illustrating one variety of "action-research."

Conflict between pairs—at work, in families, or wherever—is a ubiquitous fact of life. Addressing that fact, via both practice and theory, is consequently of great value.

Second, Robert T. Golembiewski and his colleagues detail the design and consequences of an OD effort to facilitate what was a traumatic experience for all concerned: the demotion of thirteen managers, and their assignment to work for other managers who had previously been their peers. All of the men had been satisfactory performers, but acute business conditions required major cutbacks.

"Toward Building New Work Relationships" clearly takes us to one spot where the critical action is. The goal of the demotion design was direct: to retain employees who had in the past been useful contributors to their organization, but to do so while minimizing the many personal and organizational problems that could be anticipated from demotions. Outright firing is the usual action in such cases, of course. Firing does avoid some transitional problems, but it does not acknowledge the mutual bonds of employee and organization that develop over time. So the demotion design attempts to rise above convenience and strive for according employees treatment that is both just and effective, even if not as swift and sudden as outright firing.

The demotion experience involves greater complications than third-party consultation. Demotion involves paired relationships between superior and subordinate, of course, as does the third-party design. In addition, the demotion experience touched on a host of other relationships: with family, customers, and friends, about an issue of moment to one's career. The demotion design, in short, attempted to meet a public and unattractive reality, and to salvage as much as possible for persons and their employing organization.

Third, Roger Harrison's "Role Negotiation: A Tough Minded Approach to Team Development" is applicable to a broad range of organizational situations even as it carefully seeks to restrict its arena for impact. Specifically, Harrison's design focuses on roles at work and deliberately seeks to avoid the kind of personal and interpersonal analysis that is the hallmark of the sensitivity training group.

Basically, Harrison urges that the depth of an OD intervention be carefully chosen. Very often, he notes, the effectiveness of people at work can be improved by interventions aimed at relatively shallow levels, such as their role relationships. Don't go any deeper than you need to go to do what needs doing, Harrison advises. To do otherwise is to risk inducing defensiveness, at least, and perhaps to unnecessarily open issues that go far beyond the immediate problem. Such "shallow" approaches are not aimed at resolving emotional issues between people, as an effective third-party consultation might do. The goal of role negotiation is more the satisfactory management of the consequences of such issues, rather than their resolution.

Not much is necessarily lost in this recognition that we need not always seek ultimate answers. Fortunately, for many practical purposes, all the issues between people do not have to be resolved in order for work relationships to improve. Leaving well enough alone has much to recommend it. Moreover, paradoxically, the effort at "deeper" intervention might create problems even as it seeks to raise and resolve the broad range of issues.

Fourth, "team building" is a common OD design for organizational work groups and involves complex combinations of emphasis on interpersonal relationships, structures, policies, and procedures, as well as on roles. William J. Crockett describes and illustrates that type of design in his "Team Building: One Approach to Organization Development." It often is a much "deeper" intervention than the role negotiation design just introduced.

Crockett's focus is the first team-building effort in the U.S. Department of State, perhaps the first in any public agency. In this particular, business organizations had a long lead. Several of them had been team building for years.

Crockett's case is not distinguishable from other efforts in businesses and charitable organizations. After considerable early doubt, team members came to make constructive responses to the data that they themselves had all along, and which the team-building design helped them mobilize.

Fifth, a growing number of OD interventions make policies or procedures their independent variable. Many of the preceding designs, in contrast, focus on interaction as the independent variable.

Robert T. Golembiewski, Samuel Yeager, and Rick Hilles focus on one simple policy design that seems to have profound consequences for employees, especially in connection with the degree of freedom available at work. Their selection, "One Avenue for Expressing Central OD Values: Some Attitudinal and Behavioral Consequences of a Flexi-Time Installation," deals with a design that is widely applicable in industrial as well as administrative or service organizations. Basically, Flexi-Time allows employees to exercise greater control over two ubiquitous choices about work: when it begins, and when it ends. As such, Flexi-Time is consistent with a variety of OD values that emphasize individual self-control and self-responsibility at work. Approaching such values in the present case, as well as in almost all other cases that have been studied, seems to generate a host of positive consequences for employees at little or no cost to the organization. That is an attractive combination.

Conveniently, also, the Flexi-Time design is relatively unobtrusive. No special skills are required of employees, and individuals can choose to participate or not, whenever they wish. These two features can be major stumbling blocks in other OD designs, such as team development or role negotiation. And serious ethical and practical issues may be involved in "encouraging" certain learning skills that some employees reject, or in variously coercing those who do not choose to participate in other OD designs. Flexi-Time nicely finesses these troublesome ethical and practical issues, although Flexi-Time clearly does not permit the degree of choice or freedom to act associated with various approaches to "participation" or "group decision-making."

Sixth, OD values also can be built into the very jobs people perform. William E. Reif and Robert M. Monczka sketch one increasingly common approach of this kind in their "Job Redesign: A Contingency Approach to Implementation." Their focus is on job enlargement, whose basic thrust is to permit greater employee control over their work while it simplifies management and supervision of employees. This is clearly an attractive combination.

Reif and Monczka are not rigid ideologs. They attempt to chart the various contingencies under which job redesign is more or less appropriate. So they propose no all-purpose remedy. Up to a substantial point, they argue, it all depends when it comes to structuring work.

Such job-related interventions are attractive in concept and intent, but their major drawback is that employees may see them as autocratic impositions to be resisted. Employees, in short, may not seem to "know what is good for them." And their opposition to *how* the design is implemented may result in a rejection of the design itself. Some OD guidelines for effective applications of approaches such as job enlargement seem clear enough, fortunately. For example,

OD approaches would emphasize employee involvement in job redesign, at both conceptual and implementation stages. One approach is to coach employees as to useful guidelines for the design of satisfying jobs, and then have the employees wholly or substantially do the redesigning themselves, perhaps subject to managerial approval.

Seventh, Management by Objectives (MBO) has been an even more common design at administrative or executive levels than job enlargement has been at operating levels. Jack E. Taylor and Elizabeth Bertinot describe one such MBO application in "An OD Intervention to Install Participative Management in A Bureaucratic Organization."

Taylor and Bertinot do us two services. They briefly describe MBO *as concept*, and brevity is sufficient because the essential ideas are quite straightforward. In addition, the authors spend useful time describing their *process of implementing* MBO. Here OD perspectives and approaches are central.

In short, MBO is an attractive concept, but its implementation often has been inadequate and even perverse. In this sense Taylor and Bertinot provide guidance about useful ways to get the best out of an attractive technique. They also put the emphasis where it belongs: much more on the implementation and much less on the concept.

Eighth, Robert Luke and his associates demonstrate how OD perspectives and values are applicable to the structural design of entire organizations. The approach of Robert A. Luke, Jr., Peter Block, Jack M. Davey, and Vernon R. Averch, which is described in "A Structural Approach to Organizational Change," has not been a favored one in OD, but many reasons suggest its potency and applicability.

Only a careful reading of Luke and colleagues' selection will reveal its multiple potency and usefulness. Summarily, however, traditional approaches to structuring organizations tend to encourage centralization. The consequences can be profound. Thus, lower-level managers might not develop attitudes and skills required for innovative and timely management in centralized organizations. Indeed, aggressive managers might be punished for showing signs of independence and initiative. When operations are stable, this condition may not be serious. When lower-level change and adaptability become necessary, however, serious difficulties can develop.

Luke and associates deal with just such a situation where managerial constants started to become galloping variables, at least for a time. The co-authors develop a useful concept for restructuring work to meet the changing demands of work, and they also detail how a sensitive OD team went about implementing its concept for structural change. Of special importance, Luke demonstrates that with care and ingenuity changing structure usually did not require that personnel be changed. If structural change implies that people will be shifted about in large numbers, or even fired, of course, resistance to structural change is highly probable.

Chapter 2

ORGANIZATION DEVELOPMENT APPLICATIONS IN SPECIFIC AGENCIES
A Growing Inventory of Public Sector Interventions

Readings

F. Gerald Brown, "SIGN: Multi-Organization Development" 19

Robert T. Golembiewski and Alan Kiepper, "MARTA: Toward An Effective, Open Giant" 81

William J. Crockett, "Team Building: One Approach to Organization Development" 36

Leonard D. Goodstein and Ronald K. Boyer, "Crisis Intervention in A Municipal Agency: A Conceptual Case History" 160

Robert T. Golembiewski and Frances Rauschenberg, "Third-Party Consultation: Principles and A Case Study of Their Violation" 118

Melvin J. Le Baron, "New Perspectives Toward More Effective Local Elected Councils and Boards" 235

Jack E. Taylor and Elizabeth Bertinot, "An OD Intervention to Install Participative Management in a Bureaucratic Organization" 313

James Kunde, "Task-Force Management in Dayton, Ohio" 219

Gerald C. Leader and Michael Brimm, "Survey Feedback and the Military" 227

W. Lynn Tanner and Muhyi A. Shakoor, "OD at the Grass Roots: First-Line Management Team-Building in A Public Housing Project" 297

Janice Kay, "Career Development for Women: An Affirmative Action First" 200

E. J. Jones, Jr., "The Prospects for Organizational Development Through Multi-Team Building" 191

Organization Development (OD) deals primarily with *application*. It is a set of techniques and methods aimed at intervention and action. Although it is undergirded with theory, values, and a growing body of data, the proof of the OD pudding is not in conceptual elegance. Nor does that proof reside in the attractiveness of OD values, although they are surely significant. Rather, the bedrock for OD is its ability to positively affect the functioning of systems, to increase productivity and to heighten employee satisfaction.

The emphasis in this second volume, then, is on OD as application. Chapter 1 introduced a large number of OD designs for learning or change. These designs illustrate the technology through which OD interventions are made. The selections in this part, further, are intended to help the reader sample the flavor of specific OD applications in particular public organizations.

Although convenient for many purposes, the reader should not make too much of this compartmentalization of parts or of books. That is to say, many of the public sector applications in this part make multiple use of the designs introduced in Chapter 1 of this volume. Indeed, the two chapters have several readings in common, each of which will be introduced here as well as in Chapter 1. And the first volume of this work provides normative and empirical support for the entire OD technology, as well as for its applications in public and business systems.

Stereotypes of Industrial Applications

To read the standard introductory text, the typical OD application industry seems stereotyped. The top management of a firm notices some deficiencies in the functioning of the human system, such as a poor intergroup collaboration, ineffective meetings, or low morale and commitment. They call in an OD consultant. The consultant gathers data by interview and/or questionnaire, and feeds it back to organization members in a series of meetings. Members diagnose their problems, and work with the consultant to plan remedial activities which may include training, team building, structural change, and so on. Voila! Functioning improves, individuals are more satisfied, and total productivity increases.

Actual Incidents Precipitating Public Applications

It is apparent from the applications described in this section that many OD projects in the public sector do not follow the "standard format." That is not remarkable, for many industrial applications do not follow the standard format either.

The selections below reflect six classes of precipitating incidents, or six motivators for OD applications in the public sector. First, in several of the selections, the reason for seeking OD assistance is a desire for improvement in the effectiveness of reasonably well-functioning organizations. F. Gerald Brown, for example, describes his work with professionally run suburban city governments in his "SIGN: Multi-Organization Development." Their overall goal seems to have been to make a relatively good situation somewhat better, both in terms of organizational performance as well as personal satisfaction. Similarly, Robert T. Golembiewski and Alan Kiepper sketch some early efforts to build a satisfying and quick-reacting agency from the ground up, as it were, in an effort to keep the collective infant from becoming just another public agency. Their "MARTA: Toward an Effective, Open Giant" details several OD designs intended to achieve that goal, and sketches some evidence suggesting the efficacy of those designs.

Second, the fat was clearly in the organizational fire in several of the other selections reprinted here. For example, William J. Crockett recounts the beginnings of a typical executive team-building program, with a typical client group. Crockett's "Team Building: One Approach to Organization Development" was introduced in Chapter 1. The only difference from many business applications was that the locus was the U.S. Department of State, which was then suffering from major managerial trauma, exacerbated by having been a favored political whipping boy for perhaps two decades. Similarly, Leonard D. Goodstein and Ronald K. Boyer consult with a city health department in crisis in their "Crisis Intervention in a Municipal Agency: A Conceptual Case History." And Robert T. Golembiewski and Frances Rauschenberg show how one OD technique can be used to deal with a conflict between members of an organization. Their "Third-Party Consultation: Principles and a Case Study of Their Violation" details a set of specific guidelines for effective interventions between conflictual pairs, and recounts a case study of how these guidelines were disregarded in one intervention in a small public agency.

Third, the precipitating issue in OD applications is often a problem in interaction, which gets reflected in low trust or interpersonal conflict. In public administration, especially where elected officials are concerned, interaction problems can achieve monumental proportions, exacerbated by the often contradictory centripetal demands of the common administrative mission and the centrifugal pull to please a constituency and thereby to retain power or to get re-elected.

So great have been these politically or institutionally reinforced problems of interaction in the public sector, in fact, that some have concluded: Public Administration is just too different for many OD designs to work as effectively as they do in the private sector.

Melvin J. Le Baron urges caution about too much despair on this critical point. His "New Perspectives Toward More Effective Local Elected Councils and Boards" stakes out two positions. Yes, there are special challenges confronting OD applications in local politics, he observes, but much can be done there to increase trust and improve problem solving by elected councils and boards. As part of the support for local governments provided by the University of Southern California versions of team building, designs are used for populations of elected officials to work on the "Five L's:"

Listening to one another

Learning from one another

Linking with each other

Leveling with others

Lauding others

In a nutshell, the purpose is to improve the process of interpersonal functioning by elected councils and boards. The reader will find much valuable detail and substance in Le Baron's text which elaborates on this skeletal description here.

Fourth, OD interventions would be limited indeed if they fixated only on problems in interaction, for management issues cover a broad range. Moreover, the solution of many problems that get reflected in unsatisfactory interaction between people does not require directly changing the character of that interaction. To illustrate, several selections below reflect an emphasis on modifying structure, in contrast to interaction. For example, Jack E. Taylor and Elizabeth Bertinot use their "An OD Intervention to Install Participative Management in a Bureaucratic Organization" to show how the technology can provide assistance to a department experiencing rapid growth. Their focus is on Management by Objectives, or MBO. Relatedly, James Kunde's "Task-Force Management in Dayton, Ohio" describes an attempt to revitalize a city government structure that had become outmoded, adapting to it a structural arrangement that had been extensively used in many high-technology settings.

Fifth, two of the selections below illustrate attempts to apply OD methods in "nontraditional" settings—in military units and public housing projects. These are the papers by: Gerald C. Leader and Michael Brimm, "Survey Feedback and the Military," and W. Lynn Tanner and Muhyi A Shakoor, "OD at the Grass Roots: First-Line Management Team-Building in A Public Housing Project." This pairing of selections is significant because it shows how OD techniques can be used at both high and low organization levels. This versatility implies the substantial potency of OD designs and technology to facilitate change and learning.

Sixth, OD efforts may be inspired by broad, social problems or quite specific organizational ones. Janice Kay's "Career Development for Women: An Affirmative Action First" illustrates the former use, and E. J. Jones, Jr. illustrates the latter use in "The Prospects for Organizational Development Through Multi-Team Building." Both Kay and Jones emphasize workshop techniques in their separate approaches to broad or specific organizational objectives.

Sources of Variation in Public Applications

It will be clear to the reader that variations among the projects described extend beyond differences in precipitating problems. We can only suggest that diversity here. The focus of intervention may vary from a single work group, to a large complex organization, to a network of several organizations. Consultants may utilize a highly structured survey-feedback technique involving prepared questionnaires, or a much less structured "process consultation" style in which the consultant creates interventions *ad hoc* in response to emerging client needs. Outcome goals may vary from ameliorating a conflict situation, to improving organizational effectiveness or changing value systems. And these differences do not even begin to exhaust the longer possible list of variants.

The applications described above also suggest why it is difficult to arrive at a precise and delimiting definition of OD. Its realm is substantial. The selections here are a reasonably good sampling of the state of the art of applied behavioral science, and the selections consequently cover a broad range.

The diversity of OD applications and designs is no fancy embroidery for its own sake. Some of the variations in approach are doubtless due to differences among consultants in their beliefs and experiences regarding which specific techniques are most useful. More significant, however, client organizations want their immediate problems addressed and resolved by specific designs which are sensitive to their specific traditions, norms, and ways of doing business. They are not interested in buying a broad and generalized organization improvement program when specific crisis points are tearing their particular system asunder. Further, most competent OD consultants are committed to a clinical approach, which implies the need to diagnose and respond to a dynamically changing system. No predetermined, "canned" program can do this. Hence the diversity of designs and applications has a very real basis in differences between individuals and organizations. Matters could be different only if major realities were neglected, or if some lock-step uniformity were somehow enforced.

Some Common Questions Regarding Public Applications

Some common questions are useful for highlighting major points of comparison among such diverse applications. For example, the following questions may be useful in analyzing and contrasting the cases that follow:

1. What symptoms/concerns in the client organization precipitated the OD effort?

2. What was the nature of the "contract" or mutual expectations between consultant and organization, and were these expectations explicit?

3. What data, if any, were utilized in the diagnosis and what inferences about basic needs/problems were made?

4. What interventions were made and what outcomes were being sought?

5. What assumptions were made about the nature of human behavior, desirable norms for interaction, and "ideal states" for organizations?

Even minor variations in how such questions are answered could patently result in major variations in OD designs and applications.

SECTION II

SIGN
Multi-Organization Development*

F. Gerald Brown

The letters SIGN stand for the Suburban Intergovernmental Network for Management Development, a consortium of the cities of Excelsior Springs, Gladstone, Grandview, Lee's Summit and Liberty, Missouri and the Center for Management Development (CMD), University of Missouri-Kansas City. SIGN was established to provide training for all five cities and a program of organization development for each. This application of O.D. is both broader and more specific than many efforts. It is broader because of the multi-city networking aspects and because the total complement of administrative, professional and technical manpower in each city was the target change group. It is specific because prior experience with the client organizations permitted advance definition of a number of specific desired training goals. The overriding objective was to increase internal organizational capability to identify, define, and work through administrative and policy issues important to the organizations' effectiveness. Training events and direct organizational interventions were selected and tailored to that end. Data from and about the specific participating individuals and organizations were the material upon which concepts and skills were tried. The end in view was always theory, perception and skill in the service of more effective action, not for their own sake.

SIGN pursued many goals at once. It is possible to separate the networking, the training and the organization development aspects from each other only conceptually. For convenience, the effort can be spoken of as taking place in two

*Reprinted with permission from the author

phases: management development followed by organization development. In practice, given the goal of O.D., the overlap was great. The networking goal was pursued indirectly throughout, but was particularly evident in the management development phase. The structure and selection of the training groups and the Advisory Committee provided the basis for networking. Management development is typically thought of as training which furthers the acquisition of appropriate attitudes, skills and knowledge on the part of individual managers with an expectation of post training application back in the organization. In this case management development training in communication skills, role development, organizational perception, group behavior, problem solving and decision-making built the network (because of the shared role concerns of the people who were involved together) and focused on real issues of the five city organizations.

The O.D. phase represented a shift not so much in kind of training experience as in format; from mixed, cross-city groups to single city groupings. The network provided a supportive backdrop that could be called upon from time to time as needed.

Identification of the Network

Networking assumes common concerns and common operations that will hold together a group of people once they have been called together and stimulated to set themselves in motion. There were two levels of selection in establishing the SIGN Network—first, the selection of the cities and secondly, the selection of the training participants. The cities were selected by the CMD staff and the city managers from two of the cities involved. The criteria for selection were that the cities be Missouri suburbs of essentially similar characteristics in terms of size, budget, form of government and degree and type of development of the city organization. In other words, they were to be city organizations with similar problems and similar resources. The number of cities was set at five to provide a critical minimum number of training participants and yet keep the number of separate city O.D. programs within workable bounds.

Selection of the training participants was done interactively by the city administrators and city managers of the participating cities and training staff. It was a process of defining the key roles in the separate organizations. Each manager was interviewed and asked to provide an organizational chart and a list of all administrative professional and technical positions "on whom you rely." These materials were circulated to all five managers and then discussed in an Advisory Committee meeting composed of the five managers and the CMD staff. During the interaction it was decided to include among the training participants the secretaries to the city managers, despite the secretaries' relatively low positional status. The pool of individuals selected included the city administrators and department heads from all functional areas—public works, fire, police, water, parks and recreation, engineering, as well as staff positions such as purchasing officer, personnel director, finance officer, city clerk, assistant city manager, city engineer and some second level positions, especially in public safety, in addition to the city administrators' secretaries. The city employment experience of participants ranged from a few months to over 30 years. There were about 12 individuals from each of the five cities. The city managers and city administrators were formed into one training group—labeled Group 1—and the remaining people were randomly assigned to Groups 2 and 3. This collection of approximately 60 people composed those who must collaborate with each other in each of the five cities for effective performance of the general management function.

Overview of Program Events

The SIGN Program events are summarized in Figure 1. Each of the three training groups went through three three-day intensive workshops together. These were designated workshops I, II, and III and covered "management styles," "group behavior" and "collaboration," respectively. Each workshop was specifically tailored for the participants in it and different trainers with different perspectives and approaches were on the staff of different workshops. No two workshops were

	Year 1			Year 2		
	Mar.	June	Sept.	Dec.	March	June
Phase I Management Development	WI-1	WII-1	WIII-1			WIV-1
	WI-2	WII-2	WIII-2			
	WI-3	WII-3		WIII-3		
Phase II Organization Development			TB-1		F-1	
				TB-2	F-2	
				TB-3		F-3
				TB-4		F-4
				TB-5		F-5 F-II5
Data Collection	QI-1			I-1 QII-1		
	QI-2			QII-2	I-2	
	QI-3			QII-3	I-3	
	QI-4			QII-4		I-4
				QII-5	I-5	

Figure 1 SIGN Program Events

exactly alike. An attempt was made to keep the same basic design and the same vocabulary so that Groups 2 and 3 would have essentially the same experiences to share.

In the structured part of Phase Two, the O.D. phase, a two-day team building event and a two-day feedback training session were held in each city. In one city an additional follow-up day was held to hear reports from task forces formed during the feedback sessions. The O.D. programs in each city then evolved in separate and distinct ways dependent upon the identified needs and the amount and kind of energy administrators, other city employees and the trainers were willing to invest.

Group 1, the group composed of the city managers, also held an additional two-day intensive training session for personnel and organizational review and consultative problem solving. This group has continued for several years as an ongoing personal support group and a vehicle for professional development and opportunistic clinicing on current pressing administrative dilemmas.

Underlying all of this training and organization development activity was a constant formal and informal process of data collection. In May of year one and again in January-February of the second year a questionnaire was administered to all available employees of the SIGN cities. (For reasons of experimental design one city was not included in the first round but all were included in the second.) The questionnaire covered motivation factors, organization renewal dimensions developed by CMD and the Likert Organization Questionnaire. The results were coded, punched to IBM cards and analyzed by computer. The Center subscribed to the local newspapers of all five SIGN cities and requested copies of council meetings, planning commission minutes and administrative documents including budgets and personnel policies. Consultants held frequent conversations on the telephone, in city offices and over lunch with the city managers, city administrators and various city employees. Finally, as part of the survey-feedback sequence, over twenty formal indepth interviews were held in each city.

Illustrative Examples of O.D. Intervention Formats Used

The formats used in SIGN were fairly formalized. Networking is not a format, but it has taken place within the management development training format. Team building, survey-feedback, task force process and consultation with individual managers and natural organizational groupings have been used. Examples will highlight some of the unique aspects of this program.

Management Development Workshops

The SIGN Management Development Workshops were intensive, three-day, non-residential workshops which can be described as structured laboratory experiences.

They were held in off-site locations with cross-city participation. The usual time-table was 9:00 a.m. through 9:00 p.m. the first two days and 9:00 a.m. through 5:00 p.m. the third day. Funding would not permit a residential program and the trainers insisted on a maximum of contact in a minimum of three days. Participants found the time frame exhausting. But the trainers question whether the necessary group development and working through of issues could have happened in less time. A large variety of structured exercises interspersed with lecturettes was used to encourage high levels of self-disclosure, as projective devices for surfacing data about the organizations and about role relationships, as formats for problem solving and as tools for conceptual learning and communication and problem solving skills development. The development of mixed inter-city, cross-functional subgroups and of single city groups and the use of pairings, small, medium-sized and total group formations was orchestrated to maximize learning and build the integration of relationships that makes up the network.

The progression of skill development and conceptual emphasis can be thought about as four sequential, overlapping and interwoven subject matter areas (See Figure 2). The first area, Area a in Figure 2, is the behavior of individuals in administered public organizations. It deals with the individual manager's own knowledge and capability as a person. One's understanding of others in the organization as individuals is also included.

Area b is working group behavior. This deals with the individual manager's role as a leader of a working group of subordinates or of peers. It also covers different types of group formats and their purposes, including the conditions of effective group decision making.

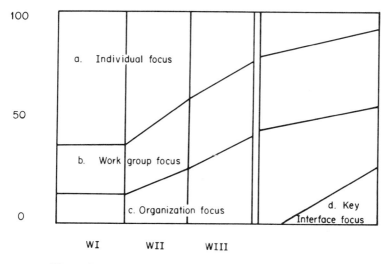

Figure 2 Progression of conceptual and skill emphasis.

The third subject matter is organization behavior and conflict management. This deals with the shared understandings of the organization by the members of it, with goals and procedures and with the individuals' abilities to confront and creatively resolve issues that may be fraught with conflict.

The final subject matter, Area d, is more significant in the O.D. phase than in management development. This is the area of interface relationships. Interface issues are questions of relationships between the organization and its environment, between important sub-units in the organization, or between a particular government and other governments.

Exercises used in the workshops included well validated questionnaire instruments such as the Styles of Management Inventory, FIRO-B, and the Reaction to Group Situation Test (RGST) which were completed, scored and discussed by participants. Other commonly available and frequently used training exercises included a Professional Life Goals Planning sequence, the New Truck Case, the NASA Moon Game, Star Power, Intergroup Competition, the Five Squares Puzzle, the Hollow Square Exercise, and the Helping Relationship Exercise (Blind Walk). Participants also developed lists of expectations, shared implementation experiences, diagnosed group climate, wrote case incidents, did Force Field Analyses of workshop and of back home problems, consulted with each other in consultation trios, role played and critiqued video tape records of their behavior in the role play and developed learning exercises for the participant group. The development of a model of one's own organization, one's role within it and one's relation to other parts of the organization using tinker toys and other projective materials proved to be a very graphic means of highlighting general management problems of structure and communications and was a powerful stimulus to discussion and improved understanding.

One exercise developed as part of SIGN Workshop I illustrates the experiential approach, the uses of data and the synergetic mixed purposes of training. "What's Important to City Employees" is an educational exercise based on information developed about the cities from the Organization Status Inventory Questionnaire, which had been administered to all employees of four of the cities prior to the workshop. The questionnaire included a ranking of work related motivational factors by all city employees. In order to teach motivational theory and bring home to the training groups the actual preferences of their own employees summarized rankings given by all sub-managerial employees were computed. They were:

1. A chance to learn new things
2. Working as part of a "team"
3. A stable and secure future
4. Opportunity for advancement
5. A chance to use my special abilities

6. A chance to benefit society

7. Variety in work assignments

8. High salary

9. Friendly and congenial associates

10. A chance to exercise leadership

11. A chance to make a contribution to important decisions

12. Freedom from pressures to conform both on and off the job

13. Freedom from supervision

14. A chance to engage in satisfying leisure activities (recreational, cultural, etc.)

15. High prestige and social status

Participants in training groups were not given the rankings directly, but were first asked to rank the factors for themselves and then to predict how their employees had ranked them. These predictions were discussed in "city groups" and a small group consensus on the predicted employee ranking agreed upon before the actual rankings were released to the group. (The reader may recognize the format as being similar to the various "decision by consensus" games such as NASA and Desert Survival.) After measuring the discrepancies between what they had predicted and what employees actually said they wanted, there followed an extremely insightful discussion in which learning about motivation took place. Personnel from one city were so disbelieving of the top ranking for "learning new things" that they asked about it back in City Hall. Upon finding the top ranking confirmed, they proceeded to start a weekly bulletin, edited by the city clerk and titled appropriately: *Learning New Things.*

Team Building

In the structured part of the O.D. phase the management teams in each city took part in a two-day intensive team building session. In planning the team building the city administrators were given a chance to pick the individuals they wanted involved in this activity. Their selections ranged from a small group of top department heads to anyone who had been through Phase I training plus a few. Such broad differences in the size and composition of management teams reflected differences in the cities and in the managerial style of the administrators. Participants from the same city, but from all three training groups came together in the team building session. Although people by now had a new common vocabulary and similar shared experience they did not necessarily have shared understandings about their roles and relationships. The team building provided an opportunity to develop such shared expectations. Exercises used in all cities included building a projective organization model as a framework for talking about roles and relationships as well as a formal negotiation exercise in which each individual wrote and exchanged specific statements of "What I need from you in order to work effectively" and then discussed the requests received.

Feedback Training

Feedback training touched a larger group of people in each organization. The particular participants who were included varied in the different cities because of the uniqueness of each organization and the differing managerial approaches taken by different city administrators. Everyone included in team building was also included in the feedback training, but in four of the five cities the feedback group was considerably larger—closer to 20 than to 10.

It will be recalled that the Organization Status Inventory Questionnaire had been administered twice before the feedback training and that there were in-depth interviews with city employees before the feedback. All of this information was summarized and printed. The motivation pattern from all cities was summarized into one handout and the organization renewal dimension plus the interview responses were placed in separate city by city handouts along with the motivation data of the particular city.

Figure 3 gives a sample of part of the questionnaire summary. The indepth interviews were summarized and particular concerns of each city abstracted. Answers to questions about goals and successes were randomized and transcribed. The responses to other questions were content analyzed and sorted into categories fitting to the particular city in question. The scope and variety of comments can be seen by looking at just the headings used in one of the cities.

City One

I. What Are The Major Operational Goals Of The City Overall?

II. What Are The Major Operational Goals Of Your Unit?

III. What One Thing Would You Point To As The Greatest Success Of The City Organization?

IV. What One Thing Would You Point To As The Greatest Success Of Your Unit?

V. General Issues

A. Planning and Goal Emphasis

B. Structure

C. Adaptability

D. Communication

E. Procedural Development

Item	Mean Four Cities	Mean Before Training	City of X After Training Percentage Distribution							Mean	Change
			HU	U	PU	NSU	PS	S	HS		
1. The ability to recruit talented manpower	4.258	4.351	01	01	13	11	42	25	06	4.901	+0.550
2. Retention of talented manpower	4.176	4.311	04	07	14	13	32	24	06	4.563	+0.252
3. The ability to respond to problems and issues in the community	4.554	4.473	06	06	15	07	31	28	07	4.648	+0.175
4. The usefulness of groups, teams, and/or committees	4.318	4.122	06	14	07	20	35	15	03	4.225	+0.103
5. Operating procedures are clear for members of the organization	4.343	4.554	03	13	15	07	28	25	08	4.549	-0.005
6. Operating units communicate with each other	4.352	4.446	03	10	06	10	38	27	07	4.789	+0.343
7. People become involved and are committed to their jobs	4.910	5.081	01	01	06	10	42	24	15	5.239	+0.158
8. Meetings and conferences are productive	4.172	3.865	03	07	10	17	35	20	08	4.676	+0.811
9. Talents and capabilities are recognized and rewarded at all levels	3.708	3.757	10	14	10	14	34	15	03	4.056	+0.299
	N = 233	N = 74								N = 71	

Figure 3 Suburban intergovernmental network. Organization status inventory questionnaire responses, Rounds I and II. (HU) highly unsuccessful; (U) unsuccessful; (PU) partially unsuccessful; (NSU) neither successful nor unsuccessful; (PS) partially successful; (S) successful; (HS) highly successful.

The headings from number V on were different for each of the different cities because the issues and their priorities were different in each city.

Feedback training took place in a location close to city hall, sometimes in a community building, sometimes in a bank board room. Each session was a day and a half in duration. During the afternoon of the first day the "action research" approach of 1) data collection, 2) feedback, and 3) action planning was explained. Participants then met in small groups and listed the questions in their minds that they hoped the data would address. The staff of CMD then presented the feedback data with handouts, visual aids, lectures, and ample opportunity for participants to question and discuss the data. In general, the second day was given over to discussion of the data, sometimes item by item, sifting of problem areas, cleaning up issues that could be solved by simple information sharing, and planning any desired action steps.

Critical Impinging Events

In SIGN the political arena and the mobility of city managers had a strong effect on the O.D. programs. Within the first year of the program three of the five city administrators had left and been replaced. Each departure was a promotion for the individual rather than a sign of political displeasure and each was soon replaced with a competent and well accepted successor. Even so, the pain of the transitions was considerable. In one city, department heads felt abandoned and angry. As they saw it, they were just beginning to work well together and the chief of the team walked out on them. Similar but less vocal fits of discouragement took place in the other two cities. Training Group 1 (the managers and administrators group) spend a large portion of its training time bringing the new members on board and recovering team building ground that had been covered previously.

In one city, an election campaign that focused on the city administrator caused the team building for that city to be postponed twice. The administrator was concerned that there was not enough openness in the organization to have a productive meeting at that particular time.

Program Direction

SIGN guidance continually came from the Advisory Committee which consisted of the city managers and city administrators and two consultants, who both convened and served as secretariat to the Committee. All questions of content, participation, trainer requirements and evaluation of the management development were discussed in this body which met every other month. Direction of O.D. in the individual cities lay in the relationship between the city administrator and CMD staff. O.D. interventions were discussed in the Advisory Committee but more with the intention of information sharing than advice seeking.

SIGN Outcomes

What products can be attributed to SIGN in the five cities?

Network

For one thing a network does exist now. Perhaps even two networks can be said to exist. There is a rather strong career support group that has developed among the five city managers. The city management profession is a lonely profession because it is the only position like it in town. The role is politically sensitive. It carries enormous responsibilities and it is enacted in the limelight of the local media. One must be careful to whom one talks about burdensome issues. On top of this, the profession is highly competitive, though city managers are often quick to deny this fact. These things being the case, it is something of an accomplishment that the five SIGN managers developed a high degree of trust in each other and quite regularly call each other and have lunch together for the purpose of talking through sensitive organizational and policy issues.

The network among other members of the training groups is less intense, but real nonetheless. Employees of a city call up employees of another department or another city, whom they now know, and ask their advice, request ordinances, copies of personnel manuals, or just talk about what is going on. In one reported case two city clerks spent several hours talking with a third city clerk about her role and how it had and would continue to change as the city grew and became more professionalized. In simple words, people from these five cities are now talking to each other.

Staff Meetings

Four of the cities have instituted regular department head-city manager staff meetings as an outgrowth of problem identification in the SIGN workshops.

Newsletters

Two cities established employee newsletters to help with their general communication problems.

Employee Councils

During the program period, three of the cities have set up elected "employee councils" to deal with general questions affecting employees and their working conditions. These were not a direct outgrowth of SIGN training or problem solving under these auspices. The idea of the employee council approach was passed along between cities and their experiences were shared during training sessions and through the network.

Collaborative Resource Decisions

As a result of ideas and collaborative skills developed during the training sessions, two cities have been able to carry out a radically changed approach to making decisions about budgetary allocations and the uses of revenue sharing. In the past, it has always been the manager's prerogative to make any cuts in proposed expenditures as he sees fit, regardless of the feelings of his subordinates. This practice has frequently left a sour taste in the mouths of those individuals who have strived hard to arrive at budget figures which they feel to be necessary, reasonable, and adequately justified from supporting data. Particularly difficult is the situation in which employees have struggled during past months to hold down costs in order to meet a particularly stringent set of spending directives; having suggestions overruled after working hard to save money tends to leave employees with a feeling of ingratitude.

To avoid these and other problems, one of the city administrators called the department heads together and presented them with the opportunity to decide among themselves, as guided by his suggestions and the stated priorities of the City Council, which programs should receive the budgetary cuts. The target figure was the elimination of $50,000 in budget requests. The task was accomplished swiftly and with great sensitivity to the overall needs of the city and the individual needs of the various municipal departments. At one point the city engineer volunteered to cut an important position out of the budget altogether as a sacrifice to other departments. The police chief would have nothing of it, insisting that this position would be important to the growth of the city's engineering programs!

As important as the chief's gesture was the reasoning behind it: he saw that the engineering programs affected the success of other municipal programs to a significant extent and were thus important to the effectiveness of the city as an operating unit. Since the total operation of local government was the true focus of the budget, so the chief reasoned, then cuts should be made in reference to that goal and not as a means of bettering some departments at the expense of others. He suggested that the engineering position should remain in the budget, and it did. Subsequently, individual department heads as well as the manager reported that this effective and forthright decision-making process could not have occurred as it did without the SIGN training.

Measured Change on Organization Renewal Variables

The instrument used to "take the temperature" of the organization, as it were, is an evolved and improved version of a CMD developed instrument used in previous O.D. programs. Two applications of the questionnaire are reported here—the one training and the one after Phase I, management development and before Phase II, individual city O.D. (See Figure 4.) Each application included all available employees in four of the cities. (Round II data are also available on the fifth city but excluded here to keep the results comparable. The data on the fifth city are even more positive than that of the four presented.) The zero point on the graph stands for "neither successful nor unsuccessful," *plus* is in the "successful" direction, and *minus* is in the "unsuccessful" direction.

Visual inspection shows that on the average the cities improved on all 21 dimensions. On several variables the cities show a dramatic improvement. Interestingly, "recruitment" is one of the strongly improved variables. Perhaps this reflects the successful selection of new city managers and several other professional positions that were filled during the year and a half.

Other dramatic improvements are found in "the ability to be informed of" and "respond to the community" and in "the understanding and implementation of policy." Several individual and group level variables show substantial change, including "the ability of people to talk openly and frankly about what they think, where they stand and what they feel," the belief that "people are backed in their efforts to do a better job," "rewarding of talent and leadership," and "the productivity and satisfaction with meetings."

The least change is "on the job commitment" variable, but that was high to begin with and remains the variable seen as most successful. "Inter-unit collaboration" presents an interesting picture. While there is improvement in this variable, it is not great. "Inter-unit communication" on the other hand began at a lower level of perceived success than "inter-unit collaboration" and ended up at a higher level. It is interesting to speculate upon the relationship between these two phenomena.

In his dissertation research on this project Dick Heimovics reduced the 21

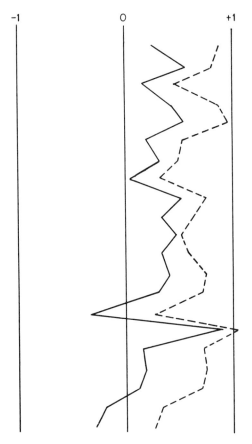

Figure 4   Organization renewal variable. Questionnaire responses—Rounds I
(——), four SIGN cities and II (- - -), four SIGN cities.

items to four dimension by factor analysis. Factor 1, which he calls "Supportive
Climate of the Organization," contains (in order of declining factor loading)
questionnaire items nos. 16, 17, 14, 1, 12 and 13. Factor 2 "Quality of Organization Information Processing" contains items 10, 7, 8, 9 and 11. Factor 3 "Use
of Groups" contains items 4, 5, 9, 15 and 6. Factor 4, "External Relationships,"
contains items 2 and 3.* These factors were then measured for carefully selected
representative individuals before and after Phase I. Figure 4 shows the dramatic

---

*Richard D. Heimovics, *A Study of Training for Organizational Change,* unpublished Doctoral Dissertation, Kansas University, Lawrence, Kansas, 1974 (pp. 167-8).

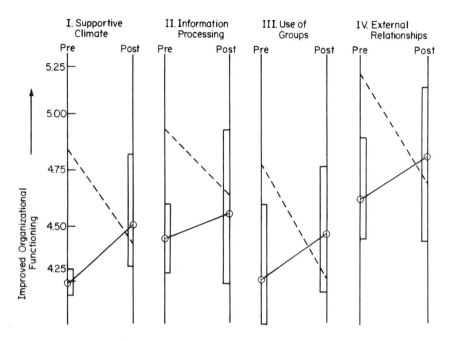

Figure 5   Pre and post scores on the four dimensions.

improvement on each factor that was demonstrated relative to matched comparison cities.

Epilogue

In the time that has passed since the end of the structured programs in the SIGN cities O.D. activities have continued, usually at a lower level but with occasional bursts of intensive effort. One city conducts regular team building events with the management team without outside consultants and another holds team building sessions about twice a year, calling upon CMD for third party facilitation. Several cross organizational one day training sessions have been held in specialized areas like personnel performance evaluation, MBO and communication. From time to time CMD staff have been called in to facilitate resolution of difficult conflict situation between two employees. But the most interesting outgrowths have been an entire department O.D. process and movements of the process upwards in all five cities to the level of the policy administrative interface.

In one city the fire chief, who had been an active participant in the city O.D. program, proposed a departmental O.D. program. Following his request, command staff and each shift were involved in several days of team building and issue identification in overlapping family groups followed by a department wide confrontation meeting that addressed several issues of command and policy. Every member of the department was involved in this process.

The SIGN program was focused at the administrative level and sponsored by the city managers with council approval but without active council participation. Throughout the structured program data collection efforts the relationship between the administrative organization and the city council was highlighted as an area of importance and concern in all of the cities. To meet this need the councils were brought into active participation in the process. A one day workshop was designed to address role relationship and mutual expectations among city council members, mayors and city managers. A majority of the membership of each of the councils and the five city managers attended the workshop. Perceived ideal role statements were exchanged and negotiated. The participants found these sessions interesting and rewarding, both personally and for the conduct of city business back at city hall. The success of the policy level workshop led to another a year later and the spread of the idea among other area councils.

It would seem from the SIGN experience that O.D. can be an effective tool for improving the organizational climate and problem solving capacity of municipal organizations. A measure of success has been achieved in each case, showing that it is possible to have O.D. in municipal government. It would appear that there are measurable and lasting effects from consistent and carefully tailored municipal behavioral science change efforts. This paper has sketched one major effort with five cities and offered a preliminary catalogue of outcomes.

Bibliography

Brown, F. Gerald and Richard Heimovics. *What Municipal Employees Want From Work, a pilot study in five suburban city governments.* Paper presented at the National Conference of the American Society for Public Administration, Los Angeles, California, April, 1973.

"What Municipal Employees Want From Work," *Kansas Government Journal,* Vol. LIX, No. 6, June, 1973, p. 261

Brown, F. Gerald and Robert J. Saunders, "KCOD and SIGN: Six Cases of Municipal O.D."; *First Tango in Boston.* (Washington, D.C.: National Training and Development Service, 1973).

Heimovics, Richard D., *A Study of Training for Organizational Change,* Lawrence, Kansas, unpublished Doctoral Dissertation, Kansas University, 1974.

Nininger, J. R., MacDonald, V. N. and McDiarmid, G. Y., *Developments in the Management of Local Government: A Review and Annotated Bibliography,* (Kingston, Canada: Queen's University, Local Government Management Project Series D Publications, December 1975).

TEAM BUILDING—ONE APPROACH TO ORGANIZATIONAL DEVELOPMENT*

William J. Crockett

The Team Meets

They could have been any business or professional group, these ten men around
the luncheon table. There was the usual banter and kidding; the good-natured
poking of fun and the quick retort. There was the obvious story and the laughter
of men at ease with one another. I tried to detect signs of strain among them but
saw none, except for my own nervousness. For this group of ten were *my* men,
men whom I had picked—men with whom I had worked and achieved. They were
all good men. Some had worked for me as long as six years, from the time that
I was first appointed by President Kennedy to be Assistant Secretary of State for
Administration early in 1961. In fact, some of the relationships went beyond
that, back to the time when I was one of them, a fellow employee in the Department of State.

Now five years later I, the Boss, and my ten key subordinates were having
lunch together before starting a series of meetings which were called "Organizational Development." The meetings would run for a day and a half or two days.
During this time we would explore our feelings and our problems of working together. In addition to the eleven of us, there were also Charles Ferguson of

*Reproduced by special permission from *The Journal of Applied Behavioral Science.* "Team
Building—One Approach to Organizational Development," by William J. Crockett. Volume
6, Number 3, pp. 291-306. Copyright © 1970 NTL Institute.

U.C.L.A. and Charles Seashore of the NTL Institute for Applied Behavioral Science, Washington, D.C. Dr. Ferguson and Dr. Seashore would meet with us and help us with the problems we would encounter.

As the luncheon drew to an end and the time for work approached, I found myself questioning the whole activity.

Could there, I wondered, be any real problems beneath the surface of our relationships that would be worth two days of our busy time away from the State Department? After all, were these men not all well adjusted, well acquainted, and quite at ease with one another? This seemed obvious from the way they had enjoyed their luncheon together. Would this kind of confrontation fracture the well-being of this group? I wondered. Would we ever have this kind of friendly, jovial, easy feeling again if we went ahead with this "team-building" exercise? And yet, I knew that there were some personal animosities among us that surfaced occasionally and, when they did, made us all uncomfortable and edgy until they were again safely tucked away from sight. Could we, I wondered, deliberately surface these feelings and then be able to handle them as a group?

How Much Risk?

I was also concerned about the other risks that a meeting like this might hold. These men were good. I needed them all. I could ill afford to lose any of them, for they did work together as well as any group with which I had ever been associated. And if, as a result of this meeting, some persons were to leave me, the price would have been too great!

I questioned also whether or not it were proper to expose the group's problems in front of two outsiders. Would these two men be trusted enough by the group for us to talk frankly and openly about our problems in front of them? Was it not true that we should not wash our dirty linen in public? Should we not try to work our problems through together without these outside consultants?

In anticipating what was to follow, I was troubled with the thought that I would be called upon to share my feelings about each of these fellows in front of the others, and later on, we would expose each of these persons before his peers. I had been taught as a manager that the boss does not discuss a man's performance, capabilities, and weaknesses in front of his peers. It just is not done. Now I suddenly realized that I would surely be called upon to do just that before the day was finished. Another strain to cause the group to fracture? Perhaps. Even more distressing to me was the thought of the honest, face-to-face evaluation which I would be expected to give on each of them. That kind of open confrontation would be the most difficult problem I personally had to face.

I also wondered about the validity of our concept of forming an Executive Group. Could I share my responsibilities and my authority with them in a group situation? We had recently reorganized my area of responsibility by eliminating, in some cases, as many as five layers of hierarchy between me and the basic program managers (personnel, budget, building, finance, accounting, audit, and so on). We must now find a means of strengthening my office, stretching it laterally rather than deepening it vertically, to enable me to cope with the many new demands that these 30 or 40 new managers, who now reported directly to me, would make upon my time. How could we organize an Executive Group that would somehow be an extension—an elongation—of "me," so that these new managers would not feel that we had freed them of an old and established bureaucracy on the one hand only to put them into a new and strange hierarchical structure on the other?[1] Could we talk openly and honestly about the issues involved? Of course, there would be opposition and hurt and doubt and questions posed for everyone. Could we really work this through at such a meeting, or would it not be easier, simpler, and better for me just to direct things to be done? After all, I did have the authority. I might even be able to "manipulate" the organization into being as I had so often done in the past when I had wanted to accomplish something difficult. Why waste all this time on such an issue when I already knew the answer I wanted?

Could We Really Level?

I wondered whether we would have the nerve—the guts—to confront one another with the personal problems (feelings) that were bothering us. Or would we slip off the issues and try to cover up the difficulties as we had so often done in the past? This group had been meeting together for years in a staff capacity. Our practice was to go around the table each morning, talk about the problems of the day, and discuss the issues. Some of those ten would always be silent. Some would have ideas on almost any subject. Some would talk superficially about the problems which were in another's area of responsibility. But in the end, all would give way to me, the boss, to make the final decision and determine what to do. They did not act as a group, nor were they much interested as a group in the total problems I faced. Each problem, no matter how complex for me, was for each of them very simple. It was either his to handle or it was someone else's. And if it was someone else's the others had no interest; nor did one man want anyone else involved if it was his. Would they, could they, really become deeply involved with complex issues that cut across the lines of each one's responsibility? Could these individuals help me perform the complex integrative process of management? And, more importantly, would each one be able to take criticism and suggestions and ideas from the others on problems which each considered to be within his own responsibility? If anything was apparent to me about the group it was their lack of commitment to the entire Organizational Development program we had mounted some months before.[2]   Each person in the group fiercely defended his own piece of the program, even at the expense of the others. Could they gain commitment to the whole from such a meeting as this?

I also wondered about the data that my good friend Chuck Ferguson had collected from the group. He had maintained that we needed a method of "deep sensing" within this group to discover the subsurface feelings that might be different from those on the surface. Some of these men had come to me privately, saying, "Do you really want him to dredge into the depths of all our feelings about one another and about you? Isn't it being disloyal for us to tell him of our problems and of our feelings for you? Does it serve any purpose for these problems to be brought out into the open and exposed? In fact, is he not *creating* problems for us when he digs as deeply as he has done into the problems we have as a group together?" And, of course, while assuring them they would not be disloyal to talk honestly and that these were things that we wanted to get out onto the table, I had my secret doubts about whether this were really the way to develop an organization. Now I had the sinking feeling that these two days could really end up in "group destruction" rather than in "group growth."

These were some of the feelings and questions that went 'round and 'round within me as we were finishing our lunch. And yet I knew that, according to the Theory at least, it would come out all right in the end, and something good would be the result.

Finally, the lunch ended and we filed into the conference room away from telephones and papers to confront the evidence that Chuck Ferguson and Charlie Seashore had gathered about us. We were ready to start our first session of "Organizational Development" or "Team Building."

The Group Has the Data

In accord with the design for the meeting, the two behavioral scientists interviewed all the persons who reported directly to me in order to get data that we would use in our off-site conference together. Interviews were conducted informally and in a friendly atmosphere, but they probed very deeply into each person's relationships and feelings for each of the others in the group and with me. Searching questions were asked. What are the real problems of getting the job done? What problems do each of the members cause you in getting your job done? What are the problems that the boss has caused in the group? What are the personal problems, the personality problems, and the real life business problems that are destructive to the group? What are the deep interpersonal feelings? Is there confrontation? How are differences handled in the group when they come up? Is there conflict? Are you interested in participating in others' areas of responsibility? Is there any feedback to members who get out of line or who have problems? Is there a spirit of help and coaching within the group? Is there a spirit of trust and caring in the group? What are the group norms; what will the group tolerate? And there were many, many other questions as well.

When the meeting started, Chuck put all of us in a large circle—a common shape within T Groups—and talked to us about the agenda and the procedures for the next two days. He said that he would present the data that he had developed about each of us, then each person would have a chance to comment or to talk about them, and finally others would be asked to join the discussion. Since the data were to be presented anonymously, we could start the process of seeing ourselves without creating embarrassment and animosity. This would give us the first opportunity for coaching and feedback, we were told. In this way the group would have an opportunity to work, for the very first time, on problems within the group in a nonthreatening atmosphere.

Chuck explained that we would work upon the real issues, such as how we might form the new "Executive Group," how we might make policy, and so on, as well as dealing with the specific issues identified in the data. He assured us that in all cases he and Charlie Seashore would be there to help us to work through the data that we now had about ourselves and one another. He told us that he would stop us occasionally to talk to us about Organizational Development, to ask us to look at ourselves and what we were doing to one another or what we were doing as a group, or what we were not doing as a group.

Dr. Ferguson had coded the data by number so that the various kinds of data that were similar were given the same number. One number would represent one kind of data gathered from numerous sources (persons), and another number would represent another kind of data, and so on. Thus, if more than one of us had a problem in common with others, that problem would have a common number for us all. In a group of ten there might be 20 common items—things that everyone felt about some of the others—and several individual items about various persons which no one else had felt.

The Boss Is the Hang-up

The consultant put each of our names on a large board and around each one he accumulated the numbers that related to the problems others had said that they had with that particular person. I remember seeing names going up with five or six numbers encircling them, but I certainly was not prepared to see the large cluster of numbers that went up around my name! Mr. Ferguson explained what each number meant, and I can still remember some of the ones around my name. For example: "He doesn't delegate properly." "He gives the same assignment to two or three people." "He gives contradictory instructions to different people so that there are binds within the group." "He makes unilateral decisions relating to our responsibilities without first talking them over with us." "He takes action in our areas without telling us." "We are not generally informed about what's happening in the whole group." "We are kept ignorant about one another's activities." "He doesn't like confrontation and conflict." "He can't make tough (people) decisions." "We can't get in to see him." "He sees the wrong people." "He doesn't give us his attention when we do see him." "He has too many irons in the fire at one time." "He confuses us about priorities." "He is manipulative." And more. In each case that "He" was myself! I could feel my anger rising. My feelings were really hurt at this point because I still was not convinced that any of these things were actually true despite their perception by these now-so-loyal "friends." Further, I rationalized that in their dredging for feelings and in trying to discover problems, probably these people had stretched their imaginations just to come up with something to talk about. In my first throes of resentment, I could hardly refrain from saying, "If I'm so bad, pack up and get out and I'll find others who not only can do the job but will be glad for the chance!"

But it was not all bad. Chuck drew two big symbolic climates on the board, one of sunshine and one of rain. And he wisely pointed out that the evidence on each of us was not totally rain nor totally sunshine. There was some of both for each of us.

Our Self-Images

About this time, after the session had run for an hour or more, Chuck eased the situation with a lecture. This lecture was about "the perception of self-image" as opposed to how we might be seen by others. He explained how our own perceptions might actually have little to do with reality. For example, a person could feel as right and as righteous as he wished and have absolutely pure motives when he was doing something—starting a policy or making a decision or taking a stand. But it was also true that others might see his motives and acts in an entirely different light. Thus, what really mattered was not what he thought and felt but how he appeared to others.

We came to realize that a person need not admit that anything he was doing was necessarily wrong, but that it was the wise man who could understand the way he made other people feel. If the *reasons for* what a person was doing and the *way* he was doing it were both misunderstood by his staff, and if it could be revealed to him *why* they were being misunderstood, then it might be easier for him to face the problem and talk about it and work it through and learn how to avoid being misunderstood in the future. This understanding was especially helpful to all of us in dealing with our own "self-images." For example, it came out that one of the men in the group was very resentful of me because I had singled him out in a public meeting to give him credit for a new program. I had thought

that I was doing him great honor and favor, and my motives were pure and generous. But he had felt that I was trying to say to the group that if the project
turned out to be wrong or did not work or somehow failed, that it was his idea
and, therefore, he would have to bear the blame. I was making him the scapegoat!
And while I did not have to admit to any wrongdoing in dealing with him, because
my motives were pure, I did have to admit to a better understanding of the way
he felt after seeing it through his eyes. We both perceived that our mutual failure
to talk about this at the time had permitted our relationship to fester for no real
reason. This was the spirit in which Chuck led us into the discussion of the problems we would face in our relationships with one another.

Giving and Receiving Feedback

After these kinds of discussions, we had a deeper understanding of what we could
achieve. Chuck then asked me to go around the room and tell each person how I
felt about him and what my problems were with each one. The moment I dreaded
had come! I was to confront, in public, each of these persons and reveal my feelings for them. This was to be my most difficult hour. But here again the consultants tried to give us an understanding of the deep difference between a cold, hard,
objective, critical "appraisal" by the boss on the one hand and a legitimate (even
if critical) "feedback" that is given in a climate of trust and warmth and caring,
on the other. We discussed the obligations which were imposed upon all who
opted into such a group; specifically, we were reminded of the obligation of "caring" for other group members. Members who "cared" had obligations both individually and collectively to help the others to understand how they "came
through" and "were seen," how they were "felt" and "perceived," how they
"looked," and how their actions and conduct and attitudes were helpful or were
hurtful in their communications. Each had an obligation to give and to receive
feedback, and to give coaching to the others.

Since Chuck had also interviewed me prior to the meeting, I knew that he
had my candid observations on each of the individuals. All of them were my
friends but, nevertheless, all of them had a few human weaknesses in their relationships among one another and in their relationships to me. I knew that I had
revealed these in my data. I also knew that I had never liked or felt easy with
such confrontation. I found it very difficult to express my feelings and my
thoughts about each of my men. But I had the choice of giving them honest data
about themselves or doing half a job, sliding off the issues as easily as possible
despite what I had already told Dr. Ferguson.

As I went through the difficult task of discussing with each one of them the
way he came across to me, there was not so much hurt as I had expected; strange-
ly enough, there was no anger but genuine curiosity and interest. There was a

great deal of group support, disagreement, and participation in what I was saying about each person. The discussions were animated in a give-and-take way, and my data were then often related to those which Chuck had collected from each subordinate. Caring and sharing became an exciting new game.

Working the Data

After we had gone around the room like this for a while, we decided to come back to those problems which related to me. We worked on them one by one.

For example, where one had said I did not delegate, I denied it by saying, "I am the best delegator in the Department. You all have authority. You have responsibilities in your area. And it is up to you to get them done." And then the anonymity would disappear because the person who had put this item on the list would come in hard to justify his stand. And so with illustration of time and place and circumstance he would prove when I had not delegated properly or how I would fall back after I had given them authority, or how I had made a decision unknown to them or how, before evidence had come in, I had changed their decision, and so on. This kind of confrontation only started the conversation. Chuck would not let any of us off so easily. He probed deeply. How did my action make them feel? How did they see me? What were my motives? How did this affect the group's work together? This and many more questions that he asked would give me the opportunity to reply, "Yes, but you don't realize the pressure I am under from the White House . . . or from the Congress . . . or from the Secretary. . . ." And the whole complexity of relationships, the pressures upon me, and explanations for my seemingly erratic behavior would come out. From such explanations and probings came understanding and a sense of sharing that had never before existed in the group.

After they had worked with me for awhile, someone else would say, "Well, I would like to talk about [such and such] a problem around my name because I really am not this way, either." Here again the anonymity would be dropped, because the person who had put up that item would say, "Now Mr. X, don't you remember when you did that? Don't you remember when we had this kind of problem with you in your shop? Don't you remember how you wouldn't give us the funds to get the job done? Don't you recall how you changed policies while we were in midstream and then we had to scrap all the efforts we had made to that date?" And then the general discussion would start—'round and 'round— with new appreciation for people, new insights into the problems the others faced, and a new understanding of the interlocking relationships of all the functions.

There were many job-related problems that were put on top of the table for discussion for the first time, as well as many personal relationship problems. Why do you act this way? Why don't you like me? Why do you mistrust me? What do I do that annoys you so? How can I gain your confidence? Why are you so rigid? And the amazing thing to me was that the group members were actually eagerly working on their own problems without getting angry—almost urging us, "Get on to mine. I would like to talk about the cluster around my name; and while I don't really believe it, if it's true let's talk about it and I'll try to do something about it." I could see the group, hour by hour, literally growing in trust, growing in solidity, growing in caring. They were somehow involved here with one another as they had never been involved before. In the old meetings they were just individuals attending a not too interesting discussion of another person's function. But here they were a real group facing a world of problems together.

The first night we worked until very late. No one really wanted to stop. We decided that we would come back early the next day and go on with the process which in reality had just started.

A Team Spirit Is Born

The next day's activity was interspersed with lectures and with other techniques to make the group grow in trust and in confidence, in its ability to give and receive feedback, and in its confidence to deal with confrontation and conflict. For examples, we would pair off in twos or threes to discuss the interpersonal problems we faced as they appeared on the board. We would then come back and tell the others about our findings and what we thought we could do to overcome these problems. The whole group would then be brought into the discussion, and the group members would talk about these things together. We talked about how we could work better as a group, how we could make group decisions, how we could share the problems that were coming to me, and how each member in the group could broaden his interest beyond his own specialty and responsibility so that he could accept a share in the whole group's problem. We discussed how the group could rid itself of its own individual parochialism and start a process of enlarging its interest and responsibility by working together as an extension of me. There was confrontation and conflict in the group and this was handled. There was feedback and caring, disagreements and frustrations, and these were handled. Personal animosities were probed and discussed and often settled, or at least understood. There was also creativity, and risk, and in the end there was a real sense of commitment to the principles which I at one time had thought that I might achieve more quickly by directive or more easily by manipulation.

I also realized that I had not fooled them about the real me. The group had had the data all along. But due to the climate of the group—its norms—we had not been able to be open with one another; we had not been able to face confrontation, and so the group could not share the data with me earlier. It would have hurt me too much at the time. It would have asked them to risk too much at the time. As "tough minded" as we thought our own management to have been, we soon learned that it had not been tough enough to deal with real conflict, deep personal feelings, or confrontation. Instead of this kind of confrontation's causing my leadership to dissipate, I saw a new excitement born of involvement emerging within the group. There could be no question of their total commitment to me as their leader and to the concept of the "Executive Group" which we had been discussing. Out of this meeting we all saw the phenomenon of a new group come into being before our very eyes! We were a united group—trusting and caring and sharing as never before.

These were a tough, exhausting, exciting, and fulfilling two days! But we were a team at the end and felt that we had the start of a capability of functioning as an effective Executive Group.

Action Items for the Back-Home Situation

Before breaking up for the weekend, we decided on several courses of action.

We decided that we would meet every morning to talk about the issues of the day, to decide how we would deal with them, what our actions would be, how we would proceed, and who would have the responsibility for handling each problem. In these meetings everyone would have an opportunity for input and discussion before decisions were made. In this way problems were made the responsibility of the whole group, with the whole group's having knowledge and input and commitment to the decisions that were made.

We decided to continue having a behavioral scientist (Charles Seashore) meet with us occasionally in our regular staff meetings and other work sessions so that he could observe what was going on among us, and so that he could stop the group occasionally to let us observe our own process. Certainly we knew that we would need his expertise, at least for some time.

We decided that we would come back together again at some future date to have another off-site session to review our group health and our new-found spirit of trust and caring. We came to realize that the relationships between people need maintenance to keep them working smoothly and that it cannot be something done only occasionally. We came to realize that we were embarking on a new management style, a new method of handling every day's problems, which would require a great deal from each of us—a new toughness of mind—but dispensed with a great deal of "heart." Therefore we would need a continuing process of growth and understanding if we were to succeed.

We determined that we would like to have Dr. Seashore do continuing research with members of the group and go deeper into our organization so that there would be a continuous sensing of how employees felt. By this we could have a better understanding of the attitudes of our members and of how people "down below" saw us and were reacting to us. Thus we would be able to take steps within the system to handle the problems.[3]

Several of the members of this group decided that they would like to take their own subordinate staff off-site for the same kind of Organizational Development meeting. This was courageous on their part because they had seen how difficult it had been for me, the boss; and when they went off-site with their staff they realized that they would assume "the boss" role. Yet they were willing to take the risks because of the obvious vitality of the process in bringing people together, in opening people up so that they could make contributions, in actually reducing conflict by facing it, and because of the commitment that results when people participate and become deeply involved in the management process.

We decided to explore the possibility of having other off-site Organizational Development conferences with other major areas of the Department of State for whom our group was responsible for service and with whom we interfaced. For example, we provided administrative support to all the Bureaus and Offices; and if we could take them off-site with us we might be able to learn how we looked to our clients, how they felt about us, and what, if any, the problems might be in working together.

We discussed how we could be helpful to one another in the future in the way we worked together in the organization. For example, what were the coaching opportunities we had; how could each one help the other see himself and understand how he was coming through? How could we give feedback in the future that would not hurt but would be helpful and reinforcing? We determined that we would try to receive such feedback without defensiveness. We agreed that we would not "put off" all of our process discussions for some future get-together but that we would feed this kind of information into our regular meetings so that we could deal with it on the spot since the data were there for all to see. In other words, we agreed that the group must police and reinforce and maintain the group and its members if what we had started to learn at this meeting would indeed be continued within the group. We agreed that if I did something they did not like or understand the others would bring it up for discussion.

The first attempt ever made in the State Department of bringing together a manager and his own staff to talk about their individual and group problems had come to an end. It accomplished many of the positive hopes that we had had for it. It had not gone aground. We had not risked so much as I had feared in those doubt-filled moments just before the meeting started. In other words, I believe that all of us felt that it was a worthwhile, constructive two days.

What Were the Results?

A story such as this requires a sequel—some description of what happened after the group went back to work in its real life situation. Certainly it would be erroneous to say that there were no continuing problems, because there were. The process did not guarantee an end to problems. All the old animosities were not forgotten. The process did not promise that, either. Conflicts and disagreements were still with us. But in the weeks and months that followed, the group showed a highly increased capability for getting issues out into the open, of surfacing the hidden problems, and in exposing personal animosities so that we could deal with them—in short, an increased capability to work together as a group.

It did break down the fragmentation that had previously existed. The process of welding ourselves into a total integrated management team was started. As a result, I believe there came to be a great deal more understanding of points of view, understanding of the total issues, understanding of the total problems and programs, and a greater commitment on the part of everyone to the total goals.

Also, the process did move downward in the organization and horizontally, to include other parts of the State Department. As proposed in our meetings, some of the members did take their own staffs off-site for similar meetings with similar positive results. The Assistant Secretary of State for African Affairs at this time used this same technique of going off-site with his staff to better the management and decision-making process in his bureau. The same kind of program was planned for the Latin American Bureau and other areas. Our group did meet together in a similar off-site meeting with our client organizations and gained insights into how we were creating many of our own problems.

Conclusion

The lesson that was most impressive to us all was that the so-called Theory Y style of management—management by participation—is neither soft-headed nor "easy." It is much easier to avoid confrontation by issuing orders. It is easier to avoid personal involvement and conflict by smoothing over the surface. Theory Y management is not for the executive who likes surface serenity and obsequiousness. Theory Y management is for those managers who are willing to take the gut punishment of a truly tough-minded approach to management. It is for those who believe that conflict can be handled best by confronting it openly and for those who understand that real commitment of their people can be secured only by their continuing participation in making plans and setting objectives.

Organizational Development is not a panacea but a style—a tough-minded management style—and it works!

Notes

1. Part of the State Department's reorganization called "Management by Programs and objectives" (MOP).

2. A multi-action development program called "Action for Organizational Development" (ACORD). A major part of the program was the extensive use of laboratory training and behavioral scientist consultants provided under a contract with NTL.

3. Mr. Crockett resigned from the Department of State on January 31, 1960, and the ACORD program was soon discontinued by his successor. The reasons for his action were varied but included cost, style of management, failure of the Secretary to be personally involved, and so on. The discontinuance of the program should not be interpreted as the result of an evaluative judgment of its efficacy.

LABORATORY TRAINING AND ENCOUNTER GROUPS*

William B. Eddy and Bernard Lubin

Participation in some form of intensive group learning experience is becoming increasingly commonplace. In many schools, churches, business management groups, and social service agencies, involvement in a T-group, encounter group or sensitivity training session is seen as a part of one's overall development. Such learning goals as getting to know oneself better, learning how one comes across to others, understanding more about human interaction, and getting a better feel for group operations are relevant to many vocational roles.

Two major factors seem to be accelerating the use of small face-to-face group experiences as learning vehicles: (a) the fast-changing, large, complex, and impersonal society in which we live; and (b) the increasing amount of organizational work-life that takes place in small face-to-face groups.

In regard to the former, Rogers (1968) states what he believes to be behind the rapid growth of the small group training phenomenon:

> one of the most rapidly growing social phenomena in the United States is the spread of the intensive group experience. . . . Why? I believe it is because people—ordinary people—have discovered that it alleviates their loneliness and permits them to grow, to risk, to change. It brings persons into real relationships with persons [p. 269].

*Reprinted from *Personnel and Guidance Journal,* Vol. 49, No. 8 (April, 1971) pp. 625-634. Copyright April 1971, American Personnel and Guidance Association. Reprinted with permission.

The second factor, equally compelling, is the increasing amount of the work in organizations that takes place in small, face-to-face groups (planning, decision-making, problem-solving, etc.). Organizations and individuals recognize the need for training methods that improve the functioning of these work groups. Another aspect of current organizational life is the growing regard for temporary structures—committees, project teams, task forces, conferences, consulting relationships, etc. (Bennis & Slater, 1968; Miles, 1964). It is becoming increasingly important for individuals to have the ability to move rapidly into team relationships in which there is mutual trust, adequate team spirit, and creative stimulation among members.

The counselor and personnel worker are often in a position to provide guidance and information to individuals who think they want to participate in a small group training experience. Also, an increasing number of counselors and personnel workers are attending small group training programs themselves in order to improve their group leadership skills. Because of this widespread participation, it is important to understand the differences among the various small group approaches—including their goals and methods. In this article, we will provide a brief historical perspective on small group training and working definitions for some of the more frequently mentioned types: the T-group, the encounter group, the marathon group, and the therapy group. We will also comment on some of the questions often raised regarding professional ethics in this field.

Historical Overview

Intensive small group training methods have their roots in the workshop method of the 1930's and 1940's, including the action-research methods of Kurt Lewin and the spontaneity training and role-playing methods of Moreno. The general approach did not begin with a primary focus on personality change or overcoming social and psychological isolation; rather, it started as a wedding between social action and scientific inquiry (Bunker, 1965). Its parent disciplines were adult education and the applied research interests of Lewin and some of his colleagues in social psychology—Ronald Lippitt, Leland Bradford, Kenneth Benne, and others. Their innovations were responsible for the first training workshops held, beginning in 1947, in isolated New England communities such as Bethel, Maine—"cultural islands" free from some of the usual situations in people's daily lives that pressure against change.

The National Training Laboratories (NTL), affiliated with the National Education Association, grew out of these efforts. It was found that participants learned and changed in their ability to deal with human relations problems, not only by listening to lectures and participating in role-playing but also by analyzing the here-and-now characteristics of their own conference groups. The social scientists discovered, partly by accident, that participants were very much interested in behavioral data that researchers who observed the groups collected about the group interaction. The analysis of this "process" data provided trainees a "laboratory" in which to deal more dynamically and personally with some of the human relationship issues they were studying.

Although NTL has played a major role in the evolution of group training, there have been other important influences. Group trainers with clinical and counseling backgrounds brought to NTL workshops and similar programs the skills and interests for dealing with personality variables within groups. Also, individuals with consulting and change agent skills (many of whom were members of the NTL consulting network) have applied their efforts to programs in which the goals are to effect change in the organization and the community.

In another direction, the existential-humanistic "human potential" approach has moved beyond the methods of traditional social science by employing various expressive, intrapsychic, and somato-psychologic techniques. Esalen Institute at Big Sur, California, has led in this development. (For a more comprehensive history of group training, see Benne [1964] and Bradford [1967].)

Some Definitions

It is impossible to deal with small group training and the issues and problems surrounding it as a single, general phenomenon. Widely different, experience-based training approaches are currently being conducted, and to lump them together confuses rather than simplifies. Further, the need to make decisions about the appropriateness of programs and qualifications of trainers requires the ability to differentiate between kinds of programs. It is even questionable whether the various types of small groups used for educational, training, or therapeutic purposes should be subsumed under one rubric; to do so implies more commonality than actually exists. Unfortunately, there are no generally accepted meanings for many of the terms often used. The following definitions are somewhat arbitrary but seem to mesh with the historical progression.

Sensitivity training is one of the first and most generic terms in the field. It originally referred to the small group training conducted by the National Training Laboratories. Currently, it is used by some to subsume all small group training approaches. However, most practitioners do not find it a useful term because it is frequently used so broadly (to include group therapy, for example) that it has lost its power to define. Also, training personnel whose methods are only peripherally related to the original sensitivity training approach have picked up the term and have applied it to their ventures.

We find the term *laboratory training* a more useful conceptualization; it is used to refer to an educational method that emphasizes experience-based learning activities. Participants are involved in a variety of experiences, usually including small group interaction, and their behavior provides the data for learning. Thus, laboratory training involves learning by doing. The subject matter of such programs deals with some aspect of human interaction, and the goal is to be more aware of and responsive to what is going on. A specific laboratory training program (human relations lab) may run from a few hours to two or more weeks and may contain a combination of elements designed to provide experiential learning. Although laboratory training is often used to refer to NTL-sponsored programs, we use it here to include experience-based learning approaches in general.

A basic element of most laboratories is the *T-group* (T for training). In the standard NTL-type of T-group, participants find themselves in a relatively unstructured environment in which their responsibility is to build out of their interaction a group that can help them meet their needs for support, feedback, learning, etc. The behaviors exhibited by members as they play out their roles provide the material for analysis and learning. Thus, T-group members have the opportunity of learning ways in which their behavior is seen by others in the group, the kinds of styles and roles they tend to take, their effectiveness in playing various kinds of roles, ways of being more sensitive to the feelings and behaviors of other group members, methods for understanding group behavior dynamics, etc. Time is usually provided for trainees to integrate what they have learned and plan to apply their new knowledge after the laboratory ends.

Some trainers within and outside the NTL network have evolved T-groups that provide a *personal growth* focus. Weschler, Massarik, and Tannenbaum (1962), who first described a laboratory with a "personal-interpersonal emphasis," provided the following explanation and rationale:

> Our version of sensitivity training increasingly concerns itself with strengthening of the individual in his desires to experience people and events more accurately, to a process of individual growth toward ever-increasing personal adequacy.

Encounter groups, as we define the term, refer to intensive small group experiences in which the emphasis is upon personal growth through expanding awareness, exploration of intrapsychic as well as interpersonal issues, and release of dysfunctional inhibitions. There is relatively little focus on the group as a learning instrument; the trainer takes a more active and directive role; and physical interaction is utilized. Other modes of expression and sensory exploration such as dance, art, massage, and nudity are currently being tried as a part of the encounter experience.

Marathon groups are time-extended encounter groups that use the massed experience and the accompanying fatigue to break through participants' defenses. Many organizations have sprung up around the country to offer encounter groups and related continued education programs. They often call themselves *growth centers* and view their offerings as a part of the *human potential movement.*

Comparisons with Psychotherapy Groups

Since all of the above groups, in one way or another, deal with emotional experience, the self-concept, and impressions of the behavior of others, and since they stress honest communication, the question is sometimes raised, "How do these groups differ from therapy groups?"

Lubin and Eddy (1970) have summarized the differences stated by Frank (1964):

> Therapy group members are seen by themselves and others as having psychological problems and needing help, whereas T-Group members are seen as relatively well-functioning individuals interested in improving old skills and learning new ones; attitudes which therapy attempts to modify are usually concerned with persons who are close to the patient and therefore more central and resistant to change, whereas the T-Group attempts to modify more peripheral attitudes; the therapist is a much more central person than the trainer and dependency upon him continues to be strong throughout; and the T-Group, focusing less upon the individual, evokes more moderate emotional responses.

Also, the group-focused T-group emphasizes the here-and-now of group development and transactions among its members. By contrast, the therapy group sanctions the search for factors associated with conflicts and problems in the patient's past life experiences.

Another conceptualization of the current group psychotherapy scene would be helpful at this point. Parloff (1970) suggests that the diversity of objectives among group psychotherapists can be reduced by sorting them into two broad categories: "headshrinking" and "mind-expanding." "Headshrinking objectives" are similar to the ones mentioned by Scheidlinger (1967), i.e., amelioration of suffering and restoration or repair of functioning. "Mind-expanding objectives" include heightened positive affective states, self-actualization, and self-fulfillment.

When encounter groups, marathon groups, and T-groups with a personal-interpersonal focus are compared with therapy groups which have mind-expanding objectives, fewer differences can be specified. Major distinctions that remain are:

1. T-groups with a personal-interpersonal focus, encounter groups, and marathon groups are relatively brief in duration and are time-limited.

2. The T-group with a personal-interpersonal focus usually is embedded in a larger laboratory design.

3. In general, the T-group with a personal-interpersonal focus, the encounter group, and the marathon group define members as "participants" rather than patients.

The latter distinction holds true only for the T-group with a personal-interpersonal focus, as the NTL Institute discourages participation by people who have serious emotional problems; on the other hand, psychotherapists occasionally refer patients to encounter groups and marathon groups in order to move past therapeutic impasses.

Laboratory Training and T-Groups

A participant in an NTL training laboratory will find the T-group a major component of the design, in terms of both time and involvement. If the program is a week in length, he will spend perhaps 30 hours or more in intensive discussion with about 10 other people. The trainer assigned to the group probably will open with a statement somewhat similar to this:

> This group will meet for many hours and will serve as a kind of laboratory where each individual can increase his understanding of the forces which influence individual behavior and the performance of groups and organizations. The data for learning will be our own behavior, feelings, and reactions. We begin with no definite structure or organization, no agreed-upon procedures, and no specific agenda. It will be up to us to fill the vacuum created by the lack of these familiar elements and to study our group as we evolve. My role will be to help the group to learn from its own experiences, but not to act as a traditional chairman nor to suggest how we should organize, what our procedure should be, or exactly what our agenda will include. With these few comments, I think we are ready to begin in whatever way you feel will be most helpful . . . [Seashore, 1968, p. 1].

In programs with a personal-interpersonal or "personal growth" focus, the trainer might emphasize the goal of "getting to know and understand ourselves better." If the laboratory is designed to train a specific vocational group such as managers, teachers, or ministers, the opening remarks might acknowledge the relevance that group learnings have to work "back home."

After his initial remarks, the trainer usually recedes from active leadership, and the group must proceed without the usual guidance of formal authority. As the group seeks to establish goals and procedures that are acceptable and useful to its members, to develop ways of making necessary decisions, to establish norms that support its needs and goals, and to deal with the conflicts that ensue, it experiences in "real life" many of the major dilemmas in social interaction. If members can learn, with the trainer's assistance, to examine the interaction process as it unfolds, and if they can develop a trust level that will allow them to express the emotions associated with group events, learning takes place. When the appropriate climate has developed, group members share feelings and perceptions ("feedback") regarding observed behavior in the group.

Theory and Rationale for the T-Group

There is no single theory of T-groups. What is known or hypothesized is a combination of theories, some transplanted from other settings. There are, however, several major theoretical positions which most practitioners in the field find useful and which provide a theoretical base. These include Lewin's model of attitude change (unfreezing-changing-refreezing) (Schein & Bennis, 1965), experience-based learning as contrasted with the one-way lecture approach, and overcoming emotional barriers to social learning through trust development and feedback (Lubin & Eddy, 1970).

Effectiveness of T-Groups

Do training laboratories emphasizing T-groups work? Do participants actually learn and change their real-life behavior? If so, in what ways and for how long?

In spite of the fact that there are no final answers to these questions, it is *not* true that outcome research on T-groups has been ignored. It seems safe to assert that there has been more research done on T-groups than on any other training approach. The authors of the American Psychiatric Association task force report, *Encounter Groups and Psychiatry* (1970), point out that:

> T-Groups, springing from the field of social psychology, have behind them a long tradition of research in group dynamics. No comparable body of knowledge has been generated by group therapy, a field notoriously deficient in any systematic research. Thus, what is presently known of the basic science of group psychotherapy stems almost entirely from social-psychological research with task groups and T-Groups; psychotherapy owes to the T-Group much of its systematic understanding of such factors as group development, group pressure, group cohesiveness, leadership, and group norms and values. Furthermore, T-Group research has elaborated a wealth of sophisticated research techniques and tools of which the group therapy field is now slowly availing itself [p. 19].

Bibliographies and analyses of research studies have been compiled by Stock (1964), House (1967), Campbell and Dunnette (1968), Durham, Gibb, and Knowles (1967), Buchanan (1965), and others. Undoubtedly there is disagreement about what the findings, taken together, mean. We offer the following generalizations. A Majority of participants (about 60 percent) reports strong to fairly strong positive feelings about their T-group experiences and believe they have been helped to change and improve their behavior. A minority (20 to 30 percent) reports either mild positive or neutral response, and a smaller group (10 percent or less) feels negative about the experience. The question of what happens behaviorally after a T-group experience is a most difficult one to answer. One factor that has baffled research designers is that "desired" behavior outcomes cannot be specified for all participants. Each brings his own set of needs and interests which he pursues in his own way and which he may change or add to in the course of the program. In addition, comparable indices of performance-related behavior change in the work or family setting are extremely difficult to develop. A number of studies indicates that such changes do take place with significant frequency, although not all the studies are sufficiently well designed or controlled to satisfy the rigorous researcher completely.[1]

One point seems fairly clear, however. Laboratory learnings are more likely to persist and to contribute to improvements in performance when they are supported and reinforced in the back-home situation. Employees from firms that support the general norms of laboratory training through organization development programs, or married couples who have both had successful T-group experiences, are most likely the ones who find lasting benefits.

Future trends in laboratory training will probably proceed in the direction of greater linkages between training and application. Laboratories will be augmented by further training experiences which deal with the real people, processes, and problems back home. Skills, norms, and approaches to problem-solving learned in training laboratories will be put into practice through programs at community or organizational levels.

Encounter Groups

The term *encounter group* has been used generically by some writers to refer to any group, regardless of methodology or objectives, that emphasizes intensive interaction, honest communication, and self-revelation. In this sense, all the groups described in this article can be called encounter groups. To use the term in this way, however, is to invite considerable conceptual confusion at a time when clarity is urgently needed. Part of the problem arises from the dearth of definitions about encounter groups. The literature in this area is mainly of an anecdotal nature; there has been no systematic attempt to specify methods, processes, or outcomes.

Burton (1969) states that "encounter groups have been so busy being expressive that they have had little time to look to their theories" (p. ix). After studying many different kinds of encounter groups, Lieberman, Yalom, and Miles (1970, in press) conclude that "our analysis to date strongly suggests that a view of encounter groups as a uniform activity is incorrect. It thus appears that the generic title encounter groups covers a wide range of operations by leaders that lead to many kinds of group experiences, and perhaps to many types of learnings."

Despite the lack of stated theory and the diversity of leader styles, various types of encounter groups seem to share a general view of man that grows out of the existentialist-humanist tradition: "Encounter group practitioners believe that man functions at a small fraction of his potential and that methods which remove blockages and release this potential enable him to integrate at substantially higher levels of functioning" (Lubin & Eddy, 1970). Most encounter group leaders would agree with this statement by Gibb and Gibb (1968):

> People can grow. Man's potential for growth is vast and, as yet, relatively unexplored. In his inner depth—in his *essential* reality—man is capable of giving and receiving warmth, love, and trust. He is moving toward interdependence and confrontation. Growth is a kind of freeing of this inner self of these internal processes—an emergence and fulfillment of an unguessed inner potential. Growth is a process of fulfilling, realizing, emerging, and becoming [p. 101].

Encountering methods are designed to facilitate the freeing of growth processes in a rapid manner and to circumvent defenses. Some of the methods used by various leaders are deepening of sensory awareness, muscular tension and relaxation, guided fantasy, nonverbal games, physical contact, meditation, symbolic movement, etc. Any attempt to list the methods used will of necessity by incomplete because encounter group leaders are continuously trying out new methods.

In general, cognitive activity or conceptualization of experience in encounter groups is devalued. Departures from "experience" generally are viewed as intellectual defensive maneuvers. The major exception is reported by Ellis (1969) who champions both affect and cognition.

The encounter group leader occupies a very central position in the group's activities and experience. The leader's situation bears many resemblances to that of the psychodrama director, alternately suggesting activities, concentrating his and the group's attention on various members (Haigh, 1968), regulating the time spent in various activities, etc.

Encounter groups resemble the mind-expanding (Parloff, 1970) forms of group therapy in the depth and extent of personal change that is sought, the pressure toward total self-disclosure, and the leader's centrality. Many people attend encounter groups expecting to achieve peak experiences (Maslow,

1962); these expectations are aroused by promotional material and lay literature.

Research on the effectiveness of encounter groups is almost totally nonexistent. This lack is due only partly to the newness of the field; until very recently many practitioners took the position that the outcome of encounter groups was self-evident and did not need formal evaluation. Bach (1967, 1968a) reports two studies on his marathon groups, but the reports neither compare the effectiveness of the marathon technique against other techniques nor do they contain comparison with nontreated controls. Also, duration of effect is not studied. Even though data were collected at the end of the group experience, these seem to be process rather than outcome studies. Elsewhere, Bach (1968b) has indicated that he is planning long-term follow-ups on group members. Also, the previously cited study by Lieberman et al. should provide much needed data on the effectiveness of the various encounter group methods.

Professional and Ethical Issues

During its earlier years, the laboratory training field did not encounter many problems related to maintaining standards for trainer preparation and behavior. Summer internship programs followed by co-training assignments provided an avenue of induction for the modest number of newcomers to the field. Most entered with doctorates in applied psychology or education. This situation has changed dramatically. It is no overstatement to assert that the situation regarding standards for training is in complete disarray.

No one knows how many T-groups, encounter groups, marathons, therapy groups for normals, and other intensive group experiences are held weekly in the United States. Certainly the figure runs into hundreds. Some are conducted by qualified scientists who have acquired group training skills in special programs provided by NTL, universities, or other comparable organizations. Others are being conducted by behavioral scientists, including psychiatrists, clinical psychologists, counselors, and others without special training who assume that their therapeutic skills are sufficient. And many are being conducted by individuals whose background is peripheral to or outside behavioral science. In the eyes of many, laboratory training is no longer "owned" by professionals. T-groups and encounter groups—perhaps by slightly different names—are offered by a wide variety of individuals. Undoubtedly some of the "amateur" group trainers are competent and ethical and help provide participants in their groups a worthwhile experience. Others may not be competent and in conducting groups may be satisfying primarily their own needs for control, recognition, affection, etc., rather than the learning needs of participants.

One problem is that techniques of group training, like therapy, appear deceptively simple and easy to reproduce. The T-group trainer remains silent much of the time—injecting only an occasional observation or comment. Furthermore, superficial observation might suggest that the encounter group leader requires only an easily memorized catalogue of behavioral interventions. Cookbook-type manuals of exercises and encounter tapes and films have helped provide group leaders, including the marginally qualified ones, with additional tools.

The NTL Institute has never accredited or certified trainers. In granting Fellow or Associate status to behavioral scientists, it has included them in its "network" of trainers and change agents who are utilized in NTL laboratories and other programs.[2]

Negative Effects of Training

A common criticism of laboratory training is that it is potentially psychologically harmful. Stories about someone who "cracked up" while attending a laboratory program are not uncommon, and the assumption is that the T-group experience was the cause of the problem. A few large sample studies and several anecdotal reports are available. NTL Institute records indicate that of 14,200 individuals who participated in its summer human relations programs and industrial training programs between 1947 and 1968, the experience was stressful enough for 33 (2 percent) to require them to leave the program prior to its completion. Almost all of these individuals had a history of prior disturbances (*NTL Institute News and Reports,* 1969). The YMCA located four individuals who had "negative experiences" out of approximately 1,200 participants in its laboratory programs (.3 percent) (Batchelder & Hardy, 1968). Three of the four, upon follow-up, seem to have gained ultimately from the disruptive experience.

The majority of studies reports the incidence of difficulty at between .2 and .5 percent, although some have higher proportions of negative results reported. Most of these studies deal with only one or two groups, and many with situations that differ from the traditional one- or two-week "stranger" laboratory led by professionals, i.e., they refer to weekend encounter marathons, training programs for psychiatric residents, classroom-type settings, leaderless groups, etc. A summarization of the data seems to indicate that laboratory training should *not* be viewed as a benign and foolproof method. In residential programs run by professionals where purposes are advertised as clearly educational rather than therapeutic, the incidence of difficulty seems quite low. On the other hand, in situations in which there is doubt about the qualifications of the trainer, the expectations of the clients, the intensity and duration of the program, and other situational pressures, there may be reason for caution.

Conclusion

The small group training field finds itself in a curious paradox. Its value system advocates an open, accepting, nonjudgmental approach. Yet it is aware of the need to protect the public and itself by seeing to the competence and appropriateness of training offered. The challenge will be to find ways of setting and maintaining viable standards and of informing the public about them, without establishing exclusive and restrictive systems.

Notes

1. Other sources on the evaluation of laboratory training include Leiberman, M. A., Yalon, I.D. and Miles, M.B. *Encounter groups: first facts.* New York: Basic Books, 1973; Schutz, W. C. Not encounter and certainly not facts: A review of *Encountergroups: first facts* by Lieberman, M. A. *et al.* In Pfeiffer, J. W. and Jones, J. E. (Eds.) *The 1974 annual handbook for group facilitators.* San Diego, Calif.: University Associates, 1974; Cooper, C. L. and Mangham, I. L. (Eds.) *T-groups: A survey of research.* New York: Wiley-Interscience, 1971.

2. An accrediting body, The International Association of Applied Social Scientists, has been organized in response to growing concerns about trainer qualifications and training standards. Group trainers, organization development practitioners and other applied behavioral scientists may seek IAASS certification by undergoing a comprehensive review of their qualifications, experience and ethics. See American Psychological Assn. New professional association formed: Focus: certification and public education. *APA Monitor,* 1971, 2 (11) 7.

References

American Psychiatric Association. *Encounter groups and psychiatry.* Report of Task Force on Recent Developments in the Use of Small Groups. Washington, D.C.: Author, 1970.

Bach, G. R. Marathon group dynamics: II. Dimensions of helpfulness: Therapeutic aggression. *Psychological Reports,* 1967, *20,* 1147-1158.

Bach, G. R. Marathon group dynamics: III. Disjunctive contacts. *Psychological Reports,* 1968, *20,* 1163-1172. (a)

Bach, G. R. Discussion of paper "Accelerated interaction" by Frederick H. Stoller. *International Journal of Group Psychotherapy,* 1968, *18,* 244-249. (b)

Batchelder, R. L., & Hardy, J. M. *Using sensitivity training and the laboratory method: An organizational case study in the development of human resources.* New York: Association Press, 1968.

Benne, K. D. History of the T-group in the laboratory setting. In L. P. Bradford, J. R. Gibb, and K. D. Benne (Eds.), *T-group theory and laboratory method: Innovation in re-education,* New York: Wiley, 1964.

Bennis, W. G., & Slater, P. E. *The temporary society.* New York: Harper and Row, 1968.

Bradford, L. P. Biography of an institution. *Journal of Applied Behavioral Science,* 1967, *3,* 127-143.

Buchanan, P. C. Evaluating the effectiveness of laboratory training in industry. *Explorations in Human Relations Training and Research,* No. 1. Washington, D.D.: National Education Association, 1965.

Bunker, D. R. Individual applications of laboratory training. *Journal of Applied Behavioral Science,* 1965, *1,* 131-148.

Burton, A. (Ed.). *Encounter: The theory and practice of encounter groups.* San Francisco: Jossey-Bass, 1969.

Campbell, J. P., & Dunnette, M. D. Effectiveness of T-group experiences in managerial training and development. *Psychological Bulletin,* 1968, *70,* 73-104.

Durham, L. E., Gibb, J. R., & Knowles, E. S. A bibliography of research: 1947-1967. In *Explorations in applied behavioral science.* Washington, D.C.: NTL Institute, 1967.

Ellis, A. The rational-emotive encounter group. In S. Burton (Ed.), *The theory and practice of encounter groups.* San Francisco: Jossey-Bass, 1969.

Frank, J. D. Training and therapy. In L. P. Bradford et al. (Eds.), *T-group theory and laboratory method.* New York: Wiley, 1964.

Gibb, J. R., & Gibb, L. Leaderless groups: Growth-centered values and potentials. In H. A. Otto and J. Mann (Eds.), *Ways of growth: Approaches to expanding awareness.* New York: Grossman, 1968.

Haigh, G. Two residential basic encounter groups. In H. A. Otto and J. Mann (Eds.), *Ways of growth: Approaches to expanding awareness.* New York: Grossman, 1968.

House, R. J. T-group education and leadership effectiveness: A review of the empirical literature and a critical evaluation. *Personnel Psychology,* 1967, *20,* 1-32.

Lieberman, M. A., Yalom, I. D., & Miles, M. D. The group experience project: A comparison of ten encounter technologies. In L. Blank, G. G. Gottsegen, and M. Gottsegen (Eds.), *Encounter confrontations in self and interpersonal awareness.* New York: Macmillan, 1970, in press.

Lubin, B., & Eddy, W. B. The laboratory training model: Rationale, method and some thoughts for the future. *International Journal of Group Psychotherapy,* 1970, *20* (3), 305-399.

Maslow, A. H. *Toward a psychology of being.* Princeton: Van Nostrand, 1962.

Miles, M. B. On temporary systems. In M. B. Miles (Ed.), *Innovation in education.* New York: Teachers College, Columbia University, 1961.

NTL Institute for Applied Behavioral Science. *Standards for the use of the laboratory method.* Washington, D.C.: Author, 1969.

NTL Institute News and Reports, 1969, *3* (4), 1.

Parloff, M. G. Assessing the effects of headshrinking and mind-expanding. *International Journal of Group Psychotherapy,* 1970, *20,* 14-24.

Rogers, C. R. Interpersonal relationships: Year 2000. *Journal of Applied Behavioral Science,* 1968, *4,* 265-280.

Scheidlinger, S. Current conceptual and methodological issues in group psychotherapy research: Introduction to panel—Part I. *International Journal of Group Psychotherapy,* 1967, *17,* 53-56.

Schein, E. H., & Bennis, W. G. *Personal and organizational change through group methods: The laboratory approach.* New York: Wiley, 1965.

Seashore, C. What is sensitivity training? *NTL Institute News and Reports,* 1968, *2,* 1-2.

Stock, D. A survey of research on T-groups. In L. P. Bradford et al. (Eds.), *T-group theory and laboratory method.* New York: Wiley, 1961.

Weschler, I. R., Massarik, F., & Tannenbaum, R. The self in process: A sensitivity training emphasis. In I. R. Weschler (Ed.), *Issues in training.* (NTL Selected Reading Series.) Washington, D.C.: National Education Association, 1962. Pp. 33-46.

ACTION TRAINING AND RESEARCH
Something Old and Something New*

Neely Gardner

In the more than three decades since action training and research was first articulated, it has been a low profile but highly effective change strategy. Action training and research has been successfully practiced by many agents of change, some of whom one would suspect have employed the process without being aware that they were doing what was called AT and R. Kurt Lewin, the pioneer and conceptualizer of action research is reported to have noted that an infinite number of people since the beginning of time had observed falling objects, but that it took the scientific intentionality of Newton to make the connection of the phenomenon with the concept of gravitation.[1] But the objects had to be falling to be observed. In like manner one could speculate that activities and norms which make action training and research a useful change process evolved out of the restive 20th century environment. The process was occurring and Kurt Lewin was there to observe, to do the conceptualizing, and to develop the theoretical foundations for action research. Action training has emerged in sharper focus since Lewin's time and has become a complementary implementation strategy.

Before describing the nature of AT and R, I think it would be helpful to explore the theoretical framework on which AT and R is predicated. While many people have contributed to the theoretical base, Kurt Lewin and Carl Rogers are, perhaps, the most influential.[2] Lewin's research provided a great

*Reprinted from *Public Administration Review,* Vol. 34, No. 2 (March/April 1974), pp. 106-115.

deal of knowledge about leadership, tension, levels of aspiration, substitution, satiation, and anger, all of which were incorporated in his field theory and his concept of force-field analysis. Carl Rogers, though not involved directly in the early group dynamics or action research formulations, has, with his work on learning and interpersonal growth, heavily influenced the direction that action training and research is taking.

Lewin asked and tried to answer: "What conditions have to be changed to bring about a given result and how can one change these conditions with the means at hand?" Lewin developed the concert of a force-field in which a given condition is the result of a multitude of forces. Some forces are driving forces, some restraining. Conduct, of a group, say, depends on the level at which the conflicting forces reach a state of equilibrium. A more or less static condition (quasi-stationary) may be thought of as a frozen linkage between forces. In this context, processes and habits are but an epiphenomenon, since the objects which should be studied are the forces. "Successful change includes, therefore, three aspects: unfreezing (if necessary) the present level, moving to the new level, and freezing group life at the new level."[3] The field in which a person operates is a psychological as well as a physical field. In Lewin's view behavior is a function of the person and his environment—$B = F(PE)$. The task of explaining behavior becomes identical with finding scientific representation of life space and determining the function which links the behavior to the life space. In examining the life space three important areas should be understood: (a) channeling—the process and path of the delivery of needed goods, services, or psychological resources; (b) gate keepers—the person or persons who influence cognitive structure, motivation (including values, needs, and obstacles); and (c) conflict in the decision situation. To move toward change it is necessary to deal with these three factors of life space through substitutability, availability of alternatives, psychological values, change of potency of the frame of reference, and belongingness.[4]

The change process would, in Lewin's view, be directed to reinforcing vectors supporting change and to neutralizing vectors opposing change.

Carl Rogers, with his propositions concerning personality and behavior, and Lewin, who is called the "practical theorist," generated theories of behavior applied to the person which are mutually reinforcing. Together they give us an estimation as to *why* the AT and R model is practical and they even go some distance toward providing the *how* of AT and R methodology.

Rogers offers a series of propositions in which he suggests the individual lives at the center of a continually changing personal world, and the individual is constantly striving for maintenance and self-enhancement. The person reacts to the environment or field as that person perceives it; therefore the way to understand an individual's behavior is from that individual's frame of reference. The person develops a concept of self and for the most part behaves in a very consistent way with this self. Some experience and the needs of the person have not been symbolized, and since these are not "owned," a state of psychological tension may be created. The more that inconsistent experiences and needs are encountered, and denied to self, the more rigidly will the individual develop a structure to maintain self. It is when there is no threat to the self structure that inconsistent experiences may be perceived, examined, and used as a basis for change. This acceptance can only grow out of the self, and when this acceptance occurs the individual tends to grow out of his introjected self and become more comfortable with a continuing organismic valuing process.[5] The Rogerian notion that human beings will strive for self-enhancement on terms that they understand is most important to the strategies used in action training and research. It involves a process of involvement, and the development of "ownership" of the product of the activity because the individual perceives the proposed activity to be enhancing to the perceived self.

There is no orthodoxy attached to action training and research. As long as the approach that is used is conditional, the particular method, if appropriate, is not of great importance.[6] Action training and research is both descriptive and rational. It is by perceiving the advantage of changing that people will change. By dispelling the tenuous base of existing norms and giving participants a common view based on new data, the environment in which action will take place can be influenced.[7] Lewin's contributions to normative re-education strategies of changing stemmed from his vision of the required relationship between action training and research, and for him this meant collaborative relationships between researchers, educators, and practitioners.[8] *In Action Training and Research the scientist and trainer (interveners) are part of the field to be examined, the problem, and the experimental solution.*

One overriding theme is derived from the Lewinian and Rogerian postulate that people are more likely to change if they participate in exploring the reasons for, and means of, change. Human beings are goal centered and will behave in ways consistent with achieving goals which meet their needs. Participative leadership is effective in setting the stage for creativity, productivity, and innovation. The action training and research process releases the interpersonal energies that are stifled in most authority-bound systems.

An Action Training and Research Approach

Figure 1 is a schematic representation of *one* way to approach action training and research. The model grows out of almost a decade of experience in using the action training and research process as a vehicle for organizational change. It is a somewhat personal model which also has been utilized by some of my colleagues and students, frequently with more success than I have had with it. As you will note from the schematic representation, there are 12 major steps in the process.

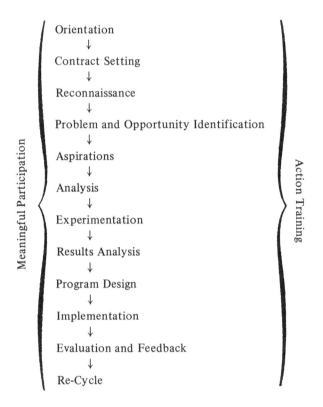

Figure 1 An action training and research process.

During each one of these steps *meaningful participation* is taking place. Also during each step there is an *action training* component for both the intervener and the client so that they may both learn as the process goes forward. I should like to run through each step with you:

Orientation

Malcolm Knowles would, I believe, call this the entry phase. This is the point of beginning, the intervention. It is at this point that we ask questions such as the following:

Are we dealing with management or with some other portion of the organization?

Do the affected persons know the action trainers and researchers are about to go to work in the organization?

Who are the clients?

Do the clients know the values held by the interveners?

To what extent do the clients understand the process that the organization is about to undertake?

What investment of resources will be required?

What are the leadership demands?

Orientation should provide a time for raising and answering questions that help in developing the level of trust between intervener and client. It is also a time for learning about the nature of the field to be examined and the manner in which the activity will be conducted. Trust must start with modeling on the part of the intervener. He is obligated to be open about his values so that he cannot in any way be charged with undertaking manipulative activities.[9] All clients should be aware that AT and R has a participative thrust and that by its very nature it tends to enhance the position of the individual and to diffuse the sources of power. My own bias is toward helping create a situation in which we consciously move toward individual freedom and effectiveness. In my terms effectiveness should be viewed from the perspective of the individual, the organization, and society.

Individual perspective—The work or community situation is effective from the perspective of the individual when it provides for:

Self enhancement through such means as

> Individual freedom
>
> Meaningful activity
>
> Participation
>
> Recognition of worth
>
> Safe and amenable work setting
>
> Needed skill and knowledge
>
> Growth opportunities
>
> Security

Organizational perspective—Effectiveness prevails from an organization perspective when the situation maintains in which the organization provides for:

Survival through

> Adequate resources
>
> Employees who accept the legitimacy of the organization's mission
>
> Supportive clients
>
> Adequate enabling linkages

*Societal perspective–*The process is effective from a societal standpoint when the outcomes contribute to society's
Quality of life which is indicated by:

> Satisfied clients
>
> Timely delivery of goods or services that are useful and economical
>
> Visibility of activities to the wider citizenry
>
> Organizational and participant operation within the range of tolerance of societal norms
>
> The presence of a choice as to whether the goods or services are wanted

After the intervener has shared values with the client and a feeling of trust has at least partially developed, the time has then come to set the contract. Many contracts have been entered into with a lack of understanding as to the nature of the proposed action and its possible consequences. In unsophisticated organizations this can be a great problem because the language used by the behavioral scientist and the language used by the practitioner frequently are not the same. When the orientation has been inadequate, the project is likely to be made more difficult, to say the least. I have a recent experience in which the entire AT and R project has been in continuous jeopardy simply because insufficient time was taken in the orientation. Questions keep recurring which should have been settled in the initial instance. Orientation or entry time is needed whether the intervener is an internal or external agent of change.

Contract Setting

When questions about the AT and R process are asked, answered, and understood, the intervener(s) can move into the contract setting phase. Essentially the contract covers resource commitment, assurance that those involved in the project will "own" their own data, agreement that communication to those affected will take place at each phase of the undertaking, agreement that the intervener will observe carefully the client/trainer confidences, and an expression of willingness on the part of the client to utilize findings to the greatest extent possible.

The contract need not be a written one, although a memorandum of understanding can be useful if drawn up in a spirit of trust. Contracts probably should be thought of as psychological contracts derived through open and tough-minded interaction. If a detail is likely to be troublesome in the future, it is probably important to make very certain that an agreement exists between client and intervener. The practice on the part of the intervener might be to focus on those issues that make the intervener anxious.[10] This practice, if followed, might avoid later stress and conflict as the project proceeds. Knowles has said that the making of the contract is so important to later transactions that the agent of change should not assume the optimistic view but should painstakingly test for agreement.[11]

During the contract setting period the participation is made meaningful to the extent that the intervener is able to model and elicit effective and authentic communication. Training at this stage addresses developing knowledge concerning issue areas and increasing the skill and willingness of clients to confront issues. Reconnaissance or "making an estimate of the situation" is undertaken only after the contract is fully negotiated.[12]

Reconnaissance

An estimate of the situation gains credence when based on data which are relevant to the change project. From these data will emerge an array of perceived opportunities, problems, and possible solutions. Participant researchers are encouraged to enter reconnaissance activities with an attitude of ignorance concerning substantive issues. The researcher will surely bring his own values and perceptions to the task. Perceived problems, opportunities, and possible solutions will also have surfaced during the entry and contract setting periods. Ideally these data are neither accepted nor rejected as they occur, but are "filed away" to be confirmed or denied by later investigation. Trainers can help client-researchers to be aware of their values and pre-conceptions so as to minimize interference with data collection.

Trainers may also help the client group explore impinging forces in the focused and diffused social environment that relate to matters under study. Information collected about environmental factors will be useful at the analysis stage.[13]

It is not absolutely necessary that clients participate in the reconnaissance activity, but from my standpoint it is highly desirable. Clients appear to receive a fair amount of education by being involved in data collection. Action training can make it possible for members of the client group to learn survey and interview methodology as well as other basic research techniques. While the performance of participant group members is somewhat less "professional" than investigation carried on by a trained behavioral scientist, there are advantages to be gained because of the access the participant has to the norms, myths, and vocabularies of the survey universe. So the client-investigator might, under some conditions, obtain better information. In any case the data he gathers educates the collector and the data also assumes a higher level of authenticity for the involved persons. Under fairly benign conditions a reasonable level of trust might be expected to grow out of the intervener-client relationship during collaboration in the investigation. It may be that involving indigenous investigators in data collection is vital to change processes involving developing countries and ghetto communities. Otherwise the data might never be secured; if secured, they might not be valid; if valid, they might not be understood.

There are many ways to collect data: group meetings, observation, interviews, and questionnaires. For a small population, meetings, team-building sessions, or workshops are useful. For larger projects involving communities, corporate structures, or major jurisdictions, a combination of methods may be called for. One excellent approach to reconnaissance grows out of the experience of the National Training and Development Service. Here training and development managers are thoroughly prepared for data gathering by providing an experience in which trainees can learn interpersonal skills. Preparation involves: learning to listen, leveling, group dynamics, team building, organization theory, project planning, change theories, learning theories, and andragogy.

Persons receiving the NTDS training have experienced high success in the conduct of AT and R projects. The trained trainers are prepared to use a wide variety of reconnaissance methods including those applicable to a more complex population.[14]

Within the last four years I have worked with such diverse organizations as the California State Compensation Insurance Fund; University of Minnesota; Advisory Commission on Intergovernmental Relations; the City of Grand Junction, Colorado; Arlington County, Virginia; and the Southern Regional Conference. In these AT and R projects we have collected data through interviews both with and without client assistance. Generally the questions posed have been broad:

What is going well in the organization that should not be changed?

What are the abrasive or problem areas that should be examined?

If you could change the organization with "a stroke of the pen," what would you do?

These questions elicit a great amount of data, some of which brings out commonly shared views, as well as views that are idiosyncratic. Items of interest are recorded immediately after the interviews, usually on 3X5 cards, one item per card. *As nearly as possible investigators record the items in the language of the person being interviewed.* Later, these cards are used during the problem and opportunity identification steps which follow.

Problem and Opportunity Identification

In this AT and R model we have waited a long time before trying to identify problems and opportunities. The first three steps have addressed climate setting, developing understanding of the process, and reconnaissance during which time data are collected. In this model the effort is to develop a "feel for the field."

So the data collected in reconnaissance are classified and tested for (a) agreement and (b) degree of importance. If the problem identification is occurring in a group which "owns" the information, the task is to develop agreement if not consensus. When working with larger populations it is useful to use a questionnaire. I like to use a questionnaire which incorporates nominal, ordinal, and interval "measures." Taking the items on the 3X5 cards developed during reconnaissance, the researchers sort, classify, arrange, and finally consolidate the items to a manageable number. Defining "manageable" may be in the eye of the beholder, since the number of items for questionnaires has ranged from 36 to 151. The researchers retain the original wording provided during the interviews. The selection is always agonizing. In the Arlington County project interviewers contacted 150 persons and developed more than 800 card items. These were consolidated to 56 items for the questionnaire. Each respondent in the study marked each item "Agree" or "Disagree." In addition, respondents indicated the level of importance that should be attached to the item. The choices were: (a) of no importance or not applicable, (b) of minor importance, (c) of average importance, (d) of considerable importance, (e) of great importance. Each choice was assigned a weight of 1 to 5 depending on the degree of perceived importance. This makes it possible to array the items in order of perceived importance and to provide a means of setting priorities for later action steps.

Questionnaires serve a number of useful purposes in the AT and R process. They communicate and educate; they let the respondents know that the data generated are being used; they help action researchers sort out and dispel (a) pluralistic ignorance and (b) conventional wisdom.

In most of the organizations with which I have worked, the interview has been conducted on a sampling basis, but in the administration of the questionnaires researchers have attempted to obtain a 100 per cent sample, with the achieved sample running about 90 per cent.[15] (In the Grand Junction project it was possible to interview virtually all of the City of Grand Junction employees.) It is my perception that the broader the base of participation in all stages of the process, the more likely is useful change to occur.

With problems and opportunities identified, the AT and R team is ready to move one step further toward change. To do this, the client group needs to agree on objectives.

Aspirations

Often, (a) determining the aspirations, (b) analyzing the data, and (c) determining the desired experimental action takes place in one workshop or training session, although the number of possibilities for interaction are no doubt as great as the trainer's ingenuity. These three phases are largely action training activities. In the Grand Junction study the entire staff of daytime employees participated in the training session. Councilmen and citizens took part in parallel sessions. There have been a large variety of configurations in other AT and R projects in which I have been involved. The process is always constrained by the practicalities of the environment.

As used here, *aspirations* refer to the results people would like to achieve as they begin to solve their problems or exploit their opportunities. One approach that works well is to convert statements taken directly from the questionnaire into *how to* statements. For example a questionnaire statement might read: "Delegate position classification to operating departments." This would be changed to reade: "*How to* bring about delegation of position classification to operating departments?"

In answering the *how to* question, participants come up with a series of *action options,* which represent their range of aspirations.

Analysis

Although any number of analytical methods might be used to examine high-priority action options, there is much to be said for the Lewin-inspired force-field analysis. In the approach I am describing, force-field analyses are developed in a workshop setting. Members of sub-groups list the driving forces (vectors) calculated to assist achieve a plus (+) valence in the force-field and the restraining forces which inhibit change, creating a minus (-) valence. Some of the vectors may require a greater amount of investigation and study. Some constraining forces, for example lack of funds, may be so compelling that attaining the action option might be difficult or even impossible.[16]

Concepts of environments described in the institution building model seem to be helpful to persons constructing force-field schemas.[17] For example: AT and R investigators look for forces in social, political, technological, and economic environments (diffused environment) for plus and minus vectors. They also look at the linkage influences between enablers, competitors, and clients and the prospective change action. If the project were taking place in a developing country, one might look for social forces pertaining to family structure, tribal groups, taboos, class structures, and role identification, among others. In regard to political forces, investigators might examine official and informal leadership in special industrial, religious, tribal, and familial special interest groups. Investigators might also wish to consider the nature of the political decision-making process, how political decisions are communicated, the sanction and reward system, and boundary maintenance mechanisms. In the area of technological forces and events, the AT and R team might look at news media, manufacturing, agriculture, merchandising, health and education for technological improvements, intrusions, and dislocations. In the area of economic forces, the AT and R client-investigators would be encouraged to consider the nature and scope of existing data concerning capital, natural resources, and income. There would also be a focus on available human resources, the nature of existing public and private enterprise, revenue and taxation systems, and development activities underway.[18]

By the end of the workshop session participants should be able to determine what significant action options seem attainable, which ones require further exploration, and which ones must be deferred until the critical constraining vector(s) is neutralized.

Experimentation

When clients agree to undertake a change, they are predicting success. Even though the change action is based on carefully developed data, the experimentation step is a logical safeguard in a process where all action is considered conditional and subject to testing. Changes initiated as action options are undertaken either on a limited "trial" basis, perhaps in the entire ortganization, or for a finite time in smaller segments of the community or jurisdiction. This trial period or limited implementation is intended to give clients an opportunity to assess the desirability of change and to correct unforeseen problems before the change is fully operative. Tentative time-limited experiments may also give participants the chance to deal with any unexpected consequences of the change action.

Clients who have conceptualized the action training and research project are also involved in the implementation and evaluation of the change action. They have participated in opportunity and problem delineation, data collection, assessment of aspiration levels, force-field analysis, and determination of the change action to be undertaken. Through these activities they have had an opportunity to understand and to invest themselves in the program. They are in a position to evaluate how the change action is working for them.

Results Analysis

At the conclusion of the trial period, this model of AT and R calls for an analysis of the results. For the most part the analysis addresses such questions as:

> Are we doing what we said we would do as well as we said we would do it?
>
> What new data do we need?
>
> How do we feel about the change action?
>
> Shall we go ahead with this change action for the next year(s)?
>
> What can we do to change the change that will make it even better?

Generally I like to see the intervener play a low-key part in the results analysis period. At this time he is most useful in training clients to understand and use AT and R methods. The relationship should approach "interdependence." The clients, in my view, should be about ready to "go it alone."

Program Design

Designing the continuing program follows the analysis of the experiment. The major attempt of the intervener during his final design stage is to keep the notion before the client group that its members are developing a "changing" program. The design of the program should reflect this changing process.

Consideration of elements in the force-field and collection of new and more sophisticated data are also factors to be incorporated in program design. New investigations may be conducted by task forces or individual experts provided their data are collected at the request of the client group with the results being shared with them. In this AT and R model expectations are that the "final" changing program design will reflect the experience of the experimental program as well as incorporate new dimensions which result from later and more detailed task group and individual studies.

Program Implementation

There may be no "elegant" way with which to introduce and implement a program. By this stage in the AT and R approach, however, it could be hoped that those affected would know about and would have participated in the decision to implement the change action. This would mean that the AT and R process had gone beyond an executive group or task force and that the participation within the organization had been very broad. They say of the elegant three star restaurant La Pyramide, in Vienne, France, that excellence is assured because "nothing is left to chance." Implementation of a change action deserves no less tenderness. Therefore, the decision to implement probably should be communicated in as many effective ways as is possible. I have seen considerable merit in utilizing the process known as the "risk" approach in disseminating information concerning change actions. The affected persons are brought together and invited to contribute (a) critical comments and (b) suggestions for overcoming problems suggested in the critical comments. It is called a "risk" approach because frequently changes are called for which are necessary or expedient and which ask for redesign or even abandonment of the proposed program. The "risk" process permits people to deal with their anxieties and to get these anxieties out in the open where they can be appropriately processed.[19] I also think that it is useful to take note in a formal or ministerial way of the adoption of the program and of the launching of its implementation. If the process has gone as planned the change action has considerable chance for success. Unfortunately, there is probably no way to foresee all of the consequences of implementation.

Evaluation and Feedback

As you will have noticed in Figure 1, the feedback loop is active in each step of the process we have outlined. Feedback implies some sort of evaluation. Evaluation flows quite naturally from the analytical process. Opportunity exists to enrich the learning and to increase the effectiveness of operations when feedback occurs during and after each AT and R collection step. In using this model we suggest that a constant and automatic feedback system be constituted (when this can be done) to provide for readjustments as the change action operates. But even with an automatic feedback system, there probably needs to be an agreed-upon evaluation date, at which time the change action is seriously and completely reviewed.

So even though evaluation and feedback activity attaches to each step, there appears to be good reason to develop a definitive process which occurs at the end of each cycle. There are a number of arguments which favor a wrap-up type of action. First, the idea of a changing organization suggests that every move is tentative, evolving, and sensitive to new inputs and perceptions. Drawing a psychological contract to review and renew the program at a specific point in time has the possibility, at least, of encouraging re-cycling. Secondly, an evaluation and review which the client-actors have set for a specific time will tend to influence timely accomplishment of stated aspirations expected from the change action. A third argument is that in the present environment no one can be completely certain of the effects of the interaction between the change undertaken and the field within which it takes place. Prudence indicates a constant wariness in this regard. Finally, the sense of involvement as well as the degree of learning that occurs among the client-actors is enhanced by re-involvement in consideration of purpose, process, and task.[20]

Evaluation and feedback may be very meaningful if participants assess the degree to which change action purposes have been accomplished, the effect of the process on the well-being of the total community or organization, the extent to which participants have grown, and the degree to which the process has contributed to the freedom and self-enhancement of involved individuals. With such a useful benediction, client-participants may be helped to a sense of closure which can lead to renewal.

Re-Cycle

In the Lewin pattern, we begin the process again. Starting with the orientation step, the process retraces the AT and R path through the steps of contract, reconnaissance, opportunity and problem identification, aspirations, and analysis. At this point the thrust of the project may be, and hopefully is, quite different from the original project. New action options should develop into innovative and creative change actions based on new data evolving from a changed environment.

The approach detailed in this essay by no means exhausts AT and R methods and strategies. As far back as 1948, Chein, Cook, and Harding described at least four approaches to action research: (a) *diagnostic,* with diagnosis being done by behavioral science specialists; (b) *participant,* with the central idea being that the people who are to take the action will be involved in the research; (c) *empirical,* with observation, recording, and analysis of data; and (d) *experimental,* with controlled research which contributes more to knowledge than to a dynamic action program.[21]

As action research emerges today, it is often a melding of all four methods, but with major emphasis on the "participant" approach. McGill has pointed out, however, that much that has been labeled action research, utilizing the diagnostic empirical and experimental approaches, has tended mostly toward research and away from social and organizational action.[22] It is suggested that the participant model represents the core of AT and R. Whatever "magic" attaches to the process seems to be generated by the involvement of those who will be affected when changes are made.

Recently, AT and R has been receiving renewed attention. The National Training and Development Service since its creation two years ago, has been investing its resources heavily in AT and R as a change strategy. At the 1973 National Conference on Public Administration in Los Angeles at least three program sessions were built around action training and research. Significant projects are underway all over the country, taking place in such diverse spots as Tacoma, South Dakota, Milwaukee, Dallas, and Arlington County, Virginia.

AT and R In Operation

Two examples of AT and R in operation might help the reader gauge the potential of the process:

Example One– In the words of Harvey Rose, here is what happened in Grand Junction, Colorado, after trainers from the NTDS Training and Development Seminar moved in:

Twenty-one men and women—public administrators from around the country—were whipped into an intellectual frenzy by NTDS and released on the unsuspecting town. Hardworking townspeople were queried, 250 valiant city employees were interviewed and examined, seven suspicious councilmen were interrogated, and one frightened city manager waited . . . waited.

The NTDS announced its survey results to manager, council, employees, and news media alike. The employees reorganized their weak representative committee into a vital research and communication tool for labor *and* management. The City Council increased the employee training budget tenfold and instructed that a "team-building" retreat be organized for council members. Further, the City Council, strengthened in its awareness of community needs, funded a new job-finding program through the Chamber of Commerce; initiated $1.5 million worth of new municipal construction, and firmed up its annexation policy—adding almost one-third its land size in only four months.[23]

Example Two—The California State Compensation Insurance Fund has been employing AT and R for the past six years. In this period of time the Fund has eliminated five layers of hierarchy; established a devolved organization which continues to move away from the bureaucratic mode toward the organic; adopted a "budgeting by objectives" or outcome budget process; dedicated itself to a Theory Y, consent model value system; learned to use the inputs of an elected employee council; started coordinating corporate activities through a management council from all district offices and home office projects; invested heavily in employee development activities; and "brought it all together" under a plural executive body which is responsible for policy direction of the Fund. While engaged in these change actions, the organization has also been innovative in new marketing and claims activities.[24]

This long-term action training and research project has been able to incorporate a wide variety of data collecting methods. Two dissertations have been completed and a third one is in progress: (a) Larry Kirkhart's "Organization Development in a Public Agency,"[25] (b) Uclu Dicle's, "Action Research and Administrative Leadership," and still to be completed, (c) Edwin Connerly's "Organizational Democracy." The first two dissertations were incorporated into the main stream of the AT and R effort and have been responsible for profound organizational and operational changes.

Other significant studies conducted in the Fund included: "Role Relations Between the Executive Committee Members and District Managers," "Role Relations Between Home Office Managers and Executive Committee Members," "Role Conflicts of Claims Managers," "Communications Patterns of District Managers," a so-called "Weed-Patch" study on budgeting by objectives, and two significant studies on "Sensing the Environment."[26] All of these studies followed areas of inquiry suggested by revolving change actions in the Fund and all were found to be useful. As an involved consultant, I am convinced that the meaningful nature of Fund participation developed a feeling of ownership around these studies.

At this point in my experience with action training and research I am somewhat hopeful about its use as a strategy of change and tend to agree with Claude Faucheux, the French social psychologist, who says, "In action training and research you not only collect information, but you shape, create, and invent social structures through the participation of people. One cannot say more, action research is bound to be of help."[27]

Notes

1. Alfred Morrow, *The Practical Theorist* (New York: Basic Books, 1958), p. 158.

2. John Collier, while associated with the Bureau of Indian Affairs, 1933-1945, conducted a form of action research, and in a concept paper entitled "United States Indian Administration as a Laboratory of Ethnic Relations," published in *Social Research*, May 1945, pp. 275-76, used the term action research to describe his methodology. Stephen Corey of Columbia Teachers' College also wrote on the use of action research in the field of education. See Stephen M. Corey, *Action Research to Improve School Practices* (New York: Bureau of Publications, Teachers' College, Columbia University, 1953). Although there were many other antecedents to the action training and research process, perhaps the most pervasive influence stems from the theoretical concepts found in the writings of John Dewey.

3. Kurt Lewin, *Field-Theory and Social Science* (New York: Harper and Brothers, 1951), p. 228.

4. *Ibid.*, p. 174-187.

5. Carl Rogers, *Client Centered Therapy* (New York: Houghton-Mifflin, 1951), pp. 483-524.

6. Isador Chein, Stuart W. Cook, and John Harding, "The Field of Action Research," *The American Psychologist*, Vol. 3, No. 43 (1948).

7. Robert Chin and Kenneth Benne, "General Strategies for Effecting Change in Human Systems," in *The Planning of Change*, Warren G. Bennis, Kenneth D. Benne, and Robert Chin (eds.) (New York: Holt, Rinehart, and Winston, Inc., 1969, 2nd ed.), p. 34.

8. *Ibid.*, p. 45

9. Wendel French, "Organization Development Objectives, Assumptions and Strategies," *California Management Review*, Vol. XII, No. 2 (Winter 1969), p. 25.

10. Neely Gardner, *Effective Use of Management Time* (Sacramento: California State Personnel Board, 1963), p. 9.

11. Malcolm Knowles, in a statement made at the National Training and Development Service Seminar, Airlie House, Va., February 1973.

12. Neely Gardner and Michael E. McGill, *Guidelines for the Training of Professional and Technical Personnel in the Administration and Management of Development Functions* (New York: Public Administration Division, Department of Economic and Social Affairs, United Nations, 1970), p. 62.

13. *Ibid.,* pp. 192-207.

14. National Training and Development Service, *Evaluation of the Aspen Training and Development Seminar for Training Managers,* Aspen, Colorado, 1972.

15. National Training and Development Service, *Report to Arlington County NTDS Action Training and Research Group,* March 1973.

16. Kurt Lewin, *Dynamic Theory of Personality* (New York: McGraw-Hill Book Company, Inc., 1931), p. 81.

17. For a recent review of institution building literature see Milton G. Blase, *Institution Building Source Book* (Beverly Hills, Calif.: Sage Publications, Inc., 1973).

18. Neely Gardner and Michael E. McGill, *Guidelines for the Training of Professional and Technical Personnel in the Administration and Management of Development Functions* (New York: Public Administration Division, Department of Economic and Social Affairs, The United Nations, 1970), p. 192-195.

19. Norman R. F. Maier, *Principles of Human Relations* (New York: John Wiley and Sons, Inc., 1952), pp. 62-73.

20. Michael E. McGill and William R. Torbert, *Devolutionary Development: An Alternative Approach to the Problem of Teams* (Dallas: Southern Methodist University, May 1972), p. 13.

21. Isador Chein, Stuart W. Cook, and John Harding, "The Field of Action Research," *The American Psychologist,* Vol. 3, No. 43 (1948), pp. 45-48.

22. Michael E. McGill, *Action Research,* dissertation, University of Southern California, 1971.

23. Harvey Rose, *Career Development Topics,* (Washington, D.C.: International City Management Association, No. 3, March 1973).

24. Neely Gardner, "Subject to Change Without Notice," paper delivered at Miami Conference, American Society for Public Administration, 1970.

25. Larry Kirkhart's dissertation covered an examination of early attempts by the State Fund to move toward a devolved organization. In addition to the contribution made by the research itself, his participation in the program influenced the development of the changing attitude within the organization.

26. Most of the studies mentioned were conducted by groups of graduate students involved in the University of Southern California MPA program.

27. In June 1968 the author had an extensive series of interviews concerning action training and research with Claude Facheaux, who was then a visiting professor at Stanford University and is presently associated with the *Centre de Recherches et D'Etudes en Dynamique Sociale* in Paris.

MARTA
Toward an Effective, Open Giant*

Robert T. Golembiewski and Alan Kiepper

In order to speed their reaction time as well as to induce an attractive quality of life, public agencies are making increasing use of the behavioral sciences. This article illustrates one such application of the "laboratory approach," whose goal was to speed the development of a managerial team and to help build a specific climate for interpersonal and intergroup relationships. The philosophy and techniques illustrated are particularly appropriate in organizations which are change-oriented and whose missions have significant developmental or research features.

Experience at MARTA (Metropolitan Atlanta Rapid Transit Authority) can be instructive to public managers, both those contemplating start-up efforts of their own, as well as those managers interested in specific applications of "organizational humanism" in public agencies.[1] Authorized by a 1971 referendum, MARTA sought to gear up quickly to launch a program whose estimated cost was $1.3 billion, and whose developmental phase was projected to cover the better part of a decade. MARTA thus qualifies as "the biggest game in town," and is in fact the largest regional public project since the early TVA days.

*Reprinted from *Public Administration Review,* Vol. 36 (January 1976) pp. 46-60.

The Force-Field at Start-up

MARTA was born in a context that was both intense and uncertain, with no prospect that things would get easier or more definite. Specifically, the challenges facing MARTA in 1973 reflected many aspects of both opportunity and danger, as well as of "hurry up" and "wait." Illustratively, MARTA more or less simultaneously had to:

> Manage and enlarge an existing bus company, using technologies that are well-established and straightforward, in general.

> Monitor and coordinate the design and construction of 69 miles of rapid-speed rail lines with associated stations, park-and-ride facilities, etc., involving technologies of sometimes-substantial indeterminacy and complexity.

> Develop a broad range of design, development, and operating capabilities as a "strong" central staff, in contrast to a staff with a narrower mission, as is the case at BART.

> Aggressively develop a transit system when funding was highly dependent on grants from federal agencies whose level of appropriations were uncertain.

> Develop fluid working relationships among a senior staff recruited nationwide only over the past few months, none of whom had experience with projects of the scale or pace of the MARTA program, and some of whom no doubt would learn relatively early that MARTA was not their cup of tea.

> Respond constructively to multiple constituencies—as represented by a MARTA Board whose directors were appointed by political bodies from four counties and from the city of Atlanta, with two counties having representation even though local elections there had rejected referenda to authorize a sales tax increment earmarked for MARTA

>> as represented by the entire state legislature, which authorized a local sales tax increment to get MARTA started, as well as a blue-ribbon committee to oversee MARTA operations

>> as represented by federal agencies which were variously regulators and dispensers of grants for mass transportation projects.

> Be open to the broadest range of local inputs as to design features, etc., within the context of the basic plan that was voted on in the referendum.

> Organize so as to effectively design and build a $1.3 billion system by 1978.

> Live within the limits of three awesome facts:

>> the MARTA system would significantly determine major aspects of the development of metro-Atlanta for decades, physically, and economically, as well as in terms of the quality of life;

any delay in developing the MARTA system would be costly, with as much as $250,000 per day in additional system costs attributable to inflation alone, not to mention the growing economic and psychologic costs of moving more people and more things with less dispatch; and

MARTA had neither taxing power nor the right of eminent domain; only the state legislature could authorize taxes, and only the several local governments could condemn property needed by MARTA

Toward an Organic Managerial System

Overall, the MARTA force-field patently was not congenial to a "standard operating procedure" approach. Considerable expenditure of socio-emotional energy at start-up thus was expended to help prepare MARTA officials to cope with certain uncertainty and permanent temporariness. The guiding model was an organic one, of MARTA as a dynamic and evolving organization with which its members and several publics could identify as an open and effective managerial system. There was no practical alternative, given that at least seven stages were envisioned in MARTA's development over a decade, beginning with the late-1972 appointment of its general manager. These stages are as follows:

Immediately, MARTA would operate and radically expand an already-extensive set of autobus routes.

As soon as possible, MARTA must develop its unique style and character, reflected not only in staff, policies, and procedures, but also in the way MARTA business was conducted.

Over its first two years, MARTA would develop detailed designs of its integrated rail/bus system, evaluate any additions to the basic referendum plan, etc.

In its second year, MARTA would get heavily into real-estate acquisition, relocation of families and businesses, and possibly even into construction for such relocation.

Within three years MARTA would transition to an emphasis on overseeing massive construction projects.

Within six to eight years MARTA would begin an equipment-testing phase.

Shortly thereafter, MARTA would have to develop into an integrated operating system of rail and bus transit.

In short, there would have to be several MARTAs, whose development would be compressed in a brief time frame. The smoothness of the unavoidable transitions would significantly influence the project's successful completion.

To help prepare for these necessary transitional shocks, learning designs

Coercive-Compromise System	Collaborative-Consensual System
Superordinate power is used to control behavior reinforced by suitable rewards and punishments.	Control is achieved through agreement on goals, reinforced by continuous feedback about results.
Emphasis on leadership by authoritarian control of the compliant and weak, obeisance to more powerful, and compromise when contenders are equal in power.	Emphasis on leadership by direct confrontation of differences and working through of any conflicts.
Disguising or suppression of real feelings or reactions, especially when they refer to powerful figures.	Public sharing of real feelings, reactions.
Obedience to the attempts of superiors to influence.	Openness to the attempts to exert influence by those who have requisite competence or information.
Authority/obedience is relied on to cement organization relationships.	Mutual confidence and trust are used to cement organization relationships.
Structure is power-based and hierarchy oriented.	Structure is task-based and solution-oriented.
Individual responsibility.	Shared responsibility.
One-to-one relationships between superior and subordinates.	Multiple-group memberships with peers, superiors, and subordinates.
Structure is based on bureaucratic model and is intendedly stable over time.	Structure emerges out of problems faced as well as out of developing consensus among members and is intendedly temporary or at least changeable.

Figure 1 Dominant characteristics of two opposed ideal managerial systems. Based on Herbert Shepard, "Changing Interpersonal and Intergroup Relationships in Organizations," in James G. March (ed.), *Handbook of Organizations* (Chicago: Rand McNally & Co., 1965), pp. 1128-31.

based on the "laboratory approach to organization development"[2] were used to accelerate the development of the MARTA managerial team, as well as to influence the style in which that team would conduct its public business. Broadly, the goal had aspects of both avoidance and approach. As much as possible, the start-up goal sought (1) to avoid the closedness and ponderousness of large-scale bureaucratic programs which tend to be hierarchy-serving and emphasize stability, and (2) to approach the openness and agile pro-activeness of an organic system which is oriented toward problem-solving and emphasizes timely change of complex, temporary systems.

Figure 1 provides substantial illustrative detail about what is to be avoided and that which is to be approached. The anti-goal was a "coercive compromise" system of management, and the thrust was toward enhancing the "collaborative-consensual" features of the MARTA managerial team.

Movement in MARTA toward the collaborative-consensual system of management was seen as requiring a long-term effort, the success of which was dependent upon behavior consistent with five basic ethical orientations characteristic of the "laboratory approach to organization development and change." These orientations could not only be "espoused," in Argyris' terms; they also had to be "operating" guides for behavior. Briefly, the five orientations require:[3]

Deep acceptance of inquiry and experimentation as the norm in relationships with others. "It is what we don't know that can destroy our relationships" could well serve as a motto. The opposed meta-value is perhaps more common and is reflected in such maxims as: "Familiarity breeds contempt." The difference between these guiding values is profound. The true acceptance of inquiry and experimentation involves a mutual accessibility of persons to one another. Such accessibility also implies a potential vulnerability to each other, as well as a real commitment to the possibility of being influenced by the other. The opposed meta-value legitimates a more distant relationship and, if only in a superficial sense, a safer one.

Such an orientation is no mere humanistic luxury in organizations like MARTA, at least in its early stages of designing and constructing a system which has numerous one-of-a-kind features. An agency with a mass-production mission could well do with far less of this spirit of inquiry and experimentation.

Expanded consciousness and recognition of choice. Patently, inquiry and experimentation would be sterile in the absence of a consciousness of the diversity of choices that exist. The linkages are direct: an expanded consciousness or awareness generates wider choices; choice permits experimentation that could lead to change or more informed decisions; and freely made choice also helps assure that the individual will own the change or decision rather than (at best) accept its imposition.

These subtle processes were seen as essential in MARTA. To suggest the point by contrast, many management teams have too narrow a view of the choices open to them, based on faulty feedback and disclosure processes. They can generate decisions that have to be constantly policed, enforced, or even continually redecided because of low commitment to them by the very decision makers who superficially acquiesced in them.[4] This implies a human tragedy, and only trouble for projects like MARTA.

Collaborative concept of authority. This is meant in two senses. In laboratory learning situations, first, the role of the participant is a far more influential one than in traditional learning situations. Second, laboratory learning situations provide an experience with collaborative authority relations that can later be approached in the "real world." Even though extreme forms of mutual influence may be seldom applicable outside of designated learning situations, more or less extensive sharing in power and authority is usually possible and is often necessary.

Experimentation with collaborative authority is no mere curiosity. Complex projects typically require substantial and subtle sharing of power and influence by wide ranges of contributors at many levels of organization. The goal is that the problem and who has the competence to deal with it will be major determinants of who seeks to influence, and whose attempts will be accepted.

"Collaborative authority" has a pleasant sound to many nowadays, but it raises a variously serious potential contradiction. In this case, for example, the general manager of MARTA stressed his *personal* responsibility for seeing that his general preference for collaborative authority did in fact work. But he also might sometimes act unilaterally—even against the consensus of those reporting to him—for various reasons, including the failure of collaborative efforts to bear timely fruit. The balance is clearly a delicate one, with intent being likely to differ from performance and with definitions of "timely" and "collaborative" probably differing in complex ways at various points in time.

Mutual helping relationships in social settings. Helping is seen as perhaps the distinctive human attribute that requires cultivation and development. Relatedly, the social setting—in contrast to a one-on-one setting—is seen as an optimal (perhaps even natural) locus for mutual helping. This world view assumes the classical concept of man as a social animal. In addition, the emphasis acknowledges the extraordinary and perhaps unique capacity of groups to induce massive forces to reinforce learning or change.

Numerous social adhesives reinforce the helping relationships stressed by the laboratory approach. For example, its learning designs tend to generate substantial (even unparalleled) exchanges of warmth, or support, between members. Such exchanges can help cement a community of learners. Similarly, the laboratory approach rests on acceptance of the other person, on what has come to be called "unconditional positive regard." Acceptance does not imply approval, but rather a concern for the person. Relatedly, designs based on the laboratory approach attempt to stress the psychological safety of participants. As two careful students note:

> People must certainly differ greatly in their ability to accept the guarantee of psychological safety. To the extent that the feeling of safety cannot be achieved—and quickly—the prime basic ingredient for this form of learning is absent. Its importance cannot be overemphasized, nor can the difficulty of its being accomplished.[5]

To be sure, much of life in organizations is narrowly self-interested and even destructive, rather than helping. The goal was to encourage greater attention to helping in MARTA than is common in many organizations. More specifically, the dual objective was to test the limits of psychological MARTA safety possible among MARTA managers, as well as to determine whether these limits could be expanded. The practical result is the exchange of minimally distorted communication which is the life-blood of effective managerial action. The main ethical product is a more humanistically oriented workplace.

Authenticity in interpersonal relationships. A final value emphasizes the expression of feelings, as well as the analysis of the behaviors inducing them. The rationale for the meta-value of authenticity has two kinds of roots. First, there are the clearly moral precepts on the theme: "To thine own self be true; thou canst not then be false to any man." Second, authenticity is seen as critical in communication. Failure to be authentic in the sense of "leveling" and "expressive feelings" so as to elicit similar behaviors from others can accumulate so much interpersonal garbage as to overburden interaction and impair rational-technical performance.

Note that being "congruent" or "authentic" is a two-way street, to contrast these notions with the cruel narcissism associated with extreme forms of "doing your own thing." Specifically, Argyris urges thinking of authenticity as an interpersonal phenomenon rather than a personal state of characteristic.[6] He conceives of human relationships as "the source of psychological life and human growth," especially because such relationships are then those in which an individual enhances personal awareness and acceptance of self and others, in ways that permit others to do the same. Consequently, for Argyris, it is no more possible to be authentic independent of others than it is possible to cooperate with yourself.

In MARTA, the costs of inauthenticity could be enormous. For any derivative lack of communication and trust would be reckoned in terms of suspicion or overcaution, delay, and eventually huge costs of lengthening schedules. Witness the related emphasis in NASA on "zero defects" at the same time that the organization gospel was: that mistakes were understandable in complex projects, up to a substantial point; that mistakes could provide valuable learning opportunities; and that in all cases it was intolerable to hide an error, for the consequences could be profoundly serious.

Learning Designs and Some Consequences

This article basically details the early learning designs used in MARTA to move toward a collaborative-consensual system, and also sketches some of the consequences of those designs over the first year. Three major elements in the learning design can be distinguished:

A. a team-building experience for the general manager and seven aids who comprised the senior staff, a linkage between the first and second tiers of management,

B. an interface experience between the senior staff and the third tier of management, and

C. an interface experience between senior staff and the MARTA Board.

Each design element was the focus of a separate three-day session held at a university center for continuing education, and each element also involved various follow-up activities.

A. Team-Building by Senior Staff

Just as the last member of the senior staff had been recruited, and while others were still settling into new homes and offices, a team-building experience was held. Its thrust is suggested by Figure 2.

Basically, the first learning design encouraged senior staff to acknowledge and deal with the products of their interactions as persons and officials. The senior staff had only a brief interactive past, so there was little unresolved socio-emotional "garbage." The focus was on the present and the future-soon-to-be-present. Team-building at once encourages almost non-stop interaction between participants, and also seems to speed up psychological time. One official reflected both aspects of the impact of team-building designs on time:

> I've learned more in three days about you guys, and more about my place on the senior staff, than I probably would have learned in three weeks back at the office, for sure, or even in three months.

> I also feel like I've been here forever, even though my calendar tells me its only been some 50 hours spread over three days.

There is ample reason to believe that such speeded-up psychological time is particularly well-spent around start-up. Simply, start-up implies a set of issues having a substantial potential for polluting the rational-technical performance of an executive team. Illustratively, these characteristics include:

> Substantial confusion about roles and relationships.

> Fairly clear understanding of immediate goals, but lack of clarity about longer-run operations, which cumulatively induce wicked double-binds: a strong desire to get on with the task, and yet a pervasive concern that precedents may be set which can mean trouble over the long run.

> Fixation on the immediate task, which often means that group maintenance activities will receive inadequate attention and individual needs will be neglected.

> A challenge to team members which will induce superior technical effort, but which may also have serious longer-run consequences for personal or family life and which in·any case probably will generate an intensity in work relationships that requires careful monitoring.

1. Any management group can improve its operations.

2. Such improvement can be critical even for a management group that is well-satisfied with its present performance, as in preparing for unpredictable stress situations.

3. An audit of interpersonal and group processes is an important way of testing for existing effectiveness, as well as of inspiring improvements. Such an audit can:

   — aid in increasing mutual understanding and empathy

   — heighten awareness of interpersonal and group processes, and so generate more realistic and detailed perceptions of "what's going on"

   — help build identification, mutual goodwill, and comradeship borne of a sometimes-intense experience

   — facilitate the development of shared perspectives and frameworks that facilitate communication

   — emphasize the importance of reality-testing based on the fullest possible expression of information, reactions, and feelings

   — build norms encouraging openness, candor, and face-to-face confrontation.

Figure 2   Brief rationale for team-building.

Confronting and Contracting—The team-building design for the senior staff—which was based on a well-known technology for behavioral change[7]— had two basic features: confronting and contracting.

Confronting refers to a complex of attitudes and behavioral skills that are seen as enhancing a management team's rational-technical performance in two basic ways. Thus such attitudes and skills can make members more aware of their socio-emotional processes, as well as more effective in their management.

"Confronting" often has a colorful press, as in versions that advertise "telling it like it is" or "letting it all hang out." As used here, however, confronting is a two-way exchange expressable in terms of four complex emphases:

1. Team members become more aware of their own reactions and feelings, as well as those of other members

2. Team members become more aware of the stimuli inducing particular reactions and feelings in themselves and others

3. Team members accept and maintain a norm which sanctions the expression of the full range of applicable information, reactions, and feelings

    4. Team members develop skills to share their concerns in ways that
        encourage similar expression by other members.

The basic vehicle[8] for focusing on confronting attitudes and behavioral
skills is a simple one based on the development and sharing of 3-dimensional
images. In this case, the general manager prepared three lists in response to these
questions:

    How do you see yourself in relation to the assistant general managers?

    How do you see your assistant general managers?

    How do you believe they see you?

As a group, the AGMs, collaboratively also developed lists in response to three
similar questions. The lists were prepared separately, and then shared. Figure 3
contains the two sets of 3-D images, edited here to clarify points unintelligible
to outsiders.

Extended discussion of the two 3-D images, with the aid of a consultant,
constituted the basic early experience with confronting, and also provided substantial skill-practice with appropriate attitudes and behaviors. Mechanically,
the procedure is simple. The two sets of 3-D images, written on large sheets of
newsprint, are taped to a wall, side-by-side. Participants survey the lists, and are
urged to ask for examples where the meaning of some item is obscure or con-
fusing. The basic ground rule to participants is that they seek to understand the
image, and to acknowledge any feelings of defensiveness or resistance but not
dwell on them. Such discussion and analysis can be both varied and intense, but
it is typically accompanied by periods of explosive laughter and friendly com-
miserating, as in a mutual reduction-of-tension.

Such designs tend to "work" for several reasons. First, basically, participants need such information, discomforting or even initially hurtful though it
may be. The senior staff's compelling concern about "the project" is implied in
their agreement, even enthusiasm, to "build a better team."

Second, participants typically understand that the best—indeed, perhaps
the only—way to raise the probability of receiving such needed information in
the future is to be accepting of the 3-D images in the present. Acceptance does
not necessarily mean agreement, be it noted. "I can understand how you see it
that way," might go such a case of acceptance without necessary agreement,
"but I hope you recognize there are many things about which reasonable people
can and do differ."

Third, confronting with 3-D images is a shared experience that can build
mutual identification and understanding, which is what many participants are
seeking. The design is accepted and valued, consequently, and in a sense made
to work.

Fourth, most individuals are uncomfortable if their verbal or non-verbal

3-D Image Prepared by Assistant General Managers	3-D Image Prepared by General Manager
I. How AGMs See General Manager	I. How General Manager Sees AGMs

I. How AGMs See General Manager

1. Unapproachable (closed door)
2. Not open
3. Dedicated
4. Determined
5. Cool under fire
6. Hard working
7. Priorities (not ordered)
8. Meticulous
9. Procrastinator
10. Too detailed
11. Sensitive
12. Organization above people
13. Tough
14. Poor delegator
15. Aloof
16. Formal
17. Highly structured personality
18. Programmed
19. Too busy
20. Violates chain of command
21. Fails to pinpoint responsibility

I. How General Manager Sees AGMs

1. Reluctant to share concerns and opinions, especially with GM
2. As disregarding opinions of others
3. Reluctant to take initiative
4. Dedicated to MARTA
5. As wanting some "answers" where none exist
6. As frustrated

II. How AGMs See Selves in Relation to GM

1. Insecure
2. Ineffective
3. Frustrated
4. Unable to perform effectively
5. Wasted and unimportant
6. Inhibited
7. Too willing to please

II. How GM Sees Self in Relation to AGMs

1. Spread too thin personally
2. As spending too little time with AGMs as group
3. As emphasizing brush-fires, without breathing room to focus on key issues
4. As too lenient with AGMs as to assignments, deadlines

III. How AGMs Believe GM Sees Them

1. Relies on group (reluctantly)
2. Trusts us, with reservations
3. Does not see us as team
4. Naive (snd sometimes we are!)
5. Sees potential in us
6. As less effective than we should be, and less effective than we can be

III. How GM Believes AGMs See Him

1. As cautious, indecisive
2. Not trusting, due to newness of relationships
3. Expressed lack of trust via deadlines, detailed reviews
4. Busy-busy, not having time for at least some AGMs

Figure 3   3-D Images that facilitated confrontation.

behavior is at some substantial variance with what they really know, believe, or feel. That lack of comfort increases sharply if the person suspects that relevant others are being similarly incongruent. The analysis of 3-D images usually helps to reduce such variance by encouraging a mutual escalation toward openness and owning. Participants typically are much concerned about what the other group or person is writing on their 3-D image in that other room, for example, for they realize that too much varnishing of the truth on their part will be painfully apparent when the 3-D images are compared. The intent is that this greater but still-tentative openness and owning will free for productive use sometimes substantial energies previously needed to repress information shared in the confrontation.

Hence confrontation designs usually leave participants with a sense that barriers are being lowered, and things are "really happening" with less effort. Consider the symbolism in these common reactions to a 3-D image exchange. "Well, that took the cork out of the bottle, and about at the right time," reports one participant. Another participant had this insightful perspective on the exchange of images:

> That's quite a load off my mind, although I didn't quite dare to put down on paper all that concerned me. I'll look for an early opportunity to make some further mileage. It was a good start, and not as tense as I had expected. I guess all of us really wanted to get over the hump of mannerly closedness, but none of us knew how or was willing to risk starting what we all were clearly eager to do. We were off-and-running on the images almost before the instructions were completed.

Fifth, substantial agreement typically exists between pairs of 3-D images, as is the case in Figure 3. This agreement almost always increases the participants' sense of mutual competence and acceptance, by confirming that one person or group shares perceptions with another as well as by signalling that a real process of exchange has been begun. Especially for a managerial team, it is both critical and comforting that its members see some important issues in similar ways, and that they also characterize the same processes in similar terms. Moreover, the resulting mutual enhancement of self-esteem can provide powerful impetus toward, as well as a solid foundation for, future communication and collaboration. In sum, the inevitable areas of major agreement on pairs of 3-D images signal that the confronted other is like the self in significant ways, which can build a sense of identification and empathy. And these, in turn, can encourage further attempts to reach and understand the other in areas where agreement or even awareness does not exist on 3-D images.

Contracting is the vehicle that seeks to assure that the sharing of 3-D images does not merely dissipate into a kind of warm glow that is quickly forgotten. Based on the 3-D images, the general manager and the group of assistant general managers each prepared "shopping lists" directed at the other. The three lists constituted responses to three questions:

1. What should you keep doing about as now?
2. What should you stop doing that you now do?
3. What should you start doing that you do not do now?

Participants were encouraged to be as specific as possible about the behaviors or attitudes in question. Not particularly helpful are such global injunctions: Be smarter!

The three lists become the bases for a complex exchange process. The key generic process follows such a form: If you want me to stop X behavior, are you willing to more of Y which is on my list of behaviors that I would like you to start performing?

The intent of contracting is transparent. The intent is to model a process that can be used back home. More immediately, the goal is to build agreement among participants about a few exchanges for openers, as it were. The process of reaching this agreement often induces forces that can later reinforce any trade-offs that are decided upon in the contracting period. The potential social power implicit in such group decision making has been amply documented by much behavioral research, beginning with such classic experiments as that by Coch and French.[9]

The specific contracts entered into by the MARTA senior staff will not be reported here, but they focused around more substantial freedom of action for the assistant general managers, which was exchanged for several items on GM's "start" list. Overall, senior staff became more aware of how their past experiences in more stable and structured local government administrative situations limited their early and resourceful responses to the novelty and quick-silveredness of the MARTA program.

Tracking Effects of the Design—The effects of the confronting and contracting among the senior staff were judged by a series of semi-structured interviews as well as by periodic administrations of a paper-and-pencil test, the Group Behavior Inventory (GBI).[10] Only the GBI will be discussed here.

The GBI, whose basic dimensions are sketched in Figure 4, proved useful in two basic ways. First, several administrations of the instrument permitted a test of whether the expected consequences of the team building did occur, for specific members of the senior staff as well as for the aggregate. Figure 4 details the effects anticipated as results of a successful team building effort, and also summarizes the actual results, using the GBI dimensions. Note that "short-run effects" compare GBI responses immediately before the team building to responses obtained two weeks later; and "longer-run effects" involved comparisons

Group Behavior Inventory Dimensions	Expected Effects of Team Building	Summaries of Actual Effects	
		Short-Run Effects	Longer-Run Effects
I. *Group Effectiveness.* This dimension describes group effectiveness in solving problems and in formulating policy through a creative, realistic team effort.	I. Increase in effectiveness is expected, but may be slow to build	I. 5/8 participants report increases	Ia. 5/8 report increases
II. *Approach to vs. withdrawal from leader.* At the positive pole of this dimension are groups in which members can establish an unconstrained and comfortable relationship with their leader—the leader is approachable.	II. Increase in approachability is probable, but may be slow to build	II. 6/8 report increases	IIa. 4/8 report increases
III. *Mutual influence.* This dimension describes groups in which members see themselves and others as having influence with other group members and the leader.	III. Substantial increase even in the short-run, which should persist; note that GM may perceive inroads on personal authority and power	III. 6/8 report increases	IIIa. 5/8 report increases
IV. *Personal involvement and participation.* Individuals who want, expect, and achieve active participation in group meetings are described by this dimension.	IV. Substantial increase even in the short-run, which should persist	IV. 7/8 report increases	IVa. 6/8 report increases

V. *Intragroup trust vs. intragroup competitiveness.* At the positive pole, this dimension depicts a group in which the members hold trust and confidence in each other.	V. Increase is expected, but may be slow to build	V. 3/8 report increases Va. 6/8 report increases
VI. *General evaluation of meetings.* This dimension is a measure of a a generalized feeling about the meetings of one's group as good, valuable, strong, pleasant, as contrasted with bad, worthless, weak, unpleasant.	VI. Increase is expected, but may be slow to build	VI. 4/8 report increases VIa. 6/8 report increases

Figure 4 GBI Dimensions, expected effects of team-building design, and summarized actual effects. GBI Dimensions based on Frank Friedlander, "The Impact of Organizational Training Laboratories upon Effectiveness and Interaction of Ongoing Work Groups," *Personnel Psychology*, Vol. 20 (Autumn 1970), p. 295.

of the benchmark GBI scores with an administration of the instrument some seven weeks after the team building began, at which time the effects of the team building become increasingly confounded by the rush of workday activities.

The GBI results are generally consistent with expectations about the effects of a successful team-building experience. Overall, that is, approximately two-thirds of the changes reported by participants are in the expected direction, and seven of the 12 aggregate comparisons achieve usually accepted levels of statistical significance. Note also that these substantial effects, if anything, understate the impact of the team building. That is, the weeks following the initial off-site session were traumatic and difficult ones that severely stressed all members of the senior staff. In addition, benchmark administrations of instruments designed to measure team-building effects often seem to reflect a kind of "rose-colored glasses" effect, either because respondents are truly optimistic, or are cautious in being open, or are simply not fully aware of the variety of magnitude of issues facing them. Post-experience scores thus often will understate actual change when they are compared to such cautious/optimistic/uninformed benchmark scores. Reinforcing this surmise is the general opinion of participants about one year later. One participant noted, to illustrate the dominant and probably universal reaction:

> You didn't promise us a rose-garden, I know. But it was quite a shock to confront an array of issues so early in the game. It violated all my governmental experience, where such confronting was done at greater leisure, and probably not at all. But I'm increasingly glad we did the team building. MARTA cannot afford to let nature take its course. There is too much to be done in a short period to risk getting sand-bagged by hoping that issues will go away if they are neglected long enough.

Second, the GBI results were also used to indicate where follow-on activity might be appropriate for individual participants. To explain, all members of the senior staff identified their completed GBI forms, which were returned to the consultant at his university address. Only aggregate results would be discussed publicly. In the two cases in which senior staff indicated by their GBI responses that the short-run effects of the team building were for them ineffectual or negative, however, the consultant contacted the respondents and sought to verify their "deviant" GBI scores.

The GBI proved sensitive in both cases. In one case, the respondent saw the initial experience as more hopeful than impactful, but certainly not harmful to his relationship with other senior staff. The second respondent reported a significant worsening of his relationships with the GM, over the interval between the first and second GBI administrations. The team-building session reinforced the AGM's perception of this rift, and did nothing to resolve what was to him a one-on-one issue not amenable to discussion in that group setting. Consultant suggested a third-party design[11] to explore these issues, which suggestion the respondent accepted. Subsequently, the two parties got together at an early date to deal with their relationship.

Note that such transactions imply significant ethical issues. In this case, basically, consultant sought to create the sense and reality of his independence in that his commitment was to facilitate MARTA's effectiveness rather than to serve as an agent of the general manager. It is easy to be self-deluding in such matters, of course. Were the subordinates under duress to accept consultant's proposal? It is at least a good sign that one AGM felt free to reject that proposal. And it is the fact that the general manager, the co-author of this paper, still is unaware of the identity of the AGM who advised that consultant's suggestion was not appropriate. Finally, both the GM and the AGM who "dealt with their relationship" perceive the outcomes to have been positive, especially so in the case of the AGM whose performance until then was unsatisfactory to him and the GM because of the growing issues between them. That AGM is now a solid performer on the senior staff, perhaps in part because of the timely suggestion to both executives which was induced by the broader OD design.

B. Two Levels of Interfaces with Department Directors

Approximately one month after the team building among senior staff, another three-day experience sought to concentrate on two sets of interfaces:

1. Between some 25 department directors and the senior staff
2. Between each assistant general manager and the cluster of directors he directly supervised.

Directors and Senior Staff—3-D images were used to explore the interface between the senior staff and the directors. Six sets of images were prepared: one by each of the five clusters of directors reporting to individual AGMs, and one by the senior staff. These were prepared in private, and then publicly shared in a large common meeting.

The sharing of 3-D images was an intense experience, in large part due to several major issues that had been generated in the early days of assembling a work force and of developing personnel policies and procedures. Illustratively, these items were included by one group of directors in their list of perceptions of the senior staff:

Some autocratic elements—dictatorial

Secretiveness—lack of communication

They have a tough job, in a rough environment, and are making good progress

Question competence level of some—admire competence of some

They earn their money.

Examples illustrating these descriptors were emphasized in an extensive public sharing period, and the associated discussion centered around several major substantive issues, mostly issues introduced by the directors.

Contracting took place at two levels. Thus the senior staff agreed to study a long list of issues, many of which were criticisms of newly instituted personnel policies and procedures. Parenthetically, some quick changes in policies and procedures were made soon after; other issues were studied over longer periods, with some changes being made later. This responsiveness no doubt reinforced the impact of this second design element.

Directors and Individual AGMs—Moreover, substantial time also was provided so that each of the five AGMs with directors reporting to them could begin some rudimentary team building in the organization cluster each supervised. Again, mutual 3-D images were developed and shared in each of the five clusters of AGMs-cum-directors. Consistently, also, contracting was encouraged between the several clusters of directors and the individual AGMs to whom each cluster reported. In addition, each cluster was mandated to provide any additional detail about the substantive issues raised in the large public meeting.

Tracking Effects of the Design—The effects of this second-level effort to develop an effective and open system in MARTA were estimated by the two administrations of the Likert (1967) "Profile of Organizational Characteristics,"[12] a simple and useful instrument. The "benchmark" administration was immediately before the organization-building session, and the post-experience administration was approximately two work weeks later. The form of the instrument used contained 18 items.

The profile has several interesting features. First, its several items can be scored along a continuum of 20 equal-appearing intervals, which are differentiated into four major systems of management:

Scores	System Descriptions	
(1-5)	System I	Exploitative-Authoritative
(6-10)	System II	Benevolent-Authoritative
(11-15)	System III	Consultative
(16-20)	System IV	Participative Group

Second, each item is anchored by four brief descriptive statements, one statement for each system. For example, one of the 18 items is: At what level in the organization are decisions formally made? The System I statement is "mostly at the top"; and the System IV statement is "throughout [the organization] but well integrated." Intermediate statements anchor Systems II and III emphasizing "some delegation" and "more delegation," respectively.

Third, the 18 profile items are intended to tap six broad phenomenal areas of organizational relevance. They are: (1) leadership (items 1-3), (2) motivation (items 4-6), (3) communication (items 7-10), (4) decisions (items 11-13), (5) goals (items 14-15), and (6) control (items 16-18).

Fourth, each profile item is scored twice. A now score reflects an estimate of the *existing* level of each item, and an ideal score on each item provides data about the *preference* of the respondent. In addition to providing useful data, the exercise is seen as meaningful for the respondent in a team-building experience. Its goal, simply, is to alert organization members to any gaps between their preferences and the interpersonal and group relationships that actually exist in their organization. This alerting can help motivate early remedial action.

Figure 5 presents data from the directors reporting to one AGM, the criterion for selection being that the design seemed *least* impactful in this case. Overall, a successful experience should move respondents' scores toward System IV, whatever their starting point.

Four points about Figure 5 deserve highlighting. First, existing interpersonal and intergroup relationships fell substantially short of where the directors preferred. See the contrast between ideal scores and the now scores on the benchmark administration of the Likert Profile. A contrast of ideal scores with post-experience now scores gathered some two weeks after the team building supports a similar conclusion, although the gap has been narrowed somewhat.

The pattern is understandable. Most directors had been hired only recently; some had been on the job only a matter of days; and a few had just been hired. These were very early days, indeed, and hectic ones.

Second, the team building seems to have moved interpersonal and group relationships in the direction preferred by the directors, even in the least-impactful case illustrated in Figure 5. No statistical tests were run due to small sample sizes of the directors reporting to each AGM, but the conclusion holds for a variety of approaches to comparing scores. Grossly, 14 of the 18 now mean scores more closely approach the benchmark ideal scores after the training than before. The pattern is similar for "large changes," defined arbitrarily as ±2 points. There are seven such large changes that move closer to the ideal scores after the training than they were before training. Only one large average change moves away from the ideal.

Third, the zigs-and-zags in Figure 5 probably understate the degree of change if anything, for at least three reasons. As was noted, Figure 5 presents data from AGM/directors cluster for which the design was *least* impactful. Moreover, there apparently is a tendency for some respondents to provide benchmark self-reports that reflect the somewhat varnished truth, as they perceive it. Alternatively or even simultaneously, team building can make participants more aware

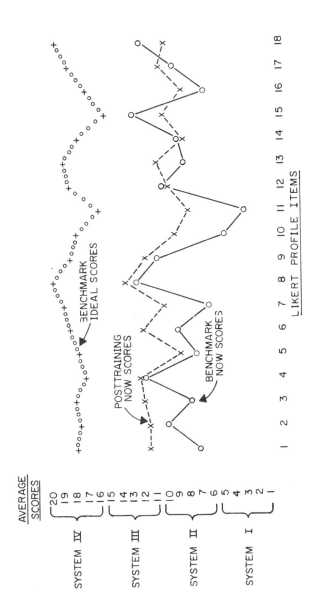

Figure 5 Changes in Likert scores among directors (N = 6) reporting to one assistant general manager.

of existing disagreements or unclarities. Illustratively, the largest deviant change in Figure 5 is for item 15, which solicits information about the degree of resistance to organization goals. This change can be explained in terms of the two possibilities above, or in terms of an actual increase in resistance generated by the team-building design. The last explanation of course, is less credible in this case because of the overall pattern of changes.

C. Linking the Board and the Senior Staff

The final design element in this first pass at institution building involved MARTA's board of directors and the senior staff. The board's members were appointed by elected officials in four counties and the City of Atlanta. The board of nine members—including two blacks—was clearly in transition. Earlier boards had been peopled by macro-prominents with independent power bases and a collective regional orientation. Over time, appointments were made from other tiers of leadership in the five jurisdictions whose political bodies named directors. Consequently, there was over time a growing responsiveness by board members to more "local" needs and aspirations. At the time of this OD design, the board had a quite substantial independence from local politics, but that relative autonomy clearly was being tested and would be substantially reduced as MARTA signed agreements with local governments and otherwise moved toward actual construction.

The board's style was to become increasingly active and involved in MARTA business as staff were selected and policies developed. Hence the especial importance of directly exposing board members to the kind of developmental experiences to which MARTA management had devoted some time and effort, with board knowledge. Moreover, the board had until then uneven but typically brief and sporadic exposure to the MARTA senior staff other than the GM. Board members desired far more contact with AGMs as a prime way of developing first-hand information about those AGMs whose policy recommendations and detailed design and construction proposals would increasingly come before the board for its action as MARTA moved toward construction. The importance of an early and mutual getting-to-know-one-another provided significant motivation for the third design element.

The design of the third stage in institution building had three prime elements, each lasting perhaps two-thirds of a day. Sequentially, the design emphasized:

> Separate meetings for board members and the senior staff, during which data about their respective internal dynamics were fed back by consultants who summarized interview and questionnaire information to serve as stimuli to encourage the two groups to evaluate their ways of relating to one another.

Two integrative experiences, the first relatively gentle and the second far more threatening:

> Board members and the senior staff independently developed verbal statements describing their concepts of MARTA's mission in some detail, which statements became objects for public sharing and comparative discussion.

> Board members and the senior staff independently developed 3-D images, and these became central stimuli for public confronting and contracting activities.

> A work session, in which matters to be publicly presented in the immediate future were discussed by the board and the senior staff in common session.

The flow of the design involving the board is direct, then. The first element stresses internal dynamics; the second encourages limited integration, consistent with the differing roles of the board and the senior staff; and the third seeks to test the usefulness of the outcomes of the first two elements in a more-or-less normal work context. There were major elements of risk and threat in dealing with the board in the confrontive spirit with which the MARTA managers sought to deal with one another. But there seemed no viable alternative to the risk and threat, given the active board role and given the style which earlier design elements had sought to foster among MARTA management.

*Tracking the Effects of the Design—*No major effort was made to measure the effects of the third design element, but two conclusions are safe enough. First, the experience was a far more critical one for the senior staff than for the board, for obvious reasons. Basically, staff was still concerned that its concept of its job might conflict with the board's view of its responsibility; and staff was unclear as to board reaction to its overall performance.

Second, reactions of participants to the design were uniformly positive, and typically emphasized the useful beginning or acceleration of processes that required nurturing over the long run. The responses of the board chairman and vice chairman are typical. They were initially positive, and remained so after nearly a year. One official observed: "Unquestionably, I considered the experience worthwhile. It afforded us an opportunity to know one another better." The other board official had a similar reaction, but stressed the need for determined follow-up after the team-building experience.

> In general, because of the difficulty in getting most people to listen, much less understand, I feel that such sessions are constructive, beneficial, and desirable. . . .

> Specifically, I feel that this particular meeting gave me an opportunity to know our board and staff members better and to more fully appreciate the special relationship between the two groups.

I'd very much like to see these sessions repeated on an annual basis
for two reasons: one, there are almost always personnel changes
each year; and two, it appears that some participants have a tendency
to forget the vital issues discussed and generally agreed upon. . . .

Conclusion

There is a revealing way of summarizing the thrust of the three-design effort toward making MARTA an open and effective giant. First, the goal was to help
build more effective teams at several levels of organization: in the board, on the
senior staff, and among directors reporting to the same AGM. This team building has an *internal* thrust, and seeks to make members of small, formal groups
more cohesive and more aware of their own dynamics. The goal is to encourage
members of these groups to be more willing to confront the differences that will
inevitably exist among themselves, encouragement deriving from the similarities
of experience and identification that are highlighted by successful team building.

Second, each of the three design elements had a major *relational* thrust.
Directly, team building can be pernicious if it merely creates strong bonds of experience, identification, and affection between the members of some group.
Team building in this sense can develop an intense sense of we-ness only at the
expense of highlighting and perhaps manufacturing a they-ness to be distinguished
from, or even opposed to. Hence the conscious effort to build cross walk experiences into the design for a more open and effective MARTA; to utilize any forces
deriving from successful team building to help bridge social and psychological
and hierarchical distance rather than to merely exaggerate that distance which is
variously normal or necessary or convenient.

This relational thrust is vital in MARTA for a very practical reason. Given
its lack of taxing and independent condemnation power, MARTA had no reasonable alternative but getting and staying in the frame of mind that doggedly seeks
the elusive reality of a complex sense of us-ness, not only inside MARTA but
also (perhaps, especially) with various units of government and a wide range of
interests.

Third, the three elements of the design also reflect an *institutional* or contextual thrust, in the form of a set of values which condition both the internal
and relational thrusts distinguished above. In Selznick's terminology, the team-
building experiences and the crosswalks between them sought to infuse MARTA
with a specific set of values. These values imply partial answers to this critical
question: To what social or moral purpose does the team-building and cross-
walking contribute?

This set of values is reflected at several levels. Thus the expectations that
the design would have relatively specific consequences, as measured by the GBI

or Likert's Profile, are at once predictions about what can be encouraged to exist as well as value judgments about the conditions whose existence is desirable in both instrumental and ethical senses. For example, movement toward System IV is desirable in at least three distinct senses. Thus participants overwhelmingly prefer System IV, as the ideal scores in Figure 5 testify, hypothetically because respondents conclude the System IV will meet their needs more than System I. Moreover, evidence seems to indicate that successful large-scale projects in fact require substantial doses of System IV philosophy and relationships.[13] Finally, System IV more closely approaches a variety of ethical guides than does System I.[14]

Care is necessary to avoid overrepresenting the narrative above. Consider the "success" of the efforts above. Several indicators imply that expected things did happen:

> Changes in the Group Behavior Inventory, overall, were not only expected but imply that a range of more effective relationships among senior staff were developed and maintained over time.

> Changes in the Likert Profile, overall, were not only expected but also move in the direction of presumptively greater effectiveness of the organization level reporting to senior staff.

> Interviews with both directors and managers, overall, indicate that most personal definitions of "success" were met.

But this article is also limited in basic ways. Thus it does not report on a "complete OD experiment," but rather a description of the character and some of the consequences of initial steps to develop a team consciousness. Relatedly, the results of the OD interventions are not expressed as *direct* management or administrative results; those results are not related to the bottom-line context of work. Those management or administrative results have to be inferred from statements of how people feel about their work and each other.

So this study reflects a pervasive in-between-ness. Some results imply that OD as a social technology has a range of predictable consequences, and hence is potent. But much still needs to be learned about the fuller range of work-related consequences of OD interventions.

Notes

1. Stephen R. Chitwood and Michael M. Harmon, "New Public Administration, Humanism, and Organization Behavior," *Public Management,* Vol. 53 (November 1971), pp. 13-22.

2. Robert T. Golembiewski, *Renewing Organizations* (Itasca, Ill.: F. E. Peacock, 1972).

3. *Ibid.,* pp. 60-68.

4. For some chilling details from the highest governmental levels, see Irving Janis, *Groupthink* (Boston: Houghton-Mifflin, 1972).

5. John P. Campbell and Marvin D. Dunnette, "Effectiveness of T-Group Experiences in Managerial Training and Development," *Psychological Bulletin,* Vol. 70 (August 1968), pp. 73-104.

6. Chris Argyris, *Interpersonal Competence and Organizational Effectiveness* (Homewood, Ill.: Dorsey Press, 1962), p. 21.

7. For details and supporting rationales, see: Golembiewski, *Renewing Organizations, op. cit.,* esp. pp. 142-155, 327-386, and 455-484; Wendel L. French and Cecil H. Bell, Jr., *Organizational Development* (Englewood Cliffs, N. J.: Prentice-Hall, 1973), esp. pp. 112-146; and Newton Margulies and John Wallace, *Organizational Change* (Glenview, Ill.: Scott, Foresman, 1973), esp. pp. 99-121.

8. As important preliminaries and reinforcers, members of the senior staff spent approximately 40 hours at off-site learning experiences being exposed to exercises/concepts relevant to group dynamics, as well as to appropriate skill practice. Most of this learning time was scheduled in one three-day period. The exercises/concepts dealt with: decision making, interpersonal openness, giving and receiving feedback, functional roles, and interpersonal orientations of senior staff. In addition, a process observer attended approximately 10 worksite meetings of the senior staff during the three-month interval following the three-day session to help reinforce real-time effort consistent with the off-site experiences.

9. Lester Coch and John R. P. French, Jr., "Overcoming Resistance to Change," *Human Relations,* Vol. 1 (December 1948), pp. 512-532.

10. Frank Friedlander, "The Impact of Organizational Training Laboratories upon Effectiveness and Interaction of Ongoing Work Groups," *Personnel Psychology,* Vol. 20 (Autumn 1970), pp. 289-307.

11. Richard E. Walton, *Interpersonal Peacemaking: Confrontations and Third-Party Consultation* (Reading, Mass.: Addison-Wesley, 1969).

12. Rensis Likert, *The Human Organization* (New York: McGraw-Hill, 1967).

13. Leonard R. Sayles and Margaret K. Chandler, *Managing Large Systems* (New York: Harper and Row, 1971); and Harvey M. Sapolsky, *The Polaris System Development* (Cambridge, Mass.: Harvard University Press, 1972).

14. Robert T. Golembiewski, *Men, Management and Morality* (New York: McGraw-Hill, 1965).

TOWARD BUILDING NEW WORK RELATIONSHIPS
An Action Design for a Critical Intervention*

Robert T. Golembiewski, Stokes B. Carrigan, Walter R. Mead,
Robert Munzenrider, and Arthur Blumberg

This study details one example of a broad family of critical interventions. The focus is on the demotion of 13 field sales managers, many of whom were senior employees. The basic intent of the intervention was to help ease the inevitable stresses on the demotees. These stresses were inherent in the diverse personal adaptations required of demotees as they changed jobs, schedules, and routines and as they modified levels of aspiration and, perhaps, self-concept. Stresses were also inherent in the need to develop viable work relations between the demotee and his new manager, who formerly had been a peer.

The intervention had both personal and organizational aspects. For the demoted men themselves, the intent was to ease what was probably a major and even painful emotional experience, as well as economically costly for most. For the organization, the intent was to preserve its valued human resources, even if it involved risking a difficult transition.

The intent of the intervention can also be suggested by two crude equations (Jones, 1968, p. 77). Equation A sketches the grim consequences to be avoided: It proposes that the imaginings or speculations induced by the demo-

*Reproduced by special permission from *The Journal of Applied Behavioral Science.* "Toward Building New Work Relationships: An Action Design for a Critical Intervention," by Robert T. Golembiewski, Walter Mead, Robert Munzenrider, and Arthur Blumberg. Volume 8, Number 2, pp. 135-148. Copyright © NTL Institute 1972.

tions, given the aloneness of the field situation and the manager's helplessness to do anything but resign, would generate immediate increases in anxiety, depression, and hostility. Such effects probably would not serve the individual positively, nor would they help him make necessary adjustments at work. In contrast,

Equation A:

(Imaginings triggered by demotion + relative aloneness + relative helplessness)
 = Initial increases in anxiety, depression, hostility

Equation B proposes to confront the imaginings induced by the demotions with the sharing of resources in a community setting in the hope that this will increase a demotee's sense of mastery over the consequences of his demotion.

Equation B:

(Imaginings triggered by demotion + community + mastery)
 = More effective coping, or reduction in initial anxiety, depression, hostility

Laboratory Approach as *Genus*

The action design for this critical intervention is based on the laboratory approach. Perhaps the term "action design" is dramatic, but we wish to distinguish the design from sensitivity training in several major senses. To illustrate these differences: the design in this case deals with a "very real" problem; the target-concerns are rooted firmly in specific organizational relationships, although the focus may extend beyond the worksite; and the thrust is toward a working resolution of major concerns that have long-run implications, rather than toward dealing with reactions and feelings in a temporary group. Despite significant differences, however, this action design and sensitivity training are viewed as *species* within the *genus* "laboratory approach."

The Demoted Population

As part of a broader reduction-in-force, 13 regional managers from the marketing department of a major firm were given a choice of accepting demotion to senior salesmen or terminating. The demotees were a heterogeneous lot. Selective data suggest the point: the managers ranged in age from 33 to 55; they had been with the company from nine to 24 years; and they had been managers for periods ranging from six months to 17 years. Moreover, although most of the demotees would suffer a major reduction in salary, reductions would range from less than $1,000 to approximately four times that amount.

Several forces-in-tension influenced the decisions of the 13 men. In favor of choosing termination were such factors as the generous separation allowances available to those with seniority. To suggest the countervailing forces: the job market was tight, the company was considered a good employer, and market conditions required cutting deeply—up to the 13 managers, all of whom were satisfactory performers.

All but two of the managers accepted the demotion. As Table 1 shows, they were given an early work-assignment intended to facilitate their making the required adaptations as effectively and quickly as possible. The demotees knew that the proposed "integrative experience," as we came to call the intervention, had been discussed with and approved by several managerial levels in the marketing department. In addition, almost all of the demotees and all of their superiors had long-standing relations of trust with four of the authors of this paper.

Broad Purposes of Design

Five broad goals of the critical intervention can be distinguished. First, the action design was intended to build on the values of the laboratory approach. The company had invested in a major way in an Organization Development program, in which an off-site sensitivity training experience was a major early learning vehicle.[1] The thrust of the initial sensitivity training experience was to help organization members in two ways: in building a specific set of norms or values into their workday relations; and in developing attitudes and behavioral skills appropriate to those norms.[2] Eighteen of the 22 participants—the 11 demotees and their immediate supervisors—had had such a learning experience earlier. The other men had their sensitivity training postponed only by the major reduction-in-force at issue here. Moreover, 19 of the men had been involved in various "team development" activities that attempted to extend the initial off-site training directly into organizational activities.

The challenge posed by the demotions was simply to apply the norms of the laboratory approach in a specific, personally and organizationally meaningful situation.

A second broad purpose was to begin developing integrative linkages at the earliest possible time after the demotion announcements.

A third purpose was to provide a specific action arena in which feelings could be expressed, *and* worked through, if possible. The working symbolism was the cauterization of a wound—not pleasant, but preferable to other possible or probable strategies. The anti-goals, things we wished to avoid, were obsessiveness and postponement of the unavoidable facing-up to new work demands, which would probably loom larger with the passage of time.

The fourth goal was to provide the demotees diverse support at a critical

Table 1

The Timing of the Action Design

Day 1	Day 2	Day 6	Day 7	Day 45
	Decision required	Three major activities	Two major activities	
Thirteen managers informed of choice	Eleven managers accept demotion.	Demotees and superiors respond to MAACL: pretest.	Demotees meet individually with their new superiors.	Demotees and superiors respond to MAACL[a]
Demotion to salesmen Termination		Demotees spend balance of day in discussion.	Demotees and superiors respond to MAACL: short posttest.	Test of persistence of changes: long posttest
If demotion accepted, an early work assignment would involve reporting to a Midwestern city for an "integrative experience" along with their new superiors.		Superiors have briefing meeting.		

[a]Multiple Affect Adjective Check List, which will be discussed shortly.

time. This support was to come from demoted peers, superiors, and the employing organization. The vicious cycle we wished to avoid can be sketched. For example, depression was an expected result of the demotions, especially for the more senior men. The consequences of believing "the organization is against me" can be both subtle and profound, especially for field salesmen. Incoming cues and messages can be misinterpreted and outgoing projections of self can trigger unintended consequences. More broadly, Kiev (1969) traces an unattractive catalog of the manifestations of depression that includes "diminished incentive, interest, morale, and ability to concentrate, feelings of alienation, inability to assume responsibility or to follow a routine, diminished ability for self-expression and self-assertiveness, decreased pride, irritation with interference, feelings of being unappreciated or worthlessness. . . . [The] psychophysiological concomitants of early depression . . . include insomnia, loss of appetite, excessive worrying, indigestion, and decline in energy."

Fifth, the integrative experience was intended to provide early data about possible adaptive difficulties for managers, demotees, and the training staff. Efforts were made to legitimize early contact from both supervisors and demotees if future help were necessary.

Characteristics of the Action Design

A simple learning design was developed to meet these multiple goals. For roughly 50 per cent of the time, demotees worked together; the rest of the time, demotees individually attempted to work through issues of concern with their new supervisors.

The first design component brought the demotees together for discussion of their concerns, problems, and needs. Approximately four hours were devoted to this exploration, with two resource persons available. The announced intent was to help prepare the demotees for the next day's sessions with their individual managers concerning work relations. This action-thrust sought to harness emotional energies to organization purposes rather than to diffuse them through sheer ventilation.

This first design component began with personal reactions to the demotions and then moved toward an emphasis on the problems perceived by demotees as relevant to developing the requisite new work relations. In the later phases, the reactions of the men to the problems expected in their new roles were stressed, as were their concerns about facing these problems. Whenever possible, different ways of coping with the problems were explored. The following list provides some flavor of the main themes dealt with, beginning with personal reactions and moving toward work-related issues:

1. Comparing experiences, especially about the diverse ways in which various relevant organizational policies were applied in their individual cases

2. Encouraging expression of anxiety or hostility about the demotions themselves or associated processes; e.g., their style or timing

3. Surfacing and testing suspicion of management, as in the concern that another personnel purge was imminent

4. Isolating and, as much as possible, working through demotees' concerns about authority dependence, as in the complaint that the demotees did not see themselves being treated as adults, or the feeling that they were men enough to take the demotions without the integrative experience

5. Dealing with a variety of issues in work relations; e.g., explaining the demotions to clients or other salesmen, in order to develop strategies and norms that would reduce the probability of avoiding issues or handling them awkwardly in the field

6. Identifying specific relevant others with whom interaction had been stressful or with whom it might prove to be so, the emphasis being on strategies for handling such interaction

Success varied from case to case, but the intentions of the resource persons were constant: to facilitate expression of feelings and reactions; to help reveal the diversity of the demotees' experiences and coping strategies; and to work toward a successful adaptation to the demands of the new job. In short, the resource persons directed attention to both "process" and "content," to use a convenient distinction. More broadly, resource persons were neither advocates of management actions nor neuters without emotional response to the sometimes tragi-comic dynamics of the demotions; they were, however, committed to helping the demotees face their demotions as clearly and as realistically as possible. Hence the resource persons considered it an open option that some demotees might decide to accept termination after the integrative experience. None of the men did so.

It is not possible to convey the diversity of the products of this first design component, but two themes provide a useful substantive summary. First, almost all demotees emphasized the positive meaning of the integrative experience, whatever its specific results. The design implied to them their value to the organization and also reflected a continuing effort to provide resources that would help them do the job. Only one of the demotees took a different approach: He resented the integrative experience as "hand-holding" and "coddling."

Second, the first component of the learning design emphasized some common elements among the demotees, as well as some differentiating factors. The training staff saw both the commonality and differentiation as being reality-based, and their conscious strategy was to avoid at all costs a strained display of ardent but feigned homogeneity or good fellowship among the demotees.

The elements of commonality that emerged in discussion among the demotees were expected ones. They included: the impact of demotion on the self; experiences with important referents, such as wives, colleagues, or salesmen from other firms; and concerns about taking on the salesman's job, "picking up the bag again" to cover a sales territory, participating in sales meetings, and so on.

The differentiating elements were harder for the men to identify openly, but they were no less clearly reality-based. For example, the demotees included both long-service employees and recent managerial appointees. On balance, the younger men could reasonably be expected to feel more optimism about being repromoted. The future for the longer-service men was far less bright, realistically, and they generally, if sometimes grudgingly, acknowledged the point. Relatedly, some men professed shock at being confronted with the choice of demotion or termination. Others maintained they had more or less expected some action, because of falling demand in the industry, or performance problems, or both. A few even expressed pleasure that the action was not so severe for them as it had been for many others affected by the major reduction-in-force.

The second component of the integrative experience extended demotee concerns into action by developing new working relations between the managers and their new subordinates in two ways. First, the managers met for some two hours to discuss the design for the next day and their role in it. The basic thrust was to empathize with how the demotees felt and to channel those feelings toward making the most successful adaptation possible.

Second, the demotees spent approximately three hours with their managers in one-to-one situations. The resource persons sat in on the dyads, as time permitted. The major concerns in the dyads were:

1. Building early supervisory relations, as in mutual pledges to work harmoniously together, which was easy enough in some cases (some demotees were able to choose their new manager)

2. Discussion of technical problems, such as going over sales territories

3. Developing strategies by which the manager and man could be mutually helpful, as in discussing ways to moderate the formation of cliques, which the demotions might encourage

4. Isolating likely problems and cementing a contract to agree to meet any such problems rapidly and mutually

Some dyads concentrated on one of these concerns; others attended to several.

Measuring Instrument

The effects of the action design were judged by changes in the Multiple Affect Adjective Check List (MAACL) developed by Zuckerman and Lubin (1965). MAACL is a brief instrument for tapping the psychological aspects of emotion; it conceives of affect, not as a trait, but as a state. That is, a time referent is specified for the respondent, who reacts as he feels "today" or "now," rather than "generally" or "occasionally." The researchers explain that the MAACL—

> was designed to fill the need for a self-administered test which would provide valid measures of three of the clinically relevant negative affects: anxiety, depression, and hostility. No attempt was made to measure positive affects, but some of the evidence indicates that the scales are bipolar, and that low scores on the full scales will indicate states of positive affect (Zuckerman and Lubin, 1965, p. 3).

Its authors characterize MAACL as "in a research phase and . . . not yet recommended for routine applied use"; however, accumulating evidence suggests its value.

The expectations in this study were direct. The demotees were expected to have high initial scores on Anxiety, Depression, and Hostility, which a successful intervention would reduce significantly. The managers were expected to have lower initial scores than the demotees and the post-treatment administration of MAACL was not expected to reveal any major score shifts, except perhaps on Anxiety. This expectation was based on the assumption that the managers, who had to develop new relations with former peers, might be somewhat anxious initially about their role in the learning design. This anxiety was expected to fall as the design unfolded, especially as it proved useful.

A third administration of MAACL was carried out by mail, approximately a month after the planned intervention, to obtain data about the persistence of any before/after changes. A potent training intervention could be expected to preserve over time any reductions in anxiety, depression, and hostility induced by the demotions, in the face of the relative isolation and threat of the field situation.

Respondents were given code numbers, which permitted comparison of before/after responses of specific individuals.[3] One of the 22 subjects did not respond to the third administration. Hence the N in several statistical tests reported below varies.

Some Major Results

Six themes emerging from the results deserve spotlighting. First, the demotees reacted strongly to the demotion, but their MAACL scores were not "unusually high." For example, the demotees initially scored higher than the managers on all three MAACL scales, the differences being statistically significant beyond the .005 level. Lubin and Zuckerman (1969, p. 483) tell us that a transformed "score of 70 is generally accepted as the point beyond which scores on a psychometric instrument are considered to be unusually high, as that point represents a score higher than that achieved by 98 per cent of the standardization sample." Only two of the 33 transformed scores for demotees on the three scales reach that level on the initial administration, but an additional eight of those transformed scores reach 60 or above.

Second, the data met all expectations concerning changes in participants in the training intervention. As Table 2 shows, demotees reported statistically significant decreases on all three scales on the second administration of the MAACL. These reductions were at least maintained through the third administration. Indeed, a comparison of the Anxiety scores on administrations 2 and 3 shows a statistically significant reduction following the earlier and major reductions.

These sudden reductions in MAACL scores and their persistence do not seem ephemeral. We do not know how long the initial high level would have been maintained in the absence of the training intervention, however.

Third, the scores of the managers showed a significant change only for Anxiety. That reduction is most easily attributed to a successful intervention,

Table 2

Overall Effects of Intervention on Three MAACL Administrations

	Mean Scale Scores, by Administrations			T Test Values for Paired Administrations		
	1	2	3	1 vs. 2	1 vs. 3	2 vs. 3
Demotees				(N = 11)	(N = 10)	(N = 10)
Anxiety	9.8	7.5	6.5	2.59**	2.74**	2.14*
Depression	17.8	14.8	13.6	2.88***	2.65**	1.09*
Hostility	9.5	7.2	7.2	2.90***	1.98**	0.15*
Managers				(N = 11)	(N = 11)	(N = 11)
Anxiety	6.3	5.3	4.6	1.24*	1.83*	0.83
Depression	9.8	9.5	9.5	0.23	0.38	0
Hostility	5.1	5.3	5.7	−.30	−.87	−.62

*$p < .05$
**$p < 0.25$
***$p < .01$

a building-down from the managers' prior concern about what the integrative experience would demand of the supervisor.

Fourth, a variety of analytical approaches established that the design had quite uniform effects for the broad range of demotees. For example, correlation analysis revealed insignificant associations between changes on the MAACL and four variables describing individual demoted managers: age, years with company, years as regional manager, and loss of salary involved in the demotion. The four individual variables were highly and positively inter-correlated. The inter-correlation matrix contains these five values: .73, .74, .83, .86, and .95, all of which attain at least the .01 level of statistical significance. In only one case in 72, however, does one of these four variables correlate significantly with any of 18 measures of outcome (the nine scores on Anxiety, Depression, and Hostility for each of the three administrations; and the nine change scores—the three MAACL scales compared pre to short post, pre to long post, and short post to long post).

Fifth, the effects on individuals also established the efficacy of the design. Comparison of the first and second MAACL administrations shows that of the 33 comparisons (11 demotees on three MAACL scales) 26 were reductions and three were no-changes in scores. In addition, no demotee had an increased score on more than one scale.

Sixth, post-experience interviews with the demotees and their managers on several levels underscored the value of the design. Many of the details cannot be revealed, since they might identify individuals. But the overall thrust of the interviews is clear. The integrative experience was considered valuable in smoothing what had been predicted to be a very stormy and costly transition. Significantly, but not conclusively, all 11 demotees were still on the job some six months later. Ten were considered to have made the transition "in great shape" or on a "more than adequate" basis, on a 20-point scale running through "adequate," "somewhat inadequate," and "critically inadequate."

Conclusion

The application of a learning design based on the laboratory approach seems, then, to have induced the intended consequences. The intervention seems to have quickly reversed emotional states that can generate consequences troublesome for the individual and the organization, specifically, scores on Anxiety, Depression, and Hostility scales were significantly reduced for a population of demoted field supervisors after the learning experience. These reductions were maintained or augmented in a third administration of the measuring instrument, given long enough after the intervention to test persistence.

The success of the learning design undoubtedly profited from earlier attempts of the host organization to develop norms, attitudes, and behavior consistent with the laboratory approach. Hence this design may not be applicable in organizations as a first-generation effort.

Methodological inelegancies prohibit attributing the effects uniquely to the learning design but the presumptive evidence is strong. For example, the initial reductions cannot easily be attributed to the passage of time. The interval between the first and second MAACL administrations was a brief one, and the demotees had patently developed and sustained high scores on the marker variables in the five or six days intervening between the demotion notices and the integrative experience.

In other senses, however, more substantial reservations must hedge attribution of the observed results to the learning design. For example, did the real magic in this case reside in the process analysis and the values of the laboratory approach? Or would *any* design have had similar effects, given that management really cared?

Only a fool or a very wise man would definitely answer these questions. The issues are incredibly complex. This pilot study at least suggests one promising extension of the laboratory approach into large organizations and urges a comparative analysis of other designs that can be safely added to the kit of the change agent.

Notes

1. For the basic design, see Golembiewski and Blumberg (1969).

2. For a listing and discussion of these values, attitudes, and behavior skills, see Golembiewski (1967).

3. On the third administration, researchers made an assignment decision in one questionable case. Statistically speaking, the assignment affects the results in only trifling ways.

References

Golembiewski, R. The laboratory approach to organization development: Schema of a method. *Public Admn. Rev.,* September 1967, *(27),* 211-220.

Golembiewski, R., & Blumberg, A. Sensitivity training in cousin groups: A confrontation design. *Train. Develpm. J.,* August 1969, 18-23.

Jones, R. M. *Fantasy and feeling in education.* New York: New York Univer. Press, 1968. P. 77.

Kiev, A. Crisis intervention in industry, p. 2. Paper delivered at Annual Meeting, New York State Society of Industrial Medicine, Occupational Psychiatry Group, December 10, 1969

Lubin, B., & Zuckerman, M. Level of emotional arousal in laboratory training. *J. Appl. Behav. Sci.,* 1969, *5* (4), 483.

Zuckerman, M., & Lubin, B. *Manual for the multiple affect adjective check
list.* San Diego, Ca.: Educational and Industrial Testing Service, 1965.

THIRD-PARTY CONSULTATION
Principles and a Case Study of Their Violation

Robert T. Golembiewski and Frances Rauschenberg

Third-party consultation is one kind of social science intervention applicable in organizations which recently has been spun off from the laboratory approach, largely through the efforts of Richard Walton.[1] Basically, the approach calls for a confrontation between two parties in interpersonal conflict, in the presence of a qualified facilitator who seeks to help the parties move toward resolution or control of their differences. Often, the confrontation *à trois* takes place after the consultant has interviewed both parties. Third-party consultations have diverse intended effects, which may be illustrated by the results of the technique's application to the three examples of interpersonal conflict introduced earlier. The results cover the range from resolution of the issues in conflict, to managing or controlling some of the consequences of issues that remained unresolved:[2]

> A recurrent conflict between two managers was based on a misunderstanding of motives with manager being suspicious that the other seeks the former's job. Third-Party consultation convinced the parties that there was a discrepancy between perceived intention and actual intention, and they developed a new understanding which eliminated that discrepancy.

> Two organization members got into a mutually destructive conflict, due to contrasting personal styles and contradictory definitions of their work roles. Third-party consultation permitted the individuals to explore these differences. No changes were made in personal styles, but the emotional conflict was reduced and the definitions of work roles were modified to reduce the contradictions.

Two managers who were directly competing for the same job pursued their mutually exclusive goals with such abandon as to support the cause of Self by undercutting Other. The Third-Party consultation helped the antagonists reach an agreement that outlawed certain destructive tactics, in the sense of an interpersonal treaty of nonagression in certain areas.

The more specific character of third-party consultation can be circumscribed in terms of four elements. *First*, the technique is a confronting one for exploring and clarifying issues in conflict, assessing the nature and magnitude of the needs or forces involved, and highlighting the feelings generated in the two parties. As Walton observes:[3]

> If well managed, the confrontation is a method: for achieving greater understanding of the nature of the basic issues and the strength of the principals' respective interests in these issues; for achieving common diagnostic understanding of the triggering events, tactics and consequences of their conflict and how they tend to proliferate symptomatic issues; for discovering or inventing control possibilities and/ or possible resolutions.

Second, the third party serves two basic functions in his role as helping the pair to confront their conflict in constructive ways. Thus he serves as a process consultant in observing the interacting pair; attempts to reflect a process orientation in his own interventions; and he also seeks to encourage the pair to increasingly respect the same values in their interactions in the learning situation as a prelude to later self-maintenance of their interaction at work. In sum, this means (to use Edgar Schein's definition again) that the consultant attempts to generate "a set of activities . . . which help the client to perceive, understand, and act upon process events which occur in the client's environment."[4] In this role, the consultant may:[5]

> Regulate interaction between pairs, as by terminating a discussion that is repetitive or counterproductive
>
> Suggest items for discussion between the pair
>
> Constantly summarize what he understands has been said or projected nonverbally by the principals, so as to clarify and perhaps even redefine issues, with the goal of increasing the consensus about what all three participants understand as the sense of ongoing communication and, hence, of increasing the credibility and reliability attributed to the communicative signs being exchanged
>
> Encourage feedback between the principals, and between the principals and himself
>
> Make observations about the processes that exist between the pair in conflict, and perhaps himself and them

Diagnose the sources of conflict

Prescribe techniques that may facilitate discussion

Suggest ways to resolve or manage the conflict

In perhaps his most crucial role, the consultant serves to encourage adherence to the values and goals of the laboratory approach. These values relate expecially to openness, willingness to risk interpersonally and to experiment, owning the conflict as well as the emotions associated with it, and acceptance of the responsibility for the consequences of the confrontation. This is not usually as difficult as it appears, because the principals often have had a T-Group experience before they begin a third-party consultation and the two parties identify their consultant with the laboratory approach. In any case, the effects are central to the success of third-party consultation. As one source explains: ". . . because of the nature of the third party's professional identity and the clients' prior experience with persons in the profession, his persence by itself tended to provide emotional support and reinvoke some of the behavioral norms which were instrumental to the conflict confrontation and resolution process."[6]

Third, since interpersonal conflicts tend to be cyclical, a major task of the third-party consultation is to isolate those factors which trigger the conflict as well as those which dampen it. Such information can serve one of two purposes. An elemental strategy for managing conflict would straightforwardly seek to minimize the occurrence of trigger events and to maximize the dampeners. Beyond that, knowledge of the specific triggers and dampeners may spotlight the causal issues which must be dealt with by any real resolution of the conflict.

Fourth, a variety of conditions seems to be necessary for a productive third-party consultation. These conditions may be sampled here briefly, since a fuller treatment with illustrations is conveniently available.[7] The conditions often can be influenced markedly by the consultant. They include:

Mutual and synchronized positive motivation by both principals seems a prerequisite, apparently in that it is a measure of willingness to invest in the confrontation and to own its consequences, both of which no doubt are powerful factors predisposing toward a successful experience.

Some balance in the power of principals in the learning situation seems important, which the consultant can help supply by interventions that help both parties get air time or that draw attention to the domination by one of the pair. E.g., the subordinate in a manager/employee pair might feel that he "will lose every time" in the learning situation as well as outside of it, in the absence of efforts by the consultant to achieve some relative balance of power or influence.

Of critical importance is the appropriate pacing of the two basic phases characteristic of third-party consultation, differentiation and integration.

These may occur several times, especially when a complex string of issues is involved.

    a. *Differentiation* often is time-consuming, as each party develops his own sense of the conflict, elaborates other differences between the two parties, and ventilates feelings and reactions toward the other. The level of tension is likely to be high.

    b. *Integration* often can occur in brief if important episodes, as in stressing the commonalities between the pair, expressing a new respect or even a mutual warmth, and moving toward commonly accepted solutions that manage or resolve the interpersonal conflict.

An intermediate tension level seems useful for learning in third-party confrontations. Low levels of tension imply low motivation; and very high levels of tension apparently bind principals in ways that confound and complicate the learning situation.

Inadequate Research Literature

No ample research literature exists that establishes the unqualified value of third-party consultation, or even the conditions under which success is probable. But the presumptive case is strong, supported as it is by some systematic research and by developing practice in a variety of organizational, institutional, and family settings, as well as by the logic of the laboratory approach developed above. Indeed, even when the goals of a specific third-party consultation are not achieved, real progress may have been made. As Walton concludes:

> The very fact of having vested personal energy in a relationship usually increases respective commitments to improve the relationship, provided there is some small basis for encouragement. Even when there is no emotional reconciliation, if the parties are able to explicitly or implicitly arrive at better coping techniques, they tend to feel more control over their interpersonal environment and less controlled by it.[8]

Whatever the case, Walton points to a number of researchable propositions with which the next developmental stage in third-party consultation must deal.

Perspectives On A Failure*

Despite the lack of explicit research, much experience implies the validity of Walton's prescriptions for effective third-party consultation. An application in a

*Written expressly for this volume by Frances Rauschenberg, a graduate student at the University of Georgia.

5-member work group which obviously failed, for example, provides patent support for Walton's approach. For many purposes, please note, the case below basically involves two overlapping pair-relationships:

A mollifying subordinate and the manager

An emotional subordinate and the manager

The intervenor, in effect, is the third party in both cases.

As part of a larger organization, the work unit was recently established to analyze policy for potential legislation. The unit's four staff members held degrees, some advanced, in the areas of political science and public administration; all had practical work experience. The unit's supervisor held a law degree and had spent two years with a law firm. The unit promised to be a compatible one that would produce quality reports.

Within three months, however, the unit was crippled by interpersonal conflict. Initially, the disagreements centered around different concepts of a satisfactory management style. The unit director took an authoritarian approach to running the division, expecting formal, written progress reports; staff members had anticipated a looser approach to structure—more brainstorming and free discussion. Problems also arose regarding each member's autonomy over projects assigned to his or her supervision. The unit director made it plain he felt he had ultimate say-so over a project; but all staff members felt their suggestions should be given equal weight in the final project.

The Third-Party Intervention

The director of the parent organization made the decision to employ a third-party consultant, at the five-month point in the unit's life. The intervenor was a member of the parent organization, although unknown to any of the staff involved.

Since the unit clearly had polarized into four (the staff) "versus" one (the supervisor), the intervenor held separate introductory meetings to determine what each "side" saw as the greatest problem facing the group. In both meetings, the intervenor acted as a sounding board, sometimes clarifying or restating an idea, but primarily playing the listener.

The first meeting was with the staff. Topics discussed were problems of miscommunication, as well as lack of communication; each member's thwarted expectations of duties and responsibilities; and perceptions of real (compared to ideal) unit organization. The four also discussed some of the degrading and critical personal remarks that were being exchanged between the director and some staff members. Silences—sometimes of several days— resulted. The problems were especially critical for one staff member, Flo. The other three had other

projects which provided them respite and shelter. Flo was on unit work full-
time, and her complaints were strongest. The other three staff sympathized with
her vulnerable position, and encouraged her to confront the supervisor while
noting they had less need to do so themselves. The four staff members worked
well together, shared similar goals for the unit, and all felt isolated from the supervisor.

There is no record of the meeting of the intervenor and the supervisor but
later recollections indicate that discussion centered on the supervisor's frustration
at being isolated and screened from *his* superiors.

The third meeting, held a few days later, was the first opportunity for the
unit to meet *in toto*. The atmosphere was strained. One of the staff members—
more experienced, and with greatest informal status—opened the meeting with
a rambling discourse about the job the unit was trying to accomplish, and how
well it was being done. He referred to recurring problems, but avoided their
personality aspects. This member later revealed his intent was to relieve obvious
tension; other staff members believed it only aggravated the situation. About 45
minutes were taken up in this way, with only minor interventions by either participants or the third-party.

Eventually, the supervisor says to the intervenor: "I am interested in knowing how Flo feels about all this." Everyone turns and looks at her.

Flo shifts uneasily in her chair. Her headache suddenly becomes a full-
blown migraine, it seems. Her thoughts are racing as she weighs alternatives:
Should she say it or not? She looks to the intervenor for encouragement, but he
is studying his cigarette with fascination.

"I must say *something*," she thinks, "or I'll regret it the rest of my life."
When she opens her mouth, she is appalled to hear a squeaky little voice emerge.
She thinks: "Can it be mine? I sound like I am going to cry! *I* know I'm not,
but everyone else looks nervous."

The words pour out. "I'll be honest: I've felt cheated in this job. You
promised some pretty great things—you said you needed someone who could do
more research than secretarial work, but I haven't seen much research yet. Some
days the only thing I come in for is to clip articles out of three newspapers and
maybe file a little. I know the menial things have to be done, too, but it seems
like that's all there is."

"I've tried to be honest about what I thought fell within the demands of
my job. Like not getting coffee for you in the morning—I think you know a lot
more about how you like your coffee than I do. And also about screening your
phone calls—no one else in the entire department has it done. I know you were
used to some of this where you worked before but things here aren't so formal.
I think you should try to fit in more with what's accepted here."

Flo is pretty elated that she's said some of these things. But by now she's
hyperventilating, so she tries a new tack. She starts to feel a little sorry for the

supervisor. "He hasn't said a word in self-defense. I'll take a little of the blame, too. It seems only fair!", she thinks.

"I know I'm stubborn and hard-to-get along with. I've refused to do things I probably should have done," she continues. "I'm feeling like a real rat."

This prompts a flurry of activity by the other staff members, the first real participation in perhaps 15 minutes. They note Flo is too hard on herself; that she has done a good job.

But the conversation soon becomes desultory. The heated invitation to confrontation seems embarrassing to all, including the intervenor. The supervisor pays virtually no attention to the emotional outburst which centered around specific personal problems that Flo has with her supervisor. Did he ask the question only for appearance? The "discussion" soon returns to its earlier orientation, centering mostly on what kinds of information were not being shared between the supervisor with the rest of the staff. The supervisor did not reveal to the staff the problems which he encountered with significant people outside the immediate unit, about which he had complained to the third-party.

The session ends after about two hours, with all members feeling there had been some initial sharing within the group. But the basic problems—vast differences in personal style and work expectations—had been ignored.

The intervenor thanks the members for their participation and indicates his availability to the group in the future, but makes no suggestion of a next meeting date. There are no additional meetings.

A Retrospective Look

This intervention seems a failure, however viewed. According to the unit's members, the "we" and "him" polarized even further after the intervention. One staff member said: "We simply gave up." The director made no further efforts at rapproachment; and the intervenor scheduled no follow-up meetings. Six months later the work unit was abolished.

Why the outcome? What follows is a personal explanation of the failure based upon failure to respect four basic elements identified by Walton as necessary for an effective third-party consultation.

i. The Technique is Confrontation not Exhortation[9]

The intervenor was perceived as more boundary-setting, or even as more hierarchy-serving, than Walton recommends. The meeting's dominant mode from the start was to do better, period. Specifically, the intervenor "helped" the supervisor more than the other four staff members by:

Restating the supervisor's views and feelings, but not those of the staff

Indicating the supervisor's interest in certain issues rather than others, yet failing to bring up the issues that had been mentioned by the four in their group session

Not encouraging or even legitimating the open discussion of the emotions and feelings that were involved

Not dealing with behavior, such as the various mechanisms that triggered conflict

Staff members sensed that confrontation would only be "allowed" to take place on certain levels. The single time a member attempted to move toward more personal issues, the effort was not reinforced. Thereafter, discussion centered on safe topics, such as ways to revise the unit's structure and improving patterns of communication.

ii. Intervenor Should Adopt a Process Orientation[10]

Walton prescribes that the third-party should adopt the same values in his personal style of confrontation that he seeks to engender in the conflictful pair. The intervenor's behavior in this case did not foster a process orientation, nor a confronting mode. Specifically, the intervenor

Did not regulate the group's interaction. He should have actively involved all members of the group instead of allowing two members of the group to dominate discussion, one of them for a 45-minute stretch.

Did not suggest topics and issues for discussion based on the fact-finding of the two introductory meetings, even though it was obvious that two very different perspectives of the unit's problems existed.

Did not attempt to deal with the conflict source, as perceived and described by staff members.

Did not "process" the "emotional outburst."

Did not reveal, or get the supervisor to reveal, that part of the supervisor's authoritarian behavior derived from the controls exercised over the supervisor by his hierarchical superiors.

This catalog implies both missed opportunities and awkward modelling by the third-party. The consultant should have reflected openness, willingness to risk and experiment, and should have encouraged owning behavior and emotions. He played an inactive, listening role. Some of the staff members showed a desire and readiness to share on a personal level, at some anticipated personal risk, but they were rebuffed by the lack of acceptance by the third-party and the supervisor.

iii. Isolate Factors which Trigger/Dampen Conflict[11]

Walton suggests that interpersonal conflict be viewed as a cyclical process. Triggering events may not actually escalate the conflict, but may cause conflictful recycling. Minimizing the events which trigger, and maximizing the issues which have a dampening effect on conflict, can break the cycle.

The intervenor made little effort to deal forthrightly with the basic causes of conflict or to discover the actions which would lead to conflict reduction. More attention was paid to preaching that the unit had to run more smoothly than to seeking elimination of problems which hindered that smoothness.

iv. Create Conditions for Productive Confrontation

Walton also prescribes that at least four elements characterize an effective third-party intervention. They are:

Equal motivation[12]

A balance of power[13]

Pacing that provides due attention to both differentiation and integration of the parties in conflict, basically in that order[14]

An appropriate level of tension[15]

The third-party consultant did not respect such elements, on balance.

First, there was no real test of participant motivation, because no choice was given. Two members probably would not have participated if an option had been available. Some members felt they had too much to lose, especially if they were honest. There were also differences in staff status which accounted for some apprehension.

Second, "balance of power" does not refer to equal status or influence among members, but to the situational balance of participation in the confrontation. The intervenor failed to ensure or even encourage each member's opportunity to participate. Therefore, most members hung back, waiting to be addressed directly. The result was domination by the director and one staff member, whose approach was to de-fuse the conflict from the first moments of the combined meeting. The other three participants grew more defensive and withdrawn as the meeting wore on, and they received no help in situationally counterbalancing the director's formal power.

Third, pacing of the confrontation requires a delicate shifting between differentiation and integration phases. Differentiation emphasizes the differences in the gorup. Integration then should follow, emphasizing the common goals and similarities. Often, there will be several cycles of differentiation ↔ integration in a third-party consultation.

Basically, the combined meeting never got very far into the sources of differentiation, probably because of the very long attempt by one staff member to emphasize integration from the start. The "emotional outburst" about the 45-minute mark probably was heightened by the delay in getting on with it. Moreover, and perhaps because of the unexpected intensity of the outburst, the consultant did not seem to know quite what to do with the emotional aspects of differentiation. In fact, he seemed to ignore and avoid attempts to deal with them. He did not seem at ease dealing with the emotional aspects of differentiation, even seemed to ignore and avoid attempts to deal with them. He did not seem at ease dealing with the personal problems and frustrations that four members had voiced to him privately as the main causes for concern. The four staff members did attempt to balance their "attacks" with integrative interchange. These latter efforts were virtually ignored by the supervisor. The intervenor did not draw attention to the lack of response from the supervisor, nor did he encourage feedback.

Fourth, the tension level in the combined meeting escalated to a point at which it was difficult for any learning to occur. One member recalled getting a migraine headache during the meeting. Yet the intervenor seemed unaware of any unusual tension, and made no efforts to discuss it.

The intervenor in this case was interviewed and his views and feelings are interesting. At his request, he was given only nominal briefing from the parent organization regarding the unit's problems. He stated his preference to observe and listen to each faction as impartially as possible. He then determined the underlying issues and formulated a strategy. He indicated that his confrontation strategy varied with each situation, the primary goal being to remain totally unbiased. He viewed the role of intervenor as a sounding board, and he comments only when he seeks clarification or sees a need to sum up what has been said. He studiously avoids the role of moderator, preferring to be inactive in structuring the discussion.

Consistent with this preferred role, the third-party did not actively encourage the transfer of confrontation values back to the worksite. Also, future dialog was made more difficult because no follow-up meeting was set. The third-party merely mentioned his future availability.

This posture about follow-up meetings seems counter-productive. One meeting on a problem of this scope scarcely scratches the surface. In this case, it only heightened the tension that the members were experiencing. The three staff members felt the single meeting actually had destructive effects. One member initially thought it was constructive, but altered that opinion after learning there would be no follow-up.

Notes

1. Richard E. Walton, "Third Party Roles in Interdepartmental Conflict," *Industrial Relations,* Vol. 7 (October, 1967), pp. 29-43; "International

Confrontation and Basic Third Party Functions: A Case Study, *"Journal of Applied Behavioral Science,* Vol. 4 (July, 1968), pp. 327-44; and *Interpersonal Peacemaking.*
For other behavioral applications of the third-party notion, see Virginia Satir, *Conjoint Family Therapy* (Palo Alto, Cal.: Behavioral Books, 1964); and L. Dave Brown, John D. Aram, and David J. Bachner, "Interorganizational Information Sharing," *Journal of Applied Behavioral Science,* Vol. 10 (December, 1974), esp. PP. 551-54.

2.   Walton, *Interpersonal Peacemaking,* pp. 6, 15-70.

3.   *Interpersonal Peacemaking: Confrontations and Third Party Consultation* (Reading, Mass.: Addison-Wesley Publishing Co., 1969), p. 95. Quoted by permission.

4.   Edgar H. Schein, *Process Consultation* (Reading, Mass.: Addison-Wesley Publishing Co., 1969), p. 9.

5.   Walton, *Interpersonal Peacemaking,* pp. 122-29.

6.   Walton, "Interpersonal Confrontation and Basic Third Party Functions," p. 327.

7.   Walton, *Interpersonal Peacemaking,* pp. 94-115.

8.   *Ibid.,* p. 95.

9.   Walton, *Interpersonal Peacemaking,* pp. 94-105.

10.   *Ibid.,* especially pp. 107-111.

11.   *Ibid.,* especially pp. 73-79.

12.   *Ibid.,* pp. 96-98.

13.   *Ibid.,* pp. 98-101.

14.   *Ibid.,* esp. pp. 105-107.

15.   *Ibid.,* pp. 111-114.

ONE AVENUE FOR EXPRESSING CENTRAL OD VALUES
Some Attitudinal and Behavioral Consequences of a Flexi-Time Installation*

Robert T. Golembiewski, Samuel Yeager, and Rick Hilles†

Despite its general emphasis on interaction and interpersonal relations, typically at higher levels of organization, a mature OD also will have to encompass interventions that are structural and apply throughout organizations. This paper seeks to contribute to that maturity by detailing the character and some of the consequences of one broadly-applicable structural intervention. The intervention is called Flexi-Time, and will be viewed from three perspectives:

As a modest step toward providing greater freedom and self-determination at work, which are central values in OD;

As a simple structural intervention that can generate substantial changes in work relationships, as well as changes in the quality of life for both employees and supervisors, which changes have often been advertised but which seldom have been dominated by research designs that seek to avoid at least the most obvious methodological difficulties

As providing a base of experience and evidence that will encourage similar applications to other kinds of work, at a broad range of organization levels.

*Reprinted from Dennis P. Slevin and Ralph H. Kilmann, editors, *The Management of Organization Design: Research and Methodology* (New York: American Elsevier Publishing Co., 1976) pp.
† The authors acknowledge the significant contribution of Munro Kagno, Promotion Research, Smith Kline Corp.

I. The Flexi-Time Model

Flexible work-hours is simple in concept, but applications must be tailored to specific worksites. The three sections below describe one such tailoring effort.

1. Flexi-Time Model

The specific version of flexible work-hours that evolved from discussions between a Personnel representative (Hilles) and R & D officials was a liberal one, as such programs go. It can be represented as an exhibit:

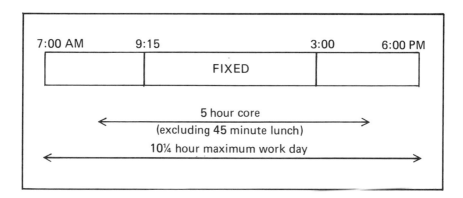

To illustrate the sense of the Flexi-Time program, an individual may start work any time between 7:00 and 9:15 a.m. and stop between 3:00 and 6:00 p.m. These hours are the flexible work hours, which the employee can choose and change from day-to-day. An employee need be at work only during the core hours.

There are some constraints on this personal and variable schedule. Each employee must work a 35-hour week. Because of wage and hour laws, weekly-roll or non-exempt employees may not work more than eight hours in any one day without being paid overtime. Therefore, a weekly-roll employee may work only one five-hour day in a week while accumulating thirty-five hours without getting into an overtime situation. Semi-monthly roll employees—who are salaried—have greater flexibility in this regard. For other details, see Appendix A.

2. Some Anticipated Advantages

Experience in other firms attributes some very real advantages to flexible working hours. Seven advantages seemed most likely in the organization studied.

Although the flexible work hour system does not explicitly provide for more work hours, it may minimize lost work hours. For example, in organizations with fixed working hours employees frequently take time off for personal business, formally or informally. Under flexible work hours time off for personal business is legitimate, but employees tend to take care of personal business on their own time.

Overtime may be reduced. Some experience indicates that flexible hours allow easy adjustments to variable work loads. Therefore, overtime compensation may be reduced.

Sick leave may be reduced. For example, individuals who oversleep can legitimately come to work, as opposed to calling in sick to avoid being recorded as late.

Productivity may increase, qualitatively and quantitatively, although this can only be measured in this case by changes in attitudes *about* productivity in the three R & D units studied here. Some evidence indicates that employees on flexible hours are more inclined to stop work only after a task has been completed, thereby reducing start-up time on the following day and avoiding down-time at the end of the workday. Moreover, flexible work hours permit an employee to plan work hours to more closely coincide with the most productive hours, as in the cases of early or late "starters."

Flexible work hours may provide a better work climate for employees, thereby resulting in improved morale.

Flexible work hours may reduce rush-hour traffic problems.

Flexible hours may provide quieter periods for more concentrated work and thought.

3. Some Potential Disadvantages

To provide some balance, the Flexi-Time intervention implies some important potential problems. Seven such disadvantages seemed of most concern:

Because core hours cover only five hours a day, informal communication such as spontaneous meetings and phone calls might be impaired.

Overtime might increase if a weekly employee's presence is routinely required on days on which salaried employees are working more than eight hours.

The positive impact of flexible hours may be diminished by the negative effects of requiring use of a time clock.

The increased flexibility enjoyed by employees may be perceived by some managers as a threat to their control.

Once employees experience flexible hours, many may not want to return to a fixed-hour system.

The cost of support services may increase.

The flexible work schedule may require increased supervisory time and may divert supervisors from more important tasks.

II. One Avenue for Expressing Central OD Values

The flexi-Time installation, more broadly, also attempted to provide a tangible avenue for expressing central OD values. To explain, the host organization had for several years sponsored OD efforts that sought to establish greater freedom and responsible self-determination at work, involving the top 6 or 7 hierarchical levels of a substantial business enterprise (Carrigan, 1973).

The values underlying such OD experiences (Golembiewski, 1972, esp. pp. 59-202) were often difficult to apply in specific cases, even though they defined the kind of workplace that virtually all employees said they desired. In this sense, the OD program in part generated a new consensus, and in part gave voice to a latent consensus, about values relevant in organization life. These values sought practical avenues for expression, but did not always find them.

Flexi-Time implies some very real attractions in this regard. The point can be illustrated by a brief contrast with "participative management" (PM), relying heavily on the fuller argument developed by Elbing, Gadon, and Gordon (1974). For present purposes, PM can be defined as including a broad range of management systems that seek to provide employees with some influence or control over the conditions or processes of their work. Many PM varieties—group decision-making, various cost-saving plans, programs for mutual influence and communicative openness, etc.—imply significant practical problems. To illustrate:

PM programs are difficult to apply in autocratic organizations, where they are most needed

PM programs can violate long-standing management norms that do not favor participation

PM programs often imply long developmental cycles, with the consequence that the effects of participation may be slow to surface, hence the enthusiasm/effort required from both management and employees may diminish too soon

PM programs imply that employees have uniformly-strong predispositions to "participate," feel safe in doing so, have the requisite skills, and will not be punished for such efforts by their managers or supervisors, which conditions may exist only variably

PM programs often are oversold by zealous managements, in which case they may be seen as having been imposed nonparticipatively and hence may be resisted by employees

PM programs often do not touch all employees, as when they involve representatives or delegates from far larger workforces

Flexi-Time applications may avoid such problems, or at least have a good chance of ameliorating some of them. To be sure, Flexi-Time is narrow in focus; but its effects seem relatively direct, definite, and tangible. Specifically, to suggest some support for the point:

> Flexi-Time is less likely to violate autocratic norms among management or employees, even though some managers may resent the loss of control over evployees involved in flexible hours and may seek to limit employee use of flexible hours

> Flexi-Time effects can be felt very early and on a day-to-day basis, as in less fighting of traffic, whatever and whether long-run benefits accrue

> Flexi-Time requires change only on a day-by-day basis, and only from those employees who desire change from normal work hours

> Flexi-Time does not require any major predisposition "to participate," or the learning of any skills

> Flexi-Time typically affects an entire workforce, or major segments of it

III. Major Features of Research Design

Readers interested in the why and how of the present Flexi-Time application can consult other sources (Golembiewski, Hilles, and Kagno, 1974). Here attention will be given only to a few major features of the research design.

Paramountly, the Flexi-Time installation was carefully limited in three especial senses. Thus the installation was a pilot application only. Moreover, the application might be temporary, and would become permanent only if results over a test-period seemed to justify it. Finally, substantial research would be devoted to the pilot application, so as to provide adequate data for an evaluation of Flexi-Time.

Some other details about the research design will be helpful. First, three organization units at one R & D field site were chosen for study, each representing a different scientific discipline. Two units, henceforth called Experimentals, had Flexi-Time installed. The third unit, the Comparisons, was used as a benchmark against which to compare the trend and magnitude of changes reported by Experimentals.

Second, both "soft" and "hard" data were gathered. Soft data involve changes in attitudes reflected on two questionnaires at three points in time. Basically, the questionnaire items sought evidence about the degree of which Flexi-Time had triggered the several anticipated advantages and disadvantages listed above. The questionnaires were administered on this approximate schedule:

Day 1	Day 15	Day 195	Day 375
Pre-test	Flexi-Time Installation	Short-post	Long-post

Company records also provide a variety of "hard" data, dealing with absenteeism, cost of support services, number of sick days, and time of arrival and departure.

Third, questionnaire data were solicited from occupants of two roles: employees and supervisors. Thus managers at several levels responded to two questionnaire forms, one as employees of the corporation and the other as supervisors of specific sections or units. Non-managers responded to only one form. These forms are referred to below as:

> Employee Form, responded to by both managerial and non-managerial personnel, whose 18 items sought such information: "What is the impact of current work-hours on your personal productivity?" The 18 items are described in Table 2.

> Managerial Form, responded to only by supervisors, whose 12 items sought such information: "What is the productivity of your employees?" The 12 items are described in Table 7.

Evidence indicates that supervisory respondents distinguished the two roles.

Note that all questionnaire items elicit responses on scales with seven equal-appearing intervals whose extreme points were anchored by such descriptions as "high" and "low." The directions of the scales were randomly reversed so as to reduce the probability of response set.

Fourth, questionnaire data were solicited only from individuals who were permanent employees during one or both of two intervals during the 375-day period of observation. In sum, the Ns are:

Total Responses to Two Questionnaire Forms

	Employee Form		Managerial Form	
	Pre-Test and Short-post	Long-post	Pre-test and Short-post	Long-post
Experimental Unit A	15	12	5	5
Experimental Unit B	21	20	6	6
Comparison Unit	21	18	4	4
Totals	57	50	15	15

Fifth, the employees performed jobs with a substantial range of abilities, training, and income. For details, see Appendix B.

IV. Three Major Analytical Tracks

Basically, the data about the effects of the Flexi-Time installation were analyzed in three distinct ways. First, all responses to the Employee Form—from both employees and supervisors—were subjected to factor analysis, and effects of the installation were interpreted in terms of the major dimensions isolated thereby.

Second, item-analysis was employed on responses to the Managerial Form. The small managerial N relative to the number of items does not permit great confidence in factor-analytical results. Hence the straightforward convention of focusing on changes in individual items, even though it requires the caution that the 12 items probably do not represent separate dimensions of reality. At an extreme, indeed, the items might only represent 12 measures of a single dimension. Item analysis, in short, might exaggerate the breadth of actual change in managerial attitudes.

Third, a variety of separate analyses were run on effects of the Flexi-Time installation, as reflected in behavioral data. The preceeding two tracks emphasized self-reports *about* attitudes or behavior, in contrast.

Some details about the factor analysis employed in the first analytical approach are vital. Specifically, all responses* by both managers and employees to the first administration of the Employee Form were factor analyzed. The conventions for assigning items to factors are straightforward. Each item was assigned to one and only one factor. Typically, this meant an item was assigned to that factor on which its loading was greatest, relative to the 6 other loadings. Every item, excluding only # 14, was assigned in this way. Item 14 was assigned to Factor III rather than IV, despite its slightly higher loading on IV. The rationale was that Item 14 contributed more to the columnar loadings on Factor III than IV.

The resulting structure was relatively "clean," as Table 1 reflects. Seven factors accounting from some 70 per cent of the variance were isolated, using a Varimax procedure after rotation with Kaiser Normalization. Specifically

Factors	Eigen Value	Per Cent Variance Accounted for	Cumulative Variance
I	3.03819	16.9%	16.9%
II	2.04730	11.4	28.3
III	1.85770	10.3	38.6
IV	1.74317	9.7	48.3
V	1.54474	8.6	56.8
VI	1.35081	7.5	64.3
VII	1.02889	5.7	70.1

*For a variety of technical reasons, some associated with analyses beyond the present one, N = 50 is the factor analysis. This N corresponds to the total number of subjects who responded to all three administrations of the Employee Form. On the Pre-test, by way of comparison, N = 57.

Table 1
Factor Loadings for 18 Items on Pre-test Responses to Employee Form (N = 50)[a]

Items	I	II	III	IV	V	VI	VII
1	**.84210**	.06753	.14990	-.07471	.08890	.06747	.05300
2	-.03415	-.01301	-.05029	-.02937	.05922	.14054	**-.86743**
3	.19456	**.67595**	-.01736	.05082	-.03688	.50026	.15465
4	-.21246	-.27815	.40254	.22444	**.56652**	-.10976	.10357
5	-.06766	**.77796**	-.01369	-.02846	.11042	-.19872	-.15386
6	.06660	.30360	**.66104**	-.07010	-.09480	.17209	.02401
7	-.13922	**.60892**	.41548	.10532	-.14728	.10434	.41178
8	-.03781	.06181	.19121	.35611	**-.54845**	-.06176	-.53486
9	-.00102	.13660	**.58134**	-.4553	.01582	.27279	-.12311
10	.27615	.03669	-.02109	.02380	-.13058	**.82829**	.00601
11	**.78383**	-.06011	.07574	.03176	-.08009	.25989	-.04358
12	.49286	-.18491	.15438	-.04502	**-.59357**	-.02109	.17877
13	-.01080	-.09462	.29782	.17568	.17471	**.65204**	-.30076
14	-.22068	-.16994	**.45948**	.47687	.01371	.10182	-.01495
15	.30851	.10542	.00100	**-.70532**	.03391	-.22414	.09763
16	.40472	.10246	.03254	.26143	**.64999**	.02665	-.10591
17	.23528	-.14024	**.82834**	.09807	.08534	-.12629	.04189
18	.13418	.21751	-.04994	**.74176**	.19600	-.01376	.03350

[a]The items assigned to each factor are underscored.

The factor analysis does double-duty. On its face, that is, the analysis establishes that the Employee Form elicits data across a substantial phenomenal range. Consistent patterns of changes across that range, or substantial parts there-of—as measured by comparing Pre-test with Short-post and Long-post administrations of the Employee Form—will imply the potency of the Flexi-Time application.

More specifically still, verbal interpretations of the individual items contributing most to the separate factors permit a tentative description of the psychological space tapped by the Employee Form. Specific predictions about expected effects of the Flexi-Time installation on each of these dimensions also can be made.

Table 2 attempts this useful if tentative mapping-cum-predictions. The verbal descriptions fit the item loadings rather comfortably, overall, even as those descriptions seem to cover a broad phenomenal range. Note that the factor descriptions are intended as statements of ideals-to-be-worked-toward. As a glance at Table 1 will establish, the loadings of items 2, 8, 12, and 15 on Factors IV, V, and VII imply the actual situation at pre-test was seen as mixed by respondents. Factor V, for example, contained negative loadings on items 8 and 12, which indicate substantial conflict over scheduling existed with both co-workers and supervisors before Flexi-Time. Similarly, Factor VI interpreted existentially implies difficulties with scheduling. The "expected effects" are based on perhaps-arbitrary but nonetheless real goals of the interveners. Specifically, for Flexi-Time to be successful, it was considered that Factor III—"Flexibility, Personal and Work-Related"—should reflect increases over time. In contrast, increases would be attractive on Factor V—"Unconflictful Worksite"—but maintenance of existing levels was acceptable.

Operationally, an individual's score on each factor of each Employee Form Administration was calculated by adding the reported scale values of each of the items assigned to any factor. For present purposes, all scores are reported as varying in the same direction.

V. Reactions in Role-as-Employee

The reactions of both managers and non-managers in their role as employees to Flexi-Time were substantially positive. Two sources of data establish the point.

1. Responses to Open-Ended Questions

At a global level, responses to open-ended questions soliciting feelings "about current work hour policy and its effect on the way you do your job" were all-but unanimously favorable. Three reactions illustrate the range and flavor of employee responses to Flexi-Time:

Table 2

Factor Descriptions and Component Items as Ideals-to-be Approached, Along with Expected Effects on Each Factor, at Three Points in Time, of Flexi-Time Installation

	Expected Effects of Flexi-Time Installation	
	Short-post vs. Pre-test and Long-post vs. Pre-test	Long-post vs. Short-post
Factor I Participative Worksite with Good Communication	increase, or at least maintain	maintain, or at least do not decrease significantly
Item 01. Substantial participation in decisions re work		
11. Good Quality of communications re work assignments		
Factor II Positive Impact of Work-Hours on Person/Productivity	increase	
Item 03. High satisfaction with work hours		
09. Lessened traffic congestion		
07. Positive Impact of work hours on personnel productivity		
Factor III Flexibility, Personal and Work-Related	increase	maintain, or at least do not decrease significantly
Item 06. Ease of attending to personal business		
09. Substantial flexibility to schedule work		
14. Ease of arranging meetings		
17. Availability of others for "spur of the moment" meetings		

Factor IV.	Reinforced Motivation to Contribute Beyond Standard	increase	maintain, or at least do not decrease significantly
	Item 15. Substantial inclination to work more than standard workweek		
	18. Good quality of support services		
Factor V.	Unconflictful Worksite	increase or at least maintain	maintain, or at least do not decrease significantly
	Item 04. Positive reaction to use of time clock		
	08. Infrequent conflict with co-workers over scheduling		
	12. Infrequent conflict with supervisors		
	16. Good quality of communication re activities in company of personal interest		
Factor VI.	Worksite Attractiveness/Availability of Human Resources	increase, or at least maintain	maintain, or at least do not decrease significantly
	Item 10. Desirability of department as place to work		
	13. Common availability of others when needed		
Factor VII.	Ease of Scheduling Work	increase, or at least maintain	maintain, or at least do not decrease significantly
	Item 02. Ease of scheduling work involving others		

Extremely favorable. It allows much more flexibility in setting up and running reactions—particularly those which involve more than 7 hours, but not overnight. I am much more willing to stay later to work up a reaction, knowing that I can leave early later in the week.

Flexible working hours—a great asset both to employees and the company alike. A very positive effect on morale and productivity.

Although I don't use the flexible hours because of a car pool I am in, I think they are excellent and I hope to use them in the future.

The only criticisms were directed at the time clock, which most saw as a perhaps-necessary evil.

Perhaps even more impressively, 8 of 18 persons from the Comparison unit who provided open-ended responses spontaneously recommended an early Flexi-Time application at their own worksite.

2. Responses to Standard Questionnaire

Responses to the Employee Form also imply that Flexi-Time contributed significantly to improvements in the quality of the work environment. The pattern is not a monolith, and it implies that elements other than Flexi-Time had significant negative effects on the quality of life at work, which were not somehow eliminated by that simple structural intervention. But Flexi-Time still had substantial impact, perhaps even an impressive impact.

Specifically, Table 3 lends support to three broad conclusions, although later fine-tuning will be necessary to pin-down some important specifics about the patterns of attitudinal change. First, Table 3 implies that the impact of Flexi-Time should be reasonably clear in comparisons of attitudinal trends in Experimental vs. Comparisons, since their pre-test attitudinal starting-points are at least similar, and usually favor the Comparisons. That is, not a single statistically significant difference exists on the 7 factors. Moreover, given typical managerial definitions of the desirable on the attitudinal items, the Experimentals had less favorable scores than the Comparisons on 4 of the 7 cases, with one additional tie.

Second, Table 3 also implies that Flexi-Time had a moderate intended impact on all respondents over the first 6 months of its application. Specifically, 4 of the 7 differences on the short-post favor the Experimentals, and two of the intended differences attain statistical significance.

Third, at T = 1 year, Table 3 reports massive changes in attitudes toward work-hour policies and their consequences. That is, 6 of the 7 differences on the Long-post are in the expected direction. Moreover, 4 of these 6 differences attain the .05 level.

Distinguishing the responses of managers and non-managers to the Employee Form seems to require no major qualification of the conclusion that responses of

Table 3

Mean Aggregate Scores, Experimentals (N = 32) vs. All Comparisons (N = 18) on Three Administrations of Employee Form

	Pre-test Scores*			Short-post Test Scores			Long-post Test Scores	
Factors	Experimentals	Comparisons	Factors	Experimentals	Comparisons	Factors	Experimentals	Comparisons
I	9.78	8.50	I	10.25	9.22	I	9.91	9.50
II	11.97	12.00	II	18.19†	13.06†	II	18.97†	13.50†
III	18.25	18.11	III	22.44†	16.39†	III	23.22†	17.44†
IV	9.19	9.33	IV	10.19†	10.33	IV	9.84	10.39
V	19.63	20.56	V	20.34	20.39	V	21.06†	19.44†
VI	10.50	11.17	VI	11.06	11.28	VI	11.09	10.17
VII	5.72	5.72	VII	6.03	5.83	VII	6.34†	5.44†

*The means vary in size due to the variable number of items defining the several factors.
†Indicates pairs of scores that attain or surpass .05 level on t-test, one tailed.

respondents in their role as employee were favorable to Flexi-Time. Over the full observational period of a year, that is, the patterns of change in Tables 4 and 5 are quite similar. Note, however, that Experimental non-managers report changes in their attitudes/behavior that occur earlier than those reported by supervisors-as-employees. A following section will specifically test the significance of these differences, which may be identified briefly. In Table 4, that is, non-managers on the short-post report 7 intended changes, 3 of which attain significance. On the long-post, an additional factor achieves the .05 level. No appreciable decay occurs between short-post and long-post, in addition. In contrast, Experimental supervisors in Table 5 report more modest changes on the short-post, which build very substantially in the second 6 months of experience with Flexi-Time. Revealingly, supervisors-as-employees report a consistent (but never statistically significant) decrease on Factor I, Participative Worksite with Good Communication. This may signal their inadequate involvement in the design of the Flexi-Time plan. In addition, supervisors-as-employees on the short-post also report lower scores on Factors IV-VII, which turn around by the long-post. Evidence to be presented later suggests that, especially on Factors V-VII, short-post responses by supervisors to the Employee Form were influenced by pressures they felt in their managerial roles.

A final note strengthens the conclusion that intended effects, on substantial balance, were generated by the Flexi-Time application. As Table 3 implies, both Comparison employees and supervisors provide stable and even deteriorating self-reports on the three administrations of the Employee Form. Specifically, Comparisons report increases/decreases in the ratio of 1/1 almost exactly. No increase or decrease attains statistical significance.

VI. Reactions of Managers

The reactions to Flexi-Time of those in supervisory roles also can be reflected in two ways: via responses to open-ended questions about work-hour policy, as well as via standard questionnaire items that solicited descriptions of broader aspects of the work environment.

Responses to Open-Ended Questions

Basically, all Experimental supervisors responded positively to the Flexi-Time program. One or two noted that it did not influence their worksite very much; and several criticized the use of the time clock. But the bulk of the responses were overwhelmingly positive, as these three illustrations establish:

Table 4

Non-managerial Experimentals, N = 21, on Three Administrations of Employee Form

Factors	Mean Aggregate Scores*			Direction of Change, and Statistical Significance of by t-test		
	Pre-test	Short-post	Long-post	Short-post vs. Pre-test	Long-post vs. Pre-test	Long-post vs. Short-post
I	8.86	9.91	9.52	increase	increase	decrease
II	11.76	18.48	18.67	increase, stat. sig.	increase, stat. sig.	increase
III	18.76	22.52	23.19	increase, stat. sig.	increase, stat. sig.	increase
IV	8.05	10.05	9.00	increase, stat. sig.	increase	decrease
V	19.43	20.76	21.43	increase	increase, stat. sig.	increase
VI	10.76	11.33	10.86	increase	increase	decrease
VII	5.66	6.14	6.38	increase	increase, stat. sig.	increase

*The means vary greatly due to the variable number of items defining the several factors.

Table 5

Managerial Experimentals, N = 11, on Three Administrations of Employee Form

Factors	Mean Aggregate Scores*			Direction of Change, and Statistical Significance of by t-test		
	Pre-test	Short-post	Long-post	Short-post vs. Pre-test	Long-post vs. Pre-test	Long-post vs. Short-post
I	11.55	10.91	10.64	decrease	decrease	decrease
II	12.36	17.64	19.55	increase, stat. sig.	increase, stat. sig.	increase, stat. sig.
III	17.27	22.27	23.27	increase, stat. sig.	increase, stat. sig.	increase, stat. sig.
IV	11.36	10.45	11.45	decrease	increase	increase
V	20.00	19.55	20.36	decrease	increase	increase
VI	10.00	10.55	11.55	increase	increase, approaches significance	increase
VII	5.82	5.82	6.27	no change	increase, approaches significance	increase

*The means vary greatly due to the variable of items defining the several factors.

I feel very positive about the current flexible hour policy. It gives me greater control over the scheduling and intermeshing of my job responsibilities with my personal external commitments. I also have found that I can now use my total working day time more effectively than in the past. Flexi-time is great! I hope it becomes permanent.

Very enthusiastic. Makes every week different. Productivity of my subordinates has not suffered from core hours—probably has increased because of better overall morale. Commuting has become easier—less time on the road—and less hectic. Occasionally, when working from 7:15 to 3:00, I find traffic almost minimal. Will find it difficult to ever return to 8:45 to 4:30 *routine*.

Excellent. At least in [my] area flexible work hours are the answer to a prayer. Employees willing to stay with long experiments pressuring them conscientiously and thoroughly—on the old system would have been rushed and maybe ruined. Employee work has improved dramatically with a parallel increase in productivity.

2. Responses to Standard Questionnaires

Interpretations of responses of the supervisors to the questionnaire items cannot be so direct. It was expected that supervisors *qua* employees would enjoy the personal benefits of Flexi-Time. But as supervisors they might see the program more in terms of its potential for inducing conflict, or for increasing the probability that some skill or service would be unavailable when needed. Hence, there were two expectations about supervisors' reactions to Flexi-Time:

As employees, supervisors were expected to show an attitudinal pattern similar to that of non-managerial personnel on short-post and long-post tests

As managers, the minimum expectation was that pre-test attitudes would not worsen over the first 6 months of the installation, and would probably improve on the long-post

The evidence supports two conclusions. First, supervisors did seem to distinguish the two roles. Second, the expectations above were generally met. The number of supervisors is small, of course. Consequently, tentativeness is appropriate in interpreting the data.

a. *Supervisors as Employees*

The evidence is convincing that responses of managers to the Employee Form do not differ significantly from those of non-managers, despite the hints in Tables 4 and 5. Table 6 takes one approach to providing such evidence. Specifically, managers and non-managers differ significantly on two factors on the

Table 6

Mean Aggregate Scores, *Experimentals Only*, Managerial (N = 11) vs. Non-Managerial Respondents (N = 21) on Three Administrations of Employee Form

	Pre-test Scores*			Short-post test Scores			Long-post Scores	
Factors	Managerial Respondents	Non-Managerial Respondents	Factors	Managerial Respondents	Non-Managerial Respondents	Factors	Managerial Respondents	Non-Managerial Respondents
I	11.55†	8.86†	I	10.91	9.91	I	10.64	9.52
II	12.36	11.76	II	17.64	18.48	II	19.55	18.67
III	17.27	18.76	III	22.27	22.52	III	23.27	23.19
IV	11.36†	8.05†	IV	10.45	10.05	IV	11.45†	9.00†
V	20.00	19.43	V	19.55	20.76	V	20.36	21.43
VI	10.00	10.76	VI	10.55	11.33	VI	11.55	10.86
VII	5.82	5.66	VII	5.82	6.14	VII	6.27	6.38

*The means vary in size due to the variable number of items defining the several factors.
†Indicates pairs of scores that attain or surpass .05 level on t-test, one-tailed.

pre-test. One of these significant differences still exists on the long-post, and that where managers report higher scores on the factor "Reinforced Motivation to Contribute Beyond Standard." The temptation to overinterpret this result will be resisted, but it is not surprising. Suffice it to conclude that Table 6 is consistent, generally, with the expectations that managers and non-managers report similar patterns of change on the Employee Form.

A similar analysis for Comparisons reveals no significant differences between managers and non-managers, on pre-test, short-post, or long-post.

b. Supervisors as Managers

Supervisors also met expectations in their responses to the Managerial Form, which contains 12 items.

The impact of Flexi-Time over its first 6 months on the attitudes of supervisors-as-managers is reflected in Tables 7 and 8. The minimum expectation about Flexi-Time was that it maintain the status quo, as supervisors view various facets of their managerial responsibilities. Hence the "desired effects" in Table 7 are usually phrased as negatives: do not lower significantly, do not increase significantly, and so on.

Table 7 implies that the minimum expectation of no deterioration on the Managerial Form was basically met. Definitely, also, supervisory attitudes did not improve substantially.

Two points underlay this conclusion. First, Table 7 indicates that Experimental and Comparison supervisors had similar pre-test profiles on the 12 Managerial items. Experimentals did provide less-favorable reports on 8 of the 12 items, but no significant differences existed. On the short-post test, the only tenable conclusion is that the perceptions of the Experimental supervisors did not deteriorate significantly in the interval between administrations of the questionnaire. Four items trend noticeably higher; two go somewhat lower; and the remainder vary in a narrow range only. No differences are statistically significant.

Second, Table 8 corroborates the conclusion that no significant deterioration in supervisory attitudes resulted from the Flexi-Time installation. Given the small Ns involved, only +, −, or 0 are used here to designate shifts in scores.

A three-step interpretation is necessary to highlight Table 8's summary of attitudinal changes 6 months after the installation. Thus no statistically significant deterioration or improvement of supervisory attitudes occurs in either Experimental unit on even one item. Moreover, although supervisors of the two experimental units patently differed, 16 of the 24 differences in pre-test vs. short-post attitudes are in the intended direction. Finally, supervisors in the Comparison unit do not consistently change their attitudes. Hence the conclusion of no deterioration in the attitudes of Experimental supervisors-as-managers, based on the data in Table 7, is not an artifact of a dramatic worsening of attitudes among supervisors in the Comparison unit.

Table 7

Summary of Differences on Pre-test vs. Short-post Supervisors in Experimental and Comparison Units, Managerial Form

Items on Managerial Form	Pre-test differences, Supervisors,* Experimentals (Es) vs. Comparisons (Cs)	Desired effect of Flexi-Time on Experimental Supervisors	Short-post differences, Supervisors,† Experimentals (Es) vs. Comparisons (Cs)
1. productivity of your employees	Es report lower productivity	do not lower significantly	Es report higher productivity
2. morale of your employees	Es report lower morale	increase	Es report higher morale
3. quality of support services	Es report better quality	do not lower significantly	Es report lower quality of services
4. degree of conflict with employees over scheduling	Es report more conflict	do not increase significantly	Es report less conflict
5. quality of communications about work assignments	Es report lower quality	do not worsen significantly	Es still report lower quality of communications
6. Flexibility to undertake projects or experiments	Es report less flexibility	do not reduce significantly	Es still report less flexibility
7. effort required to account	Es report less effort	do not increase significantly	Es now report more effort required
8. problems with other supervisors re work hours	Es report fewer problems	do not increase significantly	Es report fewer problems

9. opportunities for employees to work independently	Es report fewer opportunities	do not reduce significantly	Es still report fewer opportunities
10. effort required to schedule work assignments	Es report less effort	do not increase significantly	Es still report less effort
11. your employees' attitudes at work	Es report less positive attitudes	improve	Es report more positive employee attitudes
12. overall performance of employees	Es report lower overall performance	do not worsen significantly	Es report better overall performance

*Significance of differences was determined by t-test two-tailed. Any differences achieving the .05 level or greater is indicated by the term "significantly" in the description of effects.

†Significance of differences was determined by t-test, one-tailed. No differences attain the .05 level.

Table 8

Summary of Changes Reported by Supervisors on Managerial Form,
Short-post vs. Pre-test*

Items on Managerial Form	Experimental Unit A, Short-post vs. Pre-test N =5	Experimental Unit B, Short-post vs. Pre-test N = 6	Comparison Unit, Short-post vs. Pre-test N =4
1	+	+	−
2	+	+	−
3	−	−	+
4	+	−	−
5	0	−	0
6	+	+	−
7	+	−	+
8	0	−	−
9	+	−	+
10	+	−	+
11	0	+	−
12	0	+	−

*+ Designates a change toward a desired effect; − designates a change opposite a desired effect; 0 designates no change. No changes achieve the .05 level of statistical significance, or beyond.

To be sure, Table 8 implies some potential soft spots. Supervisors from both Experimental units report that the quality of support services has decreased somewhat in the first six months of Flexi-Time, for example. But that item—as potentially important as it can be—was the only one on which both sets of supervisors saw undesirable movement.

Approximately one year after installation, a long-post test attempted to assess whether short-post supervisory attitudes toward Flexi-Time developed into real concerns. Overall, supervisors-as-managers report impressive changes on the Managerial Form, comparing the long-post to the short-post. This pattern contrasts sharply with the no-change condition at 6 months after installation. Specifically, as Table 9 shows, 20 of the 24 changes reported by Experimental supervisors are in the desired direction, with 9 being statistically significant. Note especially that on the "worst" item, Item 8, supervisors from one experimental unit report that problems with other supervisors re work hours have remained unchanged over the first year of the Flexi-Time application, while supervisors in the other experimental unit report somewhat but not significantly greater

Table 9

Summary of Changes Reported by Supervisors on Managerial Form,
Long-post vs. Pre-test*

Items on Managerial Form	Experimental Unit A, Long-post vs. Pre-test N = 5	Experimental Unit B, Long-post vs. Pre-test N = 6	Comparison Unit, Long-post vs. Pre-test N = 4
1	+	+	−
2	+†	+†	0
3	−	+	+
4	+	+†	−
5	+	+†	−
6	+	+†	−
7	+†	+†	+
8	−	0	+
9	+	0	+
10	+†	+	+
11	+	+	−
12	+	+†	−

*+ Designates a change toward a desired effect; − designates a change opposite a desired effect; 0 designates no change.
†Designates a change that achieves the .05 level of statistical significance, or beyond, by one-tailed t-test.

problems in that regard. In contrast, Table 8 shows only 12 desired changes for Experimentals, with none achieving statistical significance, over Flexi-Time's first 6 months.

A similar analysis of Tables 8 and 9 for Comparison supervisors implies they do not change appreciably in the interval 6-12 months after the Flexi-Time installation.

An In-Process Summary

The data above support two conclusions: a potent if delayed impact of Flexi-Time on the attitudes of supervisors-as-managers; and the program's positive reception by all respondents as employees. Close observers can account for the differences between Experimentals and Comparisons in terms of no systemic variable other than the presence or absence of Flexi-Time. No doubt many other non-systemic factors do contribute to the pattern of attitudinal change. But it seems reasonable to conclude that, in this case, a structural intervention was able to trigger a variety of changes in the quality of life at the worksite, as both employees and managers viewed it.

VII. Some "Hard" Data About Flexi-Time

The impact of the Flexi-Time program also can be estimated in terms of a variety of measures of behavior, as well as via self-reports about changes in attitudes. Some observers refer to such behavioral measures as "hard," while measures of attitudes are "soft." We do not assign a somehow-different level of reality to the two kinds of data, but patent differences do exist. Thus measures of attitudes are typically "obtrusive" (Webb, Campbell, Schwartz and Sechrest, 1966), and that obtrusiveness can induce reactions in respondents that complicate interpretations of any data acquired. Moreover, measures of attitudes are more or less subject to conscious faking or to differential perceptual biases or skills of respondents (Golembiewski and Munzenrider, 1973).

Four kinds of "hard" data are available in this case. They include:

Variations in time in/time out

Changes in the amount of overtime

Changes in rates of absenteeism

Changes in cost of support services

1. Time In/Time Out

Perhaps the most obvious impact of Flexi-Time—and for some, the most worrisome—is reflected in a discrete behavior: the time people enter their worksite and when they leave. Some managers are concerned that wildly-skewed distributions may occur, creating horrendous scheduling problems.

The experience in the present firm indicates substantial but only marginal use of the Flexi-Time arrangement. Table 10 provides data from a 10-month period, with months 6-10 covering the summer vacation months. More or less, under Flexi-Time most employees keep to the standard workday of 8:45 a.m. through 4:30 p.m., ± 30 minutes. Specifically, nearly 82 per cent of the times-in during months 1-5 are recorded in the interval 8:15-9:15 in Table 10. In the summer months, the percentage drops, but only to about 75 per cent. For times-out, a little over 60 per cent are recorded as 4:00-5:00 p.m. in Table 10 for the winter months, with the figure falling only to 55 per cent in the summer months. Hence the pattern under Flexi-Time seems to be, grossly, to work later one day and leave earlier on another. Apparently only a few people check-in early and check-out early. The only noteworthy additional trend is a flattening of the distribu-

Table 10

Percentage Distributions of Time-In and Time-Out, Approximately
10,000 Employee Workdays

Times In			Times Out		
Months 1-5		Months 6-10	Months 1-5		Months 6-10
6:45 a.m.	.04%	.02%	3:00 p.m.	1.3%	2.8%
7:00	.3	.9	3:15	7.2	11.1
7:15	1.7	2.6	3:30	5.5	6.7
7:30	6.4	7.3	3:45	3.9	4.7
7:45	3.2	5.1	4:00	5.1	6.1
8:00	4.5	7.5	4:15	6.4	7.7
8:15	12.0	15.0	4:30	15.1	14.1
8:30	21.0	23.2	4:45	20.8	17.7
8:45	25.3	18.2	5:00	12.8	9.8
9:00	16.6	11.7	5:15	8.1	6.8
9:15	6.9	6.7	5:30	5.1	4.8
9:30	1.9	1.7	5:45	3.7	3.0
9:45	.1	.1	6:00	2.3	3.2
10:00 a.m.	.1	.1	6:15	1.1	.9
			6:30	.6	.4
			6:45	.4	.05
			7:00	.2	.14
			7:15	.3	.05
			after 7:30 p.m.	.3	.2

butions of both arrival and departure times on Mondays and Fridays and especially in the summer months, on which days, employees were somewhat more apt to report/depart somewhat earlier/later than on other days of the week.

2. Overtime

On the face of it, overtime decreased very sharply in the first 6 months of experience with Flexi-Time, and has stayed at the lower level for an additional 6 months. Overtime was never a big item, but it was reduced by some three-quarters.

Several factors urge against a robust conclusion on this point, however.

First, coincident with the Flexi-Time installation, management had decided to minimize overtime. Second, a major user of overtime in one Experimental unit was phased-out just before the Flexi-Time test began. Third, only about 30 per cent of the employees in the Experimental units are weekly-roll employees, and their overtime history may therefore be an unreliable indicator of Flexi-Time effects in situations where paid overtime is possible for a greater proportion of a workforce. Salaried employees, those on the semi-monthly roll, do not qualify for overtime. Fourth, the general opinion is that the Experimentals now are working on missions that have less potential for overtime.

Consequently, the decrease in overtime cannot be directly attributed to the Flexi-Time arrangement. But the program no doubt helped management work toward its policy of minimal overtime use.

3. Absenteeism

Table 11 provides summary data about absenteeism which reflect sometimes-striking changes, but whose interpretation cannot be definite. Overall, that is, total paid absences dropped by over one-third in the Experimental units, comparing the full year after the Flexi-Time installation with the prior 12 months. In contrast, a group of employees doing much the same kind of work at another company site a few miles distant, but without Flexi-Time, experienced an increase in absenteeism of some 15 per cent over a similar period. Note that the Experimentals and Comparisons started from substantially different bases, however. It is not known how much of the initial difference was due to bad medical luck, and how much was due to different employee or supervisory standards about acceptable levels of absenteeism. But it seems safe to conclude that absenteeism under Flexi-Time decreased, in the face of an increase among employees of similar skills and training without Flexi-Time.

Table 11 requires three additional points of clarification. First, the focus is on all "paid absences," whether for sick leave or other reasons. There were only 5 days of absence for which employees were not paid in the two years of observation, and they all occurred in the Comparison Group in the first year. So the reduction in "paid absences" in the Experimental unit did not result from a sudden increase in absences for which pay was denied.

Second, the "Comparison Group" in Table 11 is not the same as the "Comparison unit" referred to above. For a variety of technical reasons, meaningful retrospective absence data could not be gathered for the original Comparison unit. Fortunately, retrospective absence data were available for a substantial group of company employees at another nearby site, who also had pretty much the same skills, training, and missions as did the Experimentals. Note that both Ns in Table 11 include only those individuals in the three involved organization

Table 11

Absences in Two One-Year Periods Before and After Flexi-Time Installation

	Experimental Units N = 43		Comparison Group N = 41	
	Total Paid Absences	Absences of Single Day or Less	Total Paid Absences	Absences of Single Day or Less
Nov. 1971 - Sept. 1972	277 days	71	180 days	81
Flexi-Time introduced Oct. 1972				
Nov. 1972 - Sept. 1973	179.5 days	80	207.5 days	98
Changes	− 97.5 days	+ 9 occurrences	+ 27.5 days	+ 17 occurrences
	− 35 per cent	+ 12.7 per cent	+ 15.2 per cent	+ 21 per cent

units who were employed during the full period November 1971 through September 1973, that is, those employees about whose reactions to Flexi-Time management was most concerned. Turnover among both Experimentals and Comparisons was moderate—approximately 10 per cent per year.

Third, the expected decrease in absences of a single day or less did not occur. Short-term absences could have resulted from oversleeping before Flexi-Time, for example, and the new work hours were expected to reduce them. However, Experimentals increased such absences by nearly 13 per cent, as compared to the Comparisons who increased by 21 per cent from a somewhat-higher base.

In sum, although there is no one way to interpret the data in Table 11, the evidence implies Flexi-Time impacted on absenteeism. Employees exposed to Flexi-Time reduced their absenteeism, in the face of a substantial increase in absenteeism among employees of comparable skills, training, and pay. The expected decrease in short-term absences did not occur among Experimentals, however, although Comparisons reflected an increase that was larger by some 50 per cent.

4. Cost of Support Services

Many managerial innovations claim advantages in fact gained only by shifting costs to other parts of the system. Evidence implies that no such balloon squeezing occurred under Flexi-Time. Thus attitudinal data imply no serious by-products of Flexi-Time, such as new drains on the time of supervisors, or heightened conflict about scheduling. Moreover, it also seems that Flexi-Time has *not* resulted in increased costs of centralized support services provided to the Experimental units. These costs include personnel, as well as a variety of supplies and expenses related to day-to-day activities.

The cost can be reviewed briefly. Overall, the average number of support personnel has been reduced by approximately 15 per cent, comparing the year before vs. the year after the Flexi-Time installation. Similarly, the cost of all support services has been reduced by approximately 12 per cent. These costs include one-time charges for new equipment and new procedures that came onstream in the first year of Flexi-Time, during which period concerted efforts were being made to improve the quality of support services.

Given the usual indeterminancies, conservatively, costs for support services at least have not increased in the short-run, and substantial savings can be expected in the longer-run. Note that average employment in the two Experimental units has otherwise remained essentially stable since the Flexi-Time installation. Of course, not only Flexi-Time was impacting on support services. The campaign to improve equipment and procedures for support services also contributes to both savings and costs.

Summary

We conclude that Flexi-Time pretty much had the intended effects on the several measures used here. The usual reservations apply, of course. Thus the present sample of employees—even though it includes a substantial range of training and income—is certainly not representative of all employees performing all kinds of job-mixes. Hence caution is appropriate in extensions of the results above.

Flexi-Time, as is, has a broad but hardly universal range of potential applications in education, government, and industry. There are clearly some jobs—like security—or sets of jobs—like interfaces between quality control and production—where the present Flexi-Time model may not be appropriate. In all cases, analysis of jobs and their interdependencies is critical. And various models of Flexible work hours can be tailored to those interdependencies.

Finally, we are hesitant about applications in non-OD contexts. The magic is pretty clear not in the intervention itself. Or to make the point in another way, there is substantial potential for mischief in Flexi-Time applications. For example:

> An authoritarian management might install Flexi-Time without
> effectively gaining the support and commitment of supervisors,
> which implies long-run difficulties

The basic recommendation coming out of the successful Flexi-Time test implies the centrality of values, to cite a critical example. Thus top executives did not receive a recommendation to extend Flexi-Time to all employees. Rather they received a more permissive proposal that will allow various levels of management to adopt *some* flexible work hour program suitable to their own needs, in consultation with corporate personnel and consistent with such broad uniformities as the number of hours per workweek. The multiple intentions should be patent:

> To extend to broader ranges of employees the possibilities for greater freedom and self-determination at work implicit in flexible work hours, as illustrated by Flexi-Time
>
> But to do so while avoiding the potential expense of reducing or negating the sense of commitment or ownership or psychological success of several levels of managers
>
> And to do so while recognizing that various combinations of tasks and diverse collections of people can imply their own logic that will require various models of the core notion of flexible work hours.

Appendix A: Four Features of Flexi-Time Program

Four major features of the Flexi-Time program may be sketched briefly. First, the flexible work hour preferences of employees are *subject to work requirements of the department and to the approval of the immediate supervisor.* On occasion, the demands of the job or the preferences of a supervisor may require that certain hours be kept. This will apply particularly when an employee's work must mesh with another individual's or team's.

Second, the lunch period is not flexible.

Third, hours worked in excess of thirty-five in a week may not be "banked" for a following week.

Fourth, the test of Flexi-Time involved the accurate recording of each person's accumulated time. The hours worked by weekly-roll employees were already being recorded on a time clock, and this practice continued. An accurate record of hours worked by semi-monthly employees also was considered important, at least for the test period so that the program's effects could be accurately judged. Supervisors of the two experimental units in this case decided to use a time clock, while the comparison unit continued to use time sheets. The time cards and sheets would be summarized and submitted to appropriate supervisors. Only time cards and sheets of individuals who work less than 35 hours a week, or who have starting or quitting times inside the core day, require supervisory review.

Appendix B: Characteristics of Employees Exposed to Flexi-Time

Both hourly (weekly-roll) and salaried (semi-monthly roll) and salaried (semi-monthly roll) employees participated in the Flexi-Time research, both as experimentals and comparisons. These employees represented a substantial proportion of the corporation's workforce, using a level in the salary plan as a criterion. A few details establish the point.

Weekly-roll employees who are paid hourly. Individuals providing data here have such job-titles and representative grades in the position-classification scheme:

Job Title	Representative Weekly-Roll Grade
Senior Technologust	10
Senior Technician	8
Secretary	6
Laboratory Technician	6
Junior Technician	4
Technical Typist Clerk	4
Laboratory Helper	3

Weekly-roll grades run from 1 through 10. Consequently, responses in this study come from individuals representing much of the host firm's total hourly-job spectrum.

Approximately 32 percent of the responses in this study come from weekly-roll employees.

Semi-monthly roll employees who are salaried and "professional" or managerial. Most in the present sample have advanced degrees in scientific disciplines. Individuals providing data for this study have such job-titles and representative grades in the position-classification scheme for semi-monthlies:

Job Title	Representative Semi-monthly Roll Grade
Associate Director	8
Administrative Manager	8
Senior Investigator	6
Associate Senior Investigator	5
Scientist	3
Associate Scientist	2

Grades for salaried jobs run from 1 through 15. So responses in this study include individuals in professional and managerial jobs carrying substantial salaries and responsibilities.

References

Carrigan, Stokes. "Organization Development in A Pharmaceutical Setting." In J. Jennings Partin, ed., *Current Perspectives in Organization Development.* Reading, Mass: Addison-Wesley, 1973.

Elbing, Alvar O., Gadon, Herman, and Gordon, John R. M., "Flexible Work Hours: The Missing Link in Participative Management" (MS, 1974).

Golembiewski, Robert T. *Renewing Organizations.* Itasca, Ill.: F. E. Peacock, 1972.

Golembiewski, Robert T., Hilles, Rick, and Kagno, Munro, "A Longitudinal Study of Flexi-Time Effects: Some Consequences of An OD Structural Intervention," *Journal of Applied Behavioral Science,* Vol. 10 (December 1974), pp.

Golembiewski, Robert T., and Munzenrider, Robert. "Social Desirability as An Intervening Variable in Interpreting OD effects," *Journal of Applied Behavioral Science,* Vol. 11 (March, 1975), pp.

Webb, Eugene J., Campbell, Donald T. Schwartz, Richard D., and Sechrest, Lee. *Unobtrusive Measures: Non-reactive Research in the Social Sciences,* Chicago: Rand McNally, 1966).

CRISIS INTERVENTION IN A MUNICIPAL AGENCY
A Conceptual Case History*

Leonard D. Goodstein and Ronald K. Boyer

In the fall of 1970, the Health Department of Cincinnati was in crisis. There were a multitude of internal problems, and the Department's relationships with segments of the community were quite poor. The internal problems had led to a number of meetings of groups of dissident employees, and they had made their unhappiness with the administration of the Health Department, particularly its Commissioner, a matter of public record. An Ad Hoc Workers Council had been formed and was intent upon changing the Department and securing the termination of the Commissioner's appointment. There had been a number of resignations from the Health Department during the past months, including a special assistant to the Commissioner and an Assistant Commissioner. The circumstances surrounding both of these resignations, among others, were so unclear as to have caused much misunderstanding and suspiciousness within the Department and in the community concerning them. A number of citizens and neighborhood groups in the community, especially those that were recipients of Health Department services, had begun to voice serious discontent with the quality of services being received. These groups were insisting upon greater community involvement in the management of the Health Department, an involvement for which there was

*Reproduced by special permission from *The Journal of Applied Behavioral Science.* "Crisis Intervention in A Municipal Agency: A Conceptual Case History," by Leonard D. Goodstein and Ronald K. Boyer. Volume 8, Number 3, pp. 318-340. Copyright © 1972, NTL Institute.

no vehicle. For a period of several weeks there had been a constant series of newspaper articles and television news stories about the Health Department. Thus,
few people in Greater Cincinnati did not know that the Health Department was
in some kind of difficulty at the time consultation was requested.

Background

The Health Department of Cincinnati, an organization of over 30 employees, is
established by municipal charter and in conformance with the laws of the State
of Ohio and is generally charged with providing both health care services to the
needy and with supervising the public health aspects of the environment. The
governing Board of Health consists of five persons, each appointed by the Mayor
with the approval of the City Council for 10 years, overlapping terms. At the
time in question, the Board consisted of an aging pediatrician, who was Board
president, an aging suburban housewife (these two members had served a total
of over 30 years on the Board), a Negro physician, a dentist, and a businessman.
The latter two member were very recent appointments and had each served only
for several months.

    The Board serves without compensation and typically had met only month-
ly for a fairly brief meeting in which there was routine approval of routine items.
The only major issue that the Board had previously needed to consider was the
replacement of the Commissioner. The recent series of events, however, had
changed this pattern. There was an interminable series of meetings, both with
dissident employees and with community groups, frequently punctuated with
the politics of confrontation, high public visibility and concern over the Board's
behavior, and a tremendous drain on the members' energies. Since all of the individuals on the Board had other commitments, including extensive professional
practice and business obligations, service on the Board had become arduous and
unrewarding, a state of affairs none of the members of the Board had bargained
for in accepting an appointment.

    The Board is responsible for selecting the Health Commissioner, who is
ordinarily a physician trained in public health and epidemiology. The incumbent
at the time of the consultation was a nationally well-known public health administrator who had been on the job for approximately two years. His predecessor,
also a trained public health administrator, had resigned under pressure after a
similar, brief term of office. Prior to that the Department had been run by a
local physician for a great many years, and most of the employees of the Department had been recruited under his régime.

    In addition to the Commissioner there are three Assistant Commissioners,
one for health care, one for mental health programs, and the third for environmental protection. The Assistant Commissioner for health care had resigned

recently because she had decided that she did not care for the administrative nature of the job, but there also were unresolved personal issues between her and the Commissioner that entered into her decision. The Assistant Commissioner for mental health programs was employed only on a part-time basis and had little to do with the nonpsychiatric programs of the Department. He had played almost no role in the present difficulties. The Assistant Commissioner for environmental protection was also a part-time employee of the Department, but was rather central to the affairs of the Department. He had been in office for 18 years and had seen the comings and goings of the several different Commissioners. A well-known environmentalist, he held academic rank at the University of Cincinnati's College of Medicine and was also engaged in an extensive consulting practice. (There was also a business manager who was responsible for some aspects of routine administration and budgeting.)

The Health Department staff included a variety of professional and nonprofessional personnel, including physicians, public health nurses, public health educators, environmental sanitarians, health inspectors, secretaries, record clerks, and so on. Most of these employees were long-term civil service employees of the city whose behavior and aspirations were those typically encountered in large bureaucracies. In addition to its traditional functions of environmental supervision and providing health services, an extensive community health program had been developed through the auspices of the Pilot Cities Program by the Commissioner and a staff which he had brought in to manage this new and innovative program. There were considerable suspicion and jealousy on the part of old-line employees toward this new program: this seemed to be one of the points at issue in the crisis.

Entry

Early in September of 1970, the authors were contacted by a psychiatrist who was Assistant Commissioner for the Mental Health Programs of the Health Department. He was concerned with the tensions, problems, and discontent within the Department. Moreover, he felt a personal commitment to the Commissioner whom he both liked and respected. He was concerned about supporting the Commissioner and also with enhancing the Commissioner's effectiveness in filling his leadership role within the Health Department. His notion was that a series of workshops on intra-organization communications and leadership would serve to reduce organizational goals, and consolidate individual and organizational commitments to the delivery of high-quality health care to the community. Following some preliminary discussions with this psychiatrist, a meeting was arranged including the authors, the Health Commissioner, and the President of the Board of Health. The psychiatrist had already convinced both the Commissioner and the president of the Board of the potential utility of workshops with the Health Department. The purpose of the meeting, in their minds, was to negotiate a contract leading to the conduct of the workshops. It was agreed by the principals at this meeting to invite the authors to a special meeting of the Board of Health to draw up a contract for such a series of workshops. Some preliminary cost estimates were developed for both a diagnostic phase of inquiry and a preliminary series of workshops.

Commentary on Entry

The authors, like most citizens of Cincinnati, had been somewhat aware of the troubles in the Health Department but had no first-hand knowledge of the severity or complexity of the situation. It became immediately clear, however, in our discussion with the psychiatrist who contacted us initially, as well as in our subsequent meetings with the Commissioner and the president of the Board, that the problems of the Department had reached crisis proportions. The authors soon learned that the Board had given the Commissioner a grudging vote of confidence following receipt of an extensive list of grievances by an Ad Hoc Health Department Workers Council.

Seeing clearly that the affairs of the Health Department had become a matter of city-wide concern, it quickly became apparent to us that one of the critical issues was the deep sense of distrust around the Commissioner and his leadership role in the Department. He had become the focus of real polarization, with both sides of the polarization represented in all camps: the Department, the Board, and the community.

As the authors began to acquaint themselves with the situation in the Department through reading reports and newspaper stories and by making discreet, informal inquiries, they began to have doubts about the appropriateness of conducting communications workshops. A critical element involved in this concern was the manner in which the negotiations for the authors' services had been conducted. There had been little public discussion, either in the Board or the Department, about the need for this kind of intervention, an oversight which caused the authors no little concern about their own credibility in an already unfavorable climate of distrust and polarization.

Under conditions of extreme polarization, it is questionable whether extreme differences can be resolved in a workshop format. When circumstances have become polarized with a high degree of distrust and scapegoating, listening becomes impossible and bringing the opposed groups together is more likely to lead to "bloodshed" than increased understanding. Clearly, this is a diagnostic decision that must be made by the consultant in each case: namely, is a workshop in which the opposing sides directly confront each other more likely to lead to further polarization or can it lead to some resolution of the differences? Moreover, many of the grievances by the Ad Hoc Workers Council required action steps by the Commissioner. A workshop would not have been regarded as an appropriate response to those demands, a fact which further reduced the presumed usefulness of workshops. While there was a clear need for additional data to support the decision against conducting a workshop, this tentative decision was quickly reached by the authors, even before the contract had been agreed upon.

The authors became increasingly aware that timeliness and speed of action were absolutely critical if the crisis were to be managed in any productive fashion. At the same time, it was not at all clear to the authors what would be an appropriate set of actions to recommend for solving the crisis. The demand for prompt action coupled with a lack of clarity about what would be appropriate action seems to be one of the characteristics of crisis, one that has obvious and considerable consequences for crisis consultation.

As the authors became increasingly aware of the situation confronting the Health Department, they became increasingly convinced that any kind of intervention without extensive diagnosis would be inappropriate. They were well aware, however, that extensive data collecting in an organization is not without consequences. Nevertheless, between the time of the initial meeting with the Commissioner and the president of the Board and the next meeting with the entire Board, the authors adopted the stance that the only appropriate initial contact with the Department would be that of diagnosis and evaluation of the current situation without any necessary action steps.

It should be clear in this context that a contract for a series of workshops, with or without a preliminary diagnostic phase, could have been written and that such a series of workshops could have been attempted. Indeed, in a crisis climate the parties involved are often willing to attempt almost *anything* to reduce the conflict and restore normalcy. Presumably some consultants might have actually attempted these workshops. Based upon their prior organizational experience, however, the authors were not willing to go along with the client need in this case nor to accept their self-diagnosis for a workshop intervention. The need for competence in organizational analysis and a high level of professional integrity are underscored in this case. In retrospect, the unwillingness of the authors to conduct any workshops without a period of organizational assessment was clearly an extremely wise decision.

The authors next met with the Board and the Commissioner in a special meeting of the Board in order to explore what might be usefully attempted. The Board had some difficulty in understanding exactly what the authors meant by an "organizational diagnosis." It was pointed out to the Board that there probably was no one who knew all of the issues involved and that there was little objectivity in the various reports which had been reviewed by the Board. The authors suggested that their role might be as a diagnostic team to identify the problems facing the Department and further to serve as consultants to the Board in resolving these problems. While the Board had initially been prepared to hear a proposal for a series of workshops, they were rather easily dissuaded from this expectation after some in-depth discussion with the consultants.

There was at least one member of the Board, however, who had already reached a decision as to the only appropriate course of action—*fire the Commissioner.* The other members of the Board were more supportive of the Commissioner, especially when he was under attack by the one member. Indeed, it was clear to the consultants that the Board itself was polarized around the issue of the Commissioner and his role. Further, the Board was not processing or facing up to its internal disagreements and was being rendered ineffective in its functioning as a consequence. The poor quality of the Board's functioning, the members' inability to deal with issues openly and directly, was thus rather quickly identified by the consultants as one of the issues facing the organization.

While it was clear that the majority of the Board was supporting the Commissioner, at least for the time being, it was also rather clear that there was an uneasy tension between the Commissioner and the Board. The Commissioner's behavior toward the Board was quite proper and deferential but he was not open or informative about the real issues confronting the organization. Board members seemed perplexed and exasperated in the main toward the Commissioner. They knew that there were serious problems in the organization, were convinced that the Commissioner had a role in these problems, but were unclear about the nature of his complicity in them.

The Board then asked the Commissioner and the authors to withdraw and met in a brief executive session. They agreed to retain the services of the authors as consultants for an organizational diagnosis for a period of 60 days. It was agreed that the consultants would "conduct individual interviews and group conferences with members of the Department and certain others related to the Department and its functions." Based upon the data collected in these interviews and conferences, the consultants would develop such action plans "as they considered in their professional judgment essential to the resolution of the current organizational problems." The consultants agreed that a written report of their findings and recommendations would be available to the Board by no later than December 1, 1970.

Diagnosis

Several days after the drawing of the contract, a fact which was reported in some detail in the local press, a meeting was held of the major department heads and other significant persons in the Department of Health. The purpose of the meeting was to introduce the consultants to the Department and to request the co-operation of the Department in the diagnostic activities of the consultants. The president of the Board of Health introduced the consultants in an atmosphere of high tension, anger, and distrust.

A number of issues surfaced in the first few minutes of the meeting. Many of those present indicated that they wanted action on their previously articulated demands, not further inquiry into their merits. Others questioned the objectivity of the consultants since they would be "hired hands" of the Commissioner and the Board. Still others raised questions about the professional competence of the consultants to deal in a crisis situation in a health-care agency. The consultants tried to respond to the questions concerning their competence and objectivity, attempting to defuse the situation. It was clear, however, from the constant stream of questions that this defusing was not accomplished and that there was no resolution of the trust issue. The meeting broke up with the consultants feeling that they had failed to establish much credibility with those present at the meeting and that the trust issue would be an important one.

Recognizing that there was a good deal of mistrust of them in the Department, the consultants attempted to devise a strategy which would simultaneously give them access to those persons who had been identified as principal characters in the current crisis and, at the same time, provide an opportunity for all other interested persons to discuss in confidence their grievances and other issues with the consultants. It seemed imperative that the consultants attempt to deal with all interested parties without regard to their rank or status in the Department or their prior role in the controversy. A letter was prepared for distribution over the Commissioner's signature which spelled out a role description for the consultants and specified those mechanisms by which interested persons could arrange for a meeting or interview with the consultants. Essentially, the consultants' role was described as an "attempt to better identify and diagnose the issues and problems which have become divisive and destructive in our work," and their goal was described as promoting open and honest communication within the Department.

In response to the Commissioner's letter, the following unsigned document was circulated among the workers at the Health Department: "The Workers Council recommends that the staff *not* meet, talk, nor give any information to the two new staff psychologists. We recommend that the Commissioner and the Board of Health *meet* with these therapists, since the problems in the Health Department are their problems, not ours." In this hostile and confused atmosphere the two consultants began their diagnostic intervention into the Cincinnati Department of Health.

The consultants cleared their calendar to spend the bulk of their time on this crisis. Within several days a meeting was held with most of the department heads and assistant department heads of the Department of Health, approximately

20 in number. All of the persons present were asked to introduce themselves and describe their functional role in the Department. The consultants asked a number of questions about how their various tasks were assigned. Questions were raised about the nature of their concerns and discontents, but the quality of the responses was guarded and noninformative. The major purpose of the meeting, however was to familiarize the consultants with the administrative organization of the Department and some of the case of characters as well as to expose the consultants to this key group.

The very next day, the steering committee of the Ad Hoc Workers Council, about 20 in number, appeared for a meeting which the Commissioner had arranged. About one-half of the members of the steering committee had been present the previous day since they were either department heads or assistant heads. After a round of introductions, a senior physician arose and read a prepared statement indicating that the group had met previously and had come to a unanimous decision not to engage in any dialogue with the consultants. He indicated that they had engaged an attorney, who was not present at the meeting; and all further communications would be through him. They did indicate that they felt that the only solution to the current problems would be for the present Commissioner to resign and that they feared that any statements made to the consultants would be used against them in a vindictive and punishing way, either in the form of verbal assaults or legal attempts to remove them from their positions. They generally doubted the objectivity of the consultants and questioned whether or not they could do anything helpful in the situation anyway. The next two hours were extremely long. The consultants attempted to deal directly with each of these points and to engage the group in serious dialogue. The consultants indicated that they were open to considering that one solution to the current crisis would be for the Commissioner to resign. They were not prepared to make a recommendation on this matter at this time, they stated, but that was certainly one of the options that might come out of their diagnosis and study. Moreover, the consultants worked at clarifying the fact that they wanted to get at *issues* and did not have any reasons for reporting the specific comments of individuals.

During the course of the two hours, despite their previous decision "not to talk," many persons were won over by the open and frank manner of the consultants and their nondefensive willingness to accept the concerns and doubts about the usefulness of the consultation intervention. Moreover, the consultants indicated truthfully that they themselves had doubts regarding the extent to which they could have an impact that would be helpful in the current situation.

Turning Point

This meeting with the Ad Hoc Workers Council was a critical turning point in the consultation. The consultants felt they needed both to "buy time" and create credibility for their role, even though they themselves were uncertain about their potential influence in the crisis. Much to their own surprise, these goals were accomplished in this meeting, although there was no particular point in the meeting at which this seemed to occur, nor was there an explicit decision made to assist the consultants. Rather, individuals began to provide helpful inputs, and no additional memoranda appeared urging employees not to talk to the consultants. Following the initial difficult meeting, several members of the Workers Council voluntarily began to supply the consultants with a wide range of documents and inputs regarding the Department and their concerns. In general, those who provided information came from higher in the Department hierarchy and included about equal numbers of newer and older employees. The consultants never met or talked with the attorney engaged by the Ad Hoc Workers Council. Moreover, the consultants had no ensuing contact with the senior physician who had represented the group at the first meeting with the consultants.

A number of other diagnostic interviews were then conducted; over 100 persons were interviewed in all, either individually or in group. Among the persons interviewed were the various assistant commissioners and department heads, line workers in the Department, the Board members themselves, the Director of the Pilot Cities Program, a University of Cincinnati group which had been consulting on computer uses in the Health Department, and others. In addition, a wide range of documents about the work of the Department, letters to and from the Commissioner, documents distributed by the Ad Hoc Workers Council, newspaper clippings, and various other materials were reviewed and considered. These interviews and documents formed the data base upon which the consultants founded their conclusions and recommendations.

Commentary on Diagnosis

As Argyris (1970) notes, the primary task of an interventionist is the development of "valid and useful information." This, however, is very difficult in a crisis climate where suspicion around loyalties and intentions is high, polarization is extreme, and coalitions are forming with the intention of coopting anyone he can find to support his cause. Among the central coalitions in this situation were the Commissioner and his supporters, the Ad Hoc Workers Council, the Board of Health, and others. Another group which further complicated the situation was the local press—which had identified a newsworthy story and wanted to pursue it to wherever it might lead.

Establishing Credibility

This crisis climate seriously interfered with any information-gathering on the part of the consultants. Persons were reluctant to share data because of fear of retaliation. There were groups who wanted the consultants to meet with only those individuals who would supply the information which supported their position. The press wanted complete and open sharing at a time which the consultants felt was premature and inappropriate. Therefore, the consultants felt that the first task was not the collection of data, but the establishing of credibility with as many constituent groups as possible. Only through the development of some credibility and trust does the development of meaningful information become possible. While this is always true in a consultation process, it becomes of paramount importance in crisis consultation. The meetings, with, first, the department heads of the Health Department, and then, the Ad Hoc Workers Council, were critical points in the consultation process. The dialogue between the consultants and these two groups seemed to provide some basis for a temporary truce and for raising the trust level to one in which some collaboration on information-sharing, if not action, was possible. The factors which seemed to be most central in achieving this climate were these: the consultants were not defensive about the role of the Board or of the Health Commissioner; they were willing to entertain the possibility that one of the findings of the investigation would be that the Commissioner should resign his position; and finally, they agreed that the community might very well have a larger and more significant voice in the conduct of affairs of the Department. Within broad perspectives, these were the salient issues in the crisis.

Openness a Value

What is important to note was the consultants' agreement that these issues ought to be openly and thoroughly discussed in the system. Such discussion had not been previously legitimized. The consultants' values are to support open communication and dialogue among those persons who are vitally concerned with the issues being addressed. Their open commitment to these values in this case was undoubtedly a factor in trust building.

Paraphrasing

One technique which seemed to be of special usefulness in trust building under these crisis conditions was listening and paraphrasing. This is both especially difficult to do and critically important in crisis consultation. There is a strong tendency in crises to advocate one's own position rather than to listen, and there is also little expectation of being listened to. For example, there were a number of times during the meeting with the Workers Council when they identified specific minor administrative problems that had developed, such as reimbursement for mileage on personal automobiles, problems which they felt the consultants simply would disbelieve or fail to hear. When the consultants were able to paraphrase their understanding of the issues and the intensity of the workers' concerns, credibility and rapport were established.

The observation of the usefulness of this paraphrasing process made an important contribution to the diagnosis of the organization's problems. Out of this it became clear that many employees of the organization experienced their inputs about "problems" as not being heard or as responded to by denial: "This is not a problem."

Differentiation of Consultant Roles

During the diagnostic phase several aspects of how the consulting team operated emerged as important considerations. The personality dynamics of the two consultants and the degree and manner in which they were open about their perceptions of the issues influenced which portions of the client system trusted which consultants around which issues. For example, the consultant who had made the initial contact with the Commissioner seemed to develop a somewhat closer working relationship with him and was less open in the meetings with the Ad Hoc Workers Council. On the other hand, the second consultant was more open regarding the problems involving the Commissioner and his role in the meetings with the Ad Hoc Workers Council, and this led to his greater credibility with the latter group. Based on the perceived credibility with and support that constituent groups saw in the consultants, they made attempts to influence the individual consultants in directions that were more supportive of their own positions. For example, the second consultant received all of the telephone calls from representatives of the Ad Hoc Workers group and the first consultant received almost all of the telephone calls from the Commissioner.

What is important to note in this context is that the consultants were aware of their differentiated roles and regularly discussed how their different styles led to different levels of credibility with the various members of the client system, and consequently, how different data had become available to each of them. While there were some differences in the age and nature of consultation experiences between the consultants, these factors did not seem so critical or important as differences in personal/professional style in producing a role differentiation between the consultants. One consultant was ordinarily concerned with personal, intrapersonal, and interpersonal issues in the crisis; while the other consultant focused on organizational and intergroup issues. There did not appear to be any perceived status differences between the consultants in this intervention. They used different diagnostic frameworks for assessing and integrating the data, and this led to the exploration of differing sets of issues and actions. Such scope is possible only where the consultation team views these differences as strengths facilitating the consultation process rather than as sources of friction and competition. This conception of the team relationships was sometimes easier to accomplish in theory than in practice. The consultants were always aware of their own anxiety regarding the risks in this consultation process, particularly in this climate of crisis.

Feedback, Consultation, and Negotiations

The intensive diagnostic phase; the series of interviews, conferences, and meetings; and the readings of the documentation lasted a little over two weeks. The manifest grievances of both the employees and the community included general complaints about the failure of the Commissioner and the Board to exercise leadership, the poor communications within the Department, the inefficiency of the Department, and specific complaints about the failure to develop adequate programs in areas like VD control, school health, neighborhood health clinics, and so on. The consultants' analysis of these manifest grievances led them to the conclusion that these were in fact problems and that the responsibility for these problems was widespread.

Antipathy to Change

Among the underlying causes of these problems were a generalized resistance to change and innovation and an antipathy to any who attempted change or innovation. Further, the Department was organized as a traditional bureaucracy, which was inadequate to meet the complex urban health needs of the city. There was ineffective overcentralization and there were inadequate professional-managerial resources for the present tasks and few for long-range planning. A part-time volunteer Board of Health of only five members was simply inadequate to manage this complex, modern Department. Also interfering with the effectiveness of the Department were a series of unresolved personality conflicts, many of which involved the Commissioner.

The Commissioner's Fate

Through the course of the consultation it became increasingly apparent to the consultants that the Commissioner, because of his management style, had lost his creditability, both in the Department an in the community. This point was made in interviews even by supporters of the Commissioner and it became clear that, regardless of any recommendations which the consultants might make and regardless of the talents the Commissioner had for improving health care, his tenure in office was drawing to a close. Further, the press and other news media had helped create a climate of opinion in the community in which the Commissioner was seen as the one primarily responsible for the current situation.

During the two-week data-collection phase, as this conclusion became ever more clear, the consultants met on several different occasions with the Commissioner in order to share this conclusion with him. After several meetings, the Commissioner was convinced that his resignation would be necessary and the question arose concerning the timing of this critical act. The consultants were concerned that his resignation might so defuse the situation that the other issues which were very much part of the current problems would go unexamined in the delight and exultations following the Commissioner's decision to leave. The consultants worked closely with the Commissioner, the president of the Board, and members of the Board, with whom a number of feedback sessions were held during the week, in the timing of the announcement of the resignation in order to preserve the impact of their report.

In addition, the consultants worked together with the Commissioner and the Board in the preparation of a detailed response to the list of manifest griev-ances by the Ad Hoc Workers Council, a response which had not been previously made. The Commissioner was advised to establish a communications council within the department which would provide a vehicle for information exchange and dialogue about departmental problems.

While the consulting team was busy with its data-gathering and data analysis, the Ad Hoc Workers Council was visibly busy. They had requested time from the City Council to present their complaints about the Health Department and such time had been granted. After their initial presentation, the Council referred the matter of the Health Department to one of its standing committees, Human Re-sources, consisting of the Mayor and two other Councilmen.

The consulting team had decided that the simple issuance of a final report probably would not have the desired effect of initiating real changes in the Health Department and, further, the consultants had decided that their responsibility in this matter was to the broader community of the City, which was represented officially by the City Council. Therefore, the consultants decided to present their findings to the Council informally, through the Human Resources Commit-tee. The president of the Board of Health was asked and agreed to arrange an in-formal meeting between the consultants and the Mayor. The consultants' tenta-tive findings were shared with the Mayor and, while he was concerned about the extent and severity of the problem, he was positively impressed with the way in which the report was presented. He recognized that there was a strong data base for the findings and that the recommendations were a natural consequence of the findings. The Mayor was eager to move ahead into the action steps necessi-tated by the recommendations but first wanted the consultants to share the same feedback with the two other members of the Council's Human Resources Com-mittee.

Within the next two days a similar, informal meeting was held with the con-sultants and the three members of the Council committee. The findings and the recommendation of the consultants were reviewed. The committee was a biparti-san one, and there were obviously potent political issues involved in this contro-versy. While there was some attempt to "test" these issues with the consultants, the three Councilmen quickly became impressed with how the findings were data based and revealed a complex and difficult situation in which neither side could really "win." The Councilmen were grateful for this early sharing of the feedback by the consultants and indicated their willingness to support the recommendations.

Within one week after this meeting with the Councilmen, the final report of the consultants was submitted to the Board of Health. The day on which the report was received was the day on which the Commissioner's resignation was accepted. Within another week's time the entire Board of Health had resigned (at the request of the Mayor with the support of the rest of the City Council), and a decision had been made to seek a City Charter amendment that would change the nature and size of the Board of Health.

In the year following the final report, a new Board and Commissioner have been appointed, the Commissioner has begun a reorganization of the Department, including an expansion of the professional managerial staff, and efforts to involve the community in the affairs of the Health Department have greatly expanded. The Charter amendment expanding the Board of Health from five to nine members, shortening the term of office from ten to three years, and limiting the number of health professionals on the Board to fewer than five, was on the ballot in the November 1971 general election. With strong newspaper endorsement and no general opposition, this amendment was passed. Additional members to the expanded nine-member Board were appointed shortly after the approval of the Charter amendment.

Commentary on Feedback, Consultation, and Negotiations

In consultation it is usual to differentiate among short-term, medium-term, and long-term consequences of the consultation process. In crisis consultation, however, the intensity of the feelings involved and the strong polarization among the groups ordinarily demand such a strong focus on short-term issues and short-term solutions that longer-term issues and solutions are ignored. It should be clear from the above analysis that the root causes of the Health Department crisis were long-term and that only long-term solutions would resolve the underlying problems.

A popular short-term solution in this case would have been simply to recommend the firing of the Commissioner. There was a certain attractiveness to this proposal as it would permit the consultants to extricate themselves from a very difficult situation, it would help defuse the tremendous amounts of anger and frustration present in the organization, and it was an action which would be readily accomplished within the limitations of their contract. As attractive as this alternative appeared, however, it was clear to the consultants that the problems confronting the Department were more complex and, to quote the consultants' final report, "these problems, unless adequately resolved, will continue to plague the Department in the delivery of health services, regardless of who serves as Commissioner." The consultants' conclusion was that, while the Commissioner and his management style were important in the current crisis—and he had indeed outlived his usefulness in his present position—there were other equally important issues that needed to be addressed if the difficulties were to be resolved on a long-term basis. Under crisis conditions, it is difficult to help the client system attend to these longer-term considerations, especially when there is a convenient short-term solution available. It should be apparent, however, that long-term solutions can be contemplated only after short-term solutions have been developed and there is a reasonably high degree of confidence that these short-term solutions will work effectively.

Another important short-term issue that has to be examined in a crisis is the day-to-day workings of the organization: in other words, someone has to "mind the store." The consultants feel there always should be some public response to the manifest problems in a crisis, and some attempt must be made to open the channels of communication among the dissident groups. This was done in the present case by recommending public Board response to the grievances and the creation of the communication council. These short-term interventions were helpful in trust building and in maintaining the level of tension within the Department at a tolerable level.

Who Was the Client in This Case?

As the consultants began to draw their conclusions, one issue which continually arose was that of who was the client to whom the consulting team was finally responsible. Ordinarily in process consultation (Schein, 1969) the question of who is the client is readily apparent to both the consultant and the client system. For example, in an industrial organization the client might be the President or the Board of Directors or the Director of the Research and Development Laboratory. In any of these cases the consultants would ordinarily submit their recommendations to the client with whom they had entered into a contract and accept whatever decision or action the client might choose to make with respect to their recommendations. In the present case, however, this was not the course to be followed and the issue was not so simply resolved.

As noted above, the consultants had serious questions about the effectiveness of the Board, about the management style of the Commissioner, and about the openness of the Department as a whole. The consultants' final report was equally critical of all three parties. To whom, then, should the consultants address their report? This question became critically important when the consultants realized that they would not be comfortable in having their report gather

dust in a file cabinet and in leaving the Health Department as ineffective an organization as they had found it. While a consultant in an industrial organization
might be willing to observe that organization die through bankruptcy, it is less
easy to permit that to happen in a public service agency, particularly one committed to the delivery of health care in one's own community.

On the basis of these considerations, the consultants decided that their
primary responsibility was to the larger community—the City of Cincinnati—
rather than to the Health Department per se. The decision was not one easily
arrived at; many hours of discussion went into making it. It was recognized that
the initial contacts had been with the Commissioner and, in some ways, we were
responsible to him; without his support we would never have been involved at all.
It was also recognized that we were employees of the Board and responsible to
them. Further, we had made implicit and explicit promises to the employees of
the Department in our contacts with them, promises to help them deal effectively with their problems. The issue to some extent was how these conflicting
and discordant interests could be served simultaneously. One way of resolving
this issue, at least for the consultants, was to view their prime responsibility as
to the public whom the Department was established to serve. Since the City
Council was the official agency representing that public, it was to it the consultants decided to turn.

A Fluid Role

Sharing findings with representatives of the Council was outside the formal contract which defined the Board and Commissioner as client. The Board president
unilaterally agreed to extend the contract to include dialogue with the Council
inasmuch as he was interested in doing whatever was possible to solve what was
for him a personally difficult situation. Further, he agreed that both the political
dimensions of the crisis and any long-term solution would require political as
well as organizational changes. Prior to seeking a meeting with City Council the
consultants had informally shared the findings and their recommendations with
members of the Board and the Commissioner. Although apprehensive about
changing the contract in this fashion, the consultants saw and still see the action
as necessary and appropriate. Consultants working in public agencies may find
the nature of their role, contract, and client system to be evolutionary and fluid
rather than stable and fixed.

The experience of the consultants in this case suggests the utility of this
kind of crisis intervention in the political arena where the interventionists are
seen as objective and unbiased and are willing to operate from a data base. This
general approach has been used previously in royal commissions, "blue ribbon"
panels, and the like; but this has generally been a rather unusual role for behavioral scientists to perform, especially in a crisis.

The recommendations of the consultants, all of which have either been carried out or are being carried out, involved the resignation of the Commissioner, the reorganization of the Department, the expansion of the professional-managerial staff of the Department, and the reconstitution of the Board of Health. Acceptance of these recommendations required a careful set of negotiations, the completion of which was necessary prior to the public release of the consultants' report. These negotiations included informal information-sharing with significant power figures, preventing the recommendations from becoming partisan political issues, preparing expectations about the scope and nature of their findings and recommendations, providing "face-saving" opportunities for those who were perceived as "guilty," and generating commitment to implementing the recommendations; all of which were necessary in the opinion of the consultants to attain the long-term changes necessary to resolve the crisis. Whether or not behavioral science consultants can be similarly effective in other political systems cannot be determined. But it is clear that such a negotiation process is essential to the management of crises in the political arena.

One side effect of the negotiation process employed here was the maintenance of a cordial relationship between the consultants and all of the other protagonists. At the conclusion of the consultation there seemed to be a widespread feeling on the part of all the principals, including the Mayor, Board, City Council, Commissioner, and the Ad Hoc Workers Council, that the consultants had fulfilled the roles of unbiased, "honest brokers." Perhaps it was this shared perception of the consultants that permitted the high degree of acceptance of their findings and recommendations. On the other hand, however, the consultants have never again been used by the Department following the submission of the final report. This suggests that when crisis consultation leads to the drawing of "organizational blood," the consulting team has used up its creditability with the organization. On the other hand, perhaps not enough time has elapsed since the consultation was undertaken to warrant making so flat or sweeping a statement. The future will confirm or deny this impression.

In retrospect, it is also clear to the consultants that participation in this kind of project turns out to be heady stuff, indeed. Within a period of less than two months, the consulting team had managed to secure the resignation of the Commissioner of Health, the resignation of the entire Board of Health (the first time this had occurred in over 100 years), had the City Council pass a resolution to pursue a charter change in increase the size of the Board, and had generally changed the psychological climate of a major city agency. How the consultants managed to maintain noble disinterest in their own potency during this period of great political influence is for the reader to decide.

We have noted that there was a considerable amount of newspaper and other press coverage of the crisis in the Health Department. We would be overly modest if we did not note that the evening newspaper,[1] shortly after the final events described above, editorialized as follows: "A word of thanks is in order to psychologists Dr. Ronald K. Boyer and Dr. Leonard D. Goodstein . . . of the University of Cincinnati, for their penetrating and civic-minded studies of the inadequacies of the Health Department." Our case study ends as the editorial concluded, "Now comes the hard work of drawing up sound plans and getting on with reconstruction."

Notes

1. Cincinnati Post and Times-Star, November 20, 1970.

References

Argyris, C. *Intervention theory and method: A behavioral science view.* Reading, Mass.: Addison-Wesley, 1970.

Schein, E. H. *Process consultation: Its role in organization development.* Reading, Mass.: Addison-Wesley, 1969.

ROLE NEGOTIATION
A Tough Minded Approach to Team Development*
Roger Harrison

Getting people to work together in harmony is no easy task. Modern management techniques abound with new approaches to improving the working relationship between employees. In the United States, sensitivity training has had quite a vogue, and various techniques such as the T-group or the managerial grid have been brought forth to encourage managers to abandon their competitiveness and to create mutual trust and egalitarian approaches to decision-making.

Or managers have been urged to change their motivations from reliance upon monetary reward or punishment to more internal motivation based on intrinsic interest in the job and personal commitment to meeting work objectives: for example, in Management By Objectives and programs of job enrichment. Still other practitioners have developed purely rational approaches to group problem-solving (for example, Kepner Tregoe in the United States, and Cloverdale in Britain).

Running through these approaches is the tendency to ignore or explain away competition, conflict and the struggle for power and influence. They assume people will be cooperative and productive if they are taught how, or if the barriers to their so being are removed. These approaches may be called *tender minded* in that they see power struggles as a symptom of a managerial *mistake* rather than a basic and ubiquitous process in organizations.

*Reproduced by special permission from W. Warner Burke and H. Hornstein (eds.) *The Social Technology of Organization Development.* Copyright © NTL Learning Resources 1972.

The problem of organizational change is seen as one of *releasing* human potential for collaboration and productivity, rather than as one of controlling or checking competition for advantage and position.

However, consider the case of the production and engineering managers of a plant who had frequent disagreements over the work that was done by the latter for the former. The production manager complained that the engineering manager set maintenance priorities to meet his own convenience and reduce his own costs, rather than to make sure production targets were met. The engineering manager maintained that the production manager gave insufficient notice of jobs which could be anticipated, and the production operators cause unnecessary breakdowns by failure to carry out preventive maintenance procedures faithfully. The two men aired their dissatisfaction with one another's performance from time to time: but according to both parties, no significant change has occurred...

Or take the case of the scientist in a development department who complains of overly close supervision by his section manager. According to the scientist, the manager intervenes to change the priorities he assigns to work, or to interfere with his development of promising lines of enquiry, and to check up with insulting frequency to see whether the scientist is carrying out the manager's instructions.

The scientist is actively trying to get a transfer to another section, because he feels he cannot do a proper job with so much hampering interference from above.

On the other hand, the section manager says the scientist does competent work but is secretive and unwilling to heed advice. He fails to let the manager know what he is doing and deviates without discussion from agreements the manager thought they had reached about how the work should be carried out. The manager feels he has to spend far too much time checking up on the scientist and is beginning to wonder whether his otherwise good work is worth the trouble required to manage him.

In both of these examples, the men are concerned with either gaining increased control over the actions of the other, reducing control by the other or both. And they know it. A consultant talking to them about communication problems or target setting would no doubt be listened to politely, but in their hearts, these men would still feel it was a question of who was going to have the final say, who was going to be boss.

And, in a way, they are more intuitively right than any outside consultant could be. They know where the power and influence lie, whether people are on their side or against them. They are aware of those with whom they can be open and honest and those who will use information against them. And these concerns are much more accurate and real than an outsider's suggestions for openness and collaboration.

Knowing Where the Power and Coercion Lie

Does this mean that most behavioural science approaches to business are too optimistic? What is certain is that they fail to take into account the forces of power, competitiveness, and coercion. In this article, I shall propose a method that does work directly with these issues, a method that gets tough with the team spirit.

This program is based on role negotiation. This technique describes the process that involves changing through *negotiation* with other interested parties the *role* that an individual or group performs in the organization. By an individual's or group's *role*, I mean what activities he is supposed to perform, what decisions he can make, to whom he reports and about what and how often, who can legitimately tell him what to do and under what circumstances, and so on. Some people would say that a man's *job* is the same as what I have called his *role*, and I would partially agree with this. But what I mean by *role* includes not only the formal job description but also all the informal understandings, agreements, expectations, and arrangements with others which determine the way one person's or group's work affects or fits in with another's.

Role negotiation intervenes directly in the relationships of power, authority, and influence within the group. The change effort is directed at the work relationships among members. It avoids probing into the likes and dislikes of members for one another and their personal feelings about one another. In this it is more consonant with the task-oriented norms of business than are most other behavioural approaches.

The Fear of Touchy Emotional Confrontations

When I first developed the technique, I tried it out on a client group which was proving particularly hard to work with. They were suspicious and mistrustful of me and of each other, and said quite openly that talking about their relationships was both "irrelevant to our work problems" and "dangerous—it could split the group apart." When I introduced them to role negotiation, they saw ways they could deal with issues that were bothering them without getting into touchy emotional confrontations they could not handle. They dropped their resistance dramatically and turned to work with a will that surprised and delighted me.

I have used role negotiation successfully with top management groups, project teams, even between husbands and wives. The technique can be used with very small or quite large groups—although groups of over eight or ten should be broken down.

The technique makes one basic assumption: *most people prefer a fair negotiated settlement to a state of unresolved conflict,* and they are willing to invest some time and make some concessions in order to achieve a solution. To operate the program a modest but significant risk is called for from the participants: they must be open about the changes in behavior, authority, responsibility, etc., they wish to obtain from others in the situation.

If the participants are willing to specify concretely the changes they desire from others, then significant changes in work effectiveness can usually be obtained.

How does this program work in reality? First of all, the consultant must have the participants' sufficient confidence in his motives and competence so that they are willing at his behest to try something new and a bit strange. It also stands to reason that the consultant should know enough about the people, their work system and their relationship problems to satisfy himself that the members of the group are ready to make a real effort towards improvement. No technique will work if the clients don't trust the consultant enough to give it a fair try or if the members of the group (particularly the high influence members) devote most of their effort to maintaining the status quo. In the description that follows I am assuming that this confidence and readiness to work have been established. Although this is a rather large assumption, these problems are universal in consulting and not peculiar to role negotiation. If anything, I have found that role negotiation requires somewhat less preparation than other team development techniques I have used.

Let us say we are working with a group of five to seven people, including a manager and his subordinates, two levels in the formal organization. Once basic assumptions of trust are established, I try to get at least a day with the group away from the job location to start the role-negotiation process going. A two-day session with a commitment to follow up in three to four weeks is best. If the group is not felt to be quite prepared to undertake serious work, the session may be made longer with some trust building and diagnostic activities in the beginning, working into the role negotiation when and if the group is ready for it.

No Probing into People's Feelings

The first step in the actual role negotiation is *contract setting*. Its purpose is to make it clear between the group and the consultant what each may expect from the other. This is a critical step in the change process. It controls and channels everything that happens afterwards.

My contract is usually based on the following provisions, which should be written down, if only as a first practice step in the formal way of working which I try to establish.

It is not legitimate for the consultant to press or probe anyone's *feelings*. We are concerned about work: who does what, how and with whom. How people *feel* about their work or about others in the group is their own business, to be introduced or not according to their own judgment and desire. The expression or nonexpression of feelings is not part of the contract.

Openness and honesty about behavior are expected and essential for achieving results. The consultant will insist that people be specific and concrete in expressing their expectations and demands for the behavior of others. Each team member is expected to be open and specific about what he wants others to do *more* or *do better* or *do less* or *maintain unchanged.*

No expectation or demand is adequately communicated until it has been *written down* and is clearly understood by both sender and receiver, nor will any change process be engaged in until this has been done.

The full sharing of expectations and demands does not constitute a completed change process. It is only the precondition for change to be agreed through negotiation. It is unreasonable for anyone in the group, manager or subordinate, to expect that any change will take place merely as a result of communicating a demand or expectation. Unless a team member is willing to change his own behavior in order to get what he wants from the other(s), he is likely to waste his and the group's time talking about the issue. When a member makes a request or demand for changed behavior on the part of another, the consultant will always ask what *quid pro quo* (something for something) he is willing to give in order to get what he wants. This goes for the manager as well as for the subordinates. If the former can get what he wants simply by issuing orders or clarifying expectations from his position of authority, he probably does not need a consultant or a change process.

The change process is essentially one of bargaining and negotiation in which two or more members each agree to change behavior in exchange for some desired change on the part of the other. This process is not complete until the agreement can be *written down* in terms which include the agreed changes in behavior and make clear what each party is expected to give in return.

Threats and pressures are neither illegitimate nor excluded from the negotiation process. However, group members should realize that over-reliance on threats and punishment usually results in defensiveness, concealment, decreased communication and retaliation, and may lead to breakdown of the negotiation. The consultant will do his best to help members accomplish their aims with positive incentives wherever possible.

The Secret Game of Influence Bargaining

Each member has power and influence in the group, both positively to reward and collaborate with others, and negatively to resist, block or punish. Each uses his power and influence to create a desirable and satisfying work situation for himself. Most of the time this process is gone about secretly. People use a lot of time and energy trying to figure out how to influence another person's behavior covertly, but since they rarely are aware of others' wants and needs, their attempts fail.

Although in stable organizations, employees can learn what works on others just through trial and error over long periods of time, nowadays the fast personnel turnover makes this primitive process obsolete.

Role negotiation tries to replace this old process with a more efficient one. If one person knows because it has been made public what another's wants or intentions are, he is bound to be more effective in trying to influence that person. In addition, when someone tries to influence him, the *quid pro quo* put forward is more likely to be one he really wants or needs. I try to show my clients that by sharing the information about desires and attempts, *role negotiation increases the total amount of influence group members have on one another.*

The next stage is *issue diagnosis.* Each member spends some time thinking about the way business is conducted between himself and the others in the group. What would he change if he could? What would he like to keep as is? Who and what would have to change in order to improve things? I ask the participants to focus especially on the things which might be changed to improve their *own effectiveness,* since these are the items to be discussed and negotiated.

After he has spent twenty minutes or so thinking about these matters and perhaps making a few notes, each member fills out one Issue Diagnosis Form (like the one in Figure 1) for each other member, listing those things he would like to see the other person

1. Do more or do better
2. Do less or stop doing
3. Keep on doing, maintain unchanged

All of these messages are based on the sender's increasing his own effectiveness in his job.

These lists are exchanged so that each person has all the lists pertaining to his work behavior. Each member makes a master list for himself on a large piece of paper itemizing the behavior which each other person desires him to do *more* or *better, less* or *continue unchanged* (Figure 2). These are posted so that the entire group can peruse and refer to each list. Each member is allowed to question the others who have sent messages about his behavior, querying the what, why, and how of their requests, *but no one is allowed a rebuttal, defense or even a yes or no reply to the messages he has received.* The consultant must assure that only clarification is taking place; argument, discussion and decision making about issues must be engaged in at a later stage.

Messages from *Jim Farrell*

to *David Sills*

1. If you were to do the following
   things <u>more</u> or <u>better</u>, it would help
   me to increase my own effectiveness:

   *- Be more receptive to improvement
   suggestions from the process Engineers
   - Give help on cost control (see 2)
   - Fight harder with the G.M. to
   get our plans improved.*

2. If you were to do the following
   things <u>less</u>, or were to <u>stop</u> doing
   them, it would help me to increase
   my own effectiveness:

   *- Acting as judge and jury on cost
   control.
   - Checking up frequently on small details
   of the work.
   - Asking for so many detailed progress
   reports.*

3. The following things which you have
   been doing help to increase my own
   effectiveness, and I hope you will
   continue to do them:

   *- Passing on full information in our
   weekly meetings.
   Being available when I need to
   talk to you.*

Figure 1   Issue diagnosis form.

Defensiveness Just to Save Face

The purpose of the consultant's rather rigid and formal control on communication
is to prevent the group from having a negative problem-solving experience and
members from becoming polarized on issues or taking up extreme positions which
they will feel impelled to defend just to save face. Communication is controlled
to prevent escalation of actual or potential conflicts Channeling the energy re-

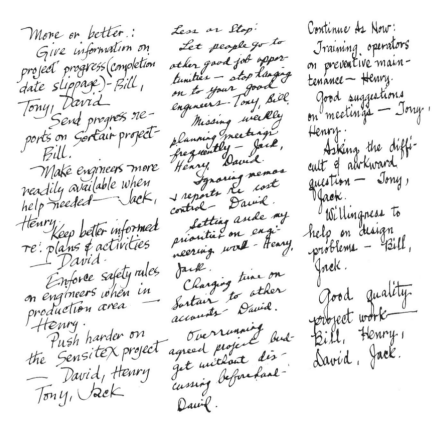

Figure 2   Summary of messages to James Farrell from other group members.

leased by the sharing of demands and expectations into successful problem solving and mutual influence is behind this strategy of control.

The consultant intervenes to inhibit hostile and destructive expression at this point and later to facilitate constructive bargaining and negotiation of mutually beneficial agreements.

This initial sharing of desires and change goals among group members leads to a point at which the team development process is most vulnerable. If sufficient anger and defensiveness are generated by the problem sharing, the consultant will not be able to hold the negative processes in check long enough for the development of the positive problem-solving spiral on which the process depends for its effectiveness. It is true that such an uncontrollable breakthrough of hostility has not yet occurred in my experience with the method. Nevertheless, concern over the negative possibilities is in part responsible for my slow, deliberate and rather formal development of the confrontation of issues within the group.

The Influence Trade

After each member has had an opportunity to clarify the messages he has received, the group selects the issues for negotiation. The consultant begins this phase by reemphasizing that unless a *quid pro quo* can be offered in return for a desired behavior change, there is little point in having a discussion about it: *unless behavior changes on both sides the most likely prediction is that the status quo will continue.*

If behavior changes merely as the result of an exchange of views between men of good will, all the better. However, one cannot count on it.

Each participant is asked to choose one or more issues on which he particularly wants to get some changes on the part of another. He is also asked to select one or more issues on which he feels it may be possible for him to move in the direction desired by others. He does this by marking his own flip chart and those of the other members. In effect, *each person indicates the issues upon which he most wants to exert influence and those on which he is most willing to accept influence.* With the help of the consultant the group then goes through the lists to select the "most negotiable issues," those where there is a combination of a high desire for change on the part of an initiator and a willingness to negotiate on the part of the person whose behavior is the target of the change attempt. The consultant asks for a group of two or more persons who are involved in one such issue to volunteer for a negotiation demonstration before the rest of the group.

The negotiation process consists of the parties making contingent offers to one another such as "If you do X, I will do Y." The negotiation ends when all parties are satisfied that they will receive a reasonable return for whatever they are agreeing to give. The consultant asks that the agreement be formalized by writing down specifically and concretely what each party is going to give and receive in the bargain (Figure 3). He also asks the participants to discuss openly what sanctions can be applied in the case of nonfulfillment of the bargain by one or another party. Often this involves no more than reversion to the status quo, but it may involve the application of pressures and penalties as well.

After the negotiation demonstration, the members are asked to select other issues they wish to work on. A number of negotiations may go on simultaneously, the consultant being involved at the request of any party to any negotiation. All agreements are published to the entire group, however, and questioned by the consultant and the other members to test the good faith and reality orientation of the parties in making them. Where agreement proves impossible, the consul-

Jim agrees to let David know as soon as agreed completion dates and cost projections look as though they won't be met, and also to discuss each project's progress fully with David on a bi-weekly basis.

In return, David agrees not to raise questions about cost details and completion dates, pending a trial of this agreement to see if it provides sufficient information soon enough to deal with questions from above.

Figure 3   Final agreement between James Farrell and David Sills.

tant and other group members try to help the parties find further incentives (positive or, less desirable, coercive) which they may bring to bear to encourage agreement.

This process is, of course, not as simple as it sounds. All kinds of difficulties can occur, from bargaining in bad faith, to refusal to bargain at all, to escalation of conflict. In my experience, however, group members tend to be rather wise about the issues they can and cannot deal with, and I refrain from publishing them to negotiate issues they feel are unresolvable. My aim is to light the sparks of team development with a successful experience which group members can look on as a fruitful way of improving their effectiveness and satisfaction.

The Consultant Withers Away

The cycle ends here. Each group must then try living with their agreements. There is always, of course, the occasion to meet later with the consultant to work out new agreements or renegotiate old ones.

Ideally, the group should learn this process so thoroughly that the consultant's role withers away. To do this, though, they must be so fully aware of the dangers and pitfalls involved in the negotiation process that a third party's arbitration is no longer needed.

So far this has not occurred in my experience. The positive results are expressed mostly in terms of less backsliding between visits than has occurred in groups where I have applied more interpersonal behavior-change methods. Role negotiation agreements have more teeth in them.

What are the advantages of role negotiation? First of all, participants seem more at home with problems of power and influence than other interpersonal issues. They feel more competent and less dependent on the consultant in dealing with the problems and so they are ready to work sooner and harder.

Furthermore, the consultant's or "referee's" amount of skill and professional training which is required to conduct role negotiation is less than for more sensitive approaches.

That does not mean that role negotiation poses no threat to organization members. The consultant asks participants to be open about matters that are often kept secret in every day life. This requires more than the normal amount of trust and confidence. If not, these matters would have been talked about before the group every got to the role negotiation.

There also seems to be some additional discomfort involved in *writing down* the changes one would like to see another make in his work behavior. Several times participants have questioned the necessity of doing this, because one feels so *exposed* when his concerns are written out for all to see, and there is the fear that others will think them silly, childish or odd (though this never seems to happen). If the matter comes up, I point out that one need not write down *all* the concerns he has, but only those he would like to work on with others at this time.

Of course, role negotiation, like any other process that changes relationships, does pose a threat to the participants. The members are never sure they will personally be better off after the change than before. In the case of role negotiation, most of these fears arise around losing power and influence, or losing freedom and becoming more controlled by others. Particular resistance to talking openly about issues occurs when someone is trying to manipulate another person to his own advantage, or when he feels that he might want to do this in the future. I think this is the main reason participants in role negotiation so often try to avoid the step of writing down their agreements. If things aren't down in black and white, they feel, it will be easier to ignore the agreement later on if it becomes inconvenient. Also, writing down agreements seems to dispel the aura of trust and good fellowship which some groups like to create on the surface and below which they engage in quite a lot of cutthroat competition.

Role negotiation is of course no panacea for power problems in groups and between people. People may bargain in bad faith; agreements once reached may be broken; circumstances and personnel may change so that the work done becomes irrelevant. Of course, these problems can exist in any group or organization. What role negotiation *does* is to try to deal with the problems directly and to identify and use constructively those areas of *mutual* advantage where both sides can benefit from discussion and agreement. These areas are almost always larger than people think they are, and when they find that they can achieve something *for* themselves by open negotiation which they could not achieve by covert competition, then the more constructive process can begin to grow.

Avoiding the Consultant's High Fees

One other likely advantage of role negotiation is the ease and economy with which it can be introduced into the firm.

One disadvantage of most behavioral approaches to team development is that the consultant's level of skill and experience must be very high indeed. Managers themselves are not confident in dealing with these issues, and because they feel uneasy in this area they reasonably want to have as much safety and skill as money can buy. This demand for skilled consultants on interpersonal and group processes has created a shortage and a meteoric rise in consulting fees. It seems unlikely that the supply will soon catch up with the demand.

The shortage of highly skilled workers in team development argues for de-skilling the requirements for effective consultant performance. I see role negotiation as a way of reducing the skill requirements for team development consultation. Preliminary results by internal consultants using the approach have been promising.

For example, one Management Development Manager teamed up with a colleague to conduct a successful role negotiation with his own top management. He reported that his main problem was getting up enough confidence to take on the job. The team development session itself went smoothly. Although I cannot say whether this experience was typical (I suspect it was not), it does lead me to hope that role negotiation will prove to be practical for use by internal consultants without professional training in the behavioral sciences.

What then are the main points about role negotiation? Firstly, role negotiation focuses on work relationshipe: what people do, and how they facilitate and inhibit one another in the performance of their jobs. It encourages participants to work with problems using words and concepts they are used to using in business. It avoids probing to the deeper levels of their feelings about one another unless this comes out naturally in the process.

Secondly, it deals directly with problems of power and influence which may be neglected by other behavioral approaches. It does not attempt to dethrone the authority in the group, but other members are helped to explore realistically the sources of power and influence available to them.

Also, unlike some other behavioral approaches to team development, role negotiation is highly action-oriented. Its aim is not just the exposing and understanding of issues as such, but achieving changed ways of working through mutually negotiated agreements. Changes brought about through role negotiation thus tend to be more stable and lasting than where such negotiated commitments are lacking.

In addition, all the procedures of role negotiation are clear and simple if a bit mechanical, and can be described to participants in advance so they know what they are getting into. There is nothing mysterious about the technique, and this reduces participants' feelings of dependency upon the special skill of the consultant.

Furthermore, role negotiation actually requires less skill from the consultant than some other behavioral approaches. Internal consultants can suitably use the technique without lengthy special training in the behavioral sciences. It can therefore be a moderate cost approach to organization change.

It's important to understand that role negotiation does not necessarily replace other "soft" behavioral approaches to organization change. Work groups can be effective and achievement-oriented and at the same time allow open and deeply satisfying interpersonal relationships.

However, resolving conflict successfully at the interpersonal level can only be done by first attacking the ever-present issues of power and influence among members. Role negotiation does this and provides a sound and effective base upon which to build more satisfying relationships.

If role negotiation is an effective first or "basic" approach to team development, it goes without saying that employee growth means moving beyond this stage into a deeper exploration of integrating work and relationships.

THE PROSPECTS FOR ORGANIZATIONAL DEVELOPMENT THROUGH MULTI-TEAM BUILDING*

E. J. Jones, Jr.

Multi-Team Building, the bringing together of three or more teams for a mutual experience in team building, has developed enough history to deserve serious attention. Over forty teams have come to the Federal Executive Institute to share in this experience. The design used for these sessions, and six distinctive qualities are reported. The educational setting, the heterogenous mixing of teams, the effect on the team leaders, the richness of the diversity, are, among other factors, reported as contributing to a better product than single team training is likely to produce.†

Conventional and Multi-Team Building

Team Building has emerged during the last five years as one of the principal strategies in the organizational development process. Among other things, it is concerned with forging a synthesis between organizational imperatives and the needs and goals of the individuals who make up human systems. It encourages the members to be more aware of the feelings of others rather than being con-

*Reprinted from *An Approach to Executive Development in Government: The Federal Executive Institute Experience,* Paul C. Buchanan, editor, (Washington, D.C.: National Academy of Public Administration, 1974), pp. 132-139.
†Appreciation is extended to George F. J. Lehner for his many contributions.

cerned almost totally with the "facts," with the technology, or with completing the task. Team building can be used as a suitable strategy for the initiation of a change effort in an organization. It has unusual potential for identifying both strengths on which the organization can build and possible limitations or barriers to its growth. A successful team building effort helps to establish effective problem solving procedures and to develop both individual and group relating skills. It may provide for a social bonding of the group, for ventilating stored up feelings in a relatively safe climate and for generating healthy new norms for the groups' interpersonal behavior.

When managers and consultants discuss strategies for executive or management improvement, team-building figures prominently. The consultant, particularly if from the behavioral sciences, is likely to offer a proposal for a team building effort as one step in a larger design to improve the operation of the system. Sometimes, this event follows individual consultation and interviews. It may be a sequel to participation of key figures in a "stranger" training event, or be used as an initial intervention with little previous collection of data or diagnosis.

Multi-team building, the process described here, is a logical outgrowth of conventional team building. For the most part, it uses OD technologies that have been applied in many other settings. What appears to make the difference is the presence of an array of teams: teams of different sizes, purposes, and personalities; teams that have had a great deal of training and those that have had none; teams that have been functioning effectively and ones that have not.

In its most simple application, multi-team calls for bringing together five to seven teams in a one-week residential workshop. The experiences reported here occurred in a setting not always feasible to reproduce. They are unusual in that generally the leader or a senior member had been through a residential long-term (eight-week) program. There was little or no direct pre-work done until the team arrived and the teams all came from agencies of the Federal Government.

Building Teams at the Federal Executive Institute

By the summer of 1973, over 1,200 senior executives had participated in the eight-week residential program of FEI. During the first year, one-week programs were initiated and one of these was devoted to Organizational Development. The workshop design used in both the eight-week and one-week programs called for organizing the "stranger" participants into work teams and attempting to demonstrate the efficacy of OD methods through a series of simulated exercises. A secondary goal of these early workshops was to help managers become more effective change agents. As a practical matter, this experience offered the executive an introduction to OD rather than an opportunity to prepare intensively for organizational change upon returning to his organization. There was an expressed need on the part of executives, to leave the Institute with a strategy to try if the opportunity presented, or at least with a preliminary plan that could be developed back home. Organizational Development was recognized as a methodology that might be helpful to the returning manager.

During the summer of 1971, the first Multi-Team Building workshop was announced. In the original brochure we said that these central concepts would be pursued:

1. The expanding of human potential as a basis for all organizational growth
2. The need for receptivity for change as well as a capability to design change at the individual, organizational, and systems levels
3. The centrality of the small face-to-face group (the team) to the overall performance of the organization
4. The potential for maximum payoff where interrelated teams share the experience

By April, 1973, the Institute had completed the seventh of these one-week programs in a series called Organizational Development and Multi-Team Building Workshop. During the two years, over forty teams and several hundred executives representing a broad spectrum of Federal agencies had participated in this training.

Certain assumptions were made in the initial design of multi-team building. Others emerged from experience as the teams have moved through the week. These include:

1. We assume that the payoff comes from building on team competencies and successes. One of the emerging dilemmas is how best to make this theory operational in ways the teams can accept and use, once back at the work place.
2. We assume that the individuals and the team will become more assured and more effective, as new competencies, both individual and team, are identified and skills sharpened.
3. We assume that where six or seven teams can meet together for a week in a residential setting, major benefits accrue. Consultants must be wise enough, of course, to help team members exploit the opportunities presented.
4. We assume that any one-week exposure is merely an opening and that if we are to build on the residential experience, much more needs to be done over an extended time.
5. We assume that most teams will need additional consultant help in developing their OD programs beyond initial team building.

6. We assume that it is imperative to develop system skills, for example, skills in making decisions, in setting goals, in evaluating programs.

7. We assume that there will be few significant changes in leadership style as a result of a team-building experience. To a large degree, we rely on increased individual and system awareness of the possible payoff or costs that accompany specific behaviors.

8. We assume that some leaders and some team members will be threatened even by a technique that has built in safety devices. To minimize this threat, the consultant is encouraged to emphasize individual and team growth. The assumption is made that every human system has many deficiencies and that placing undue stress on them is less productive than identifying and exploiting opportunities for more effective system behavior.

9. We assume that for most of these teams it is not feasible to conduct extensive data collection prior to the residential meeting. The pre-work is done at the training site.

Design for First 2½ Days

The design calls for a one-week program in which about 60 executives in six or eight teams meet in two major formations. We start the week by asking the executives to examine their expectations about the experience they are entering. Specifically, they are asked to score the expectations on a seven-point scale. They are asked to discuss these with a neighbor and after a few minutes share some of the things that influenced their ratings. The facilitator proceeds through a series of induction exercises designed to help the participant identify learning needs and to develop feelings of contact with and acceptance for other participants.

At this first meeting, the group is divided into eight-person Executive Learning Teams and asked to complete a work project within a limited time (2-3 hours). These assigned tasks vary, generally requiring each group to present a 5-7 minute skit, or to design, construct, and present a collage. Either activity is then subjected to a careful within-group examination of the processes which have been followed in meeting the assigned task. Thus, in the first hours of the training, participants are asked to experience a new mode of learning, make initial contact with seven or eight other executives, make a presentation to the entire workshop, and examine their own behavior and that of others when asked to complete an unusual task while working with strangers.

The second module of the workshop looks at ways to increase personal effectiveness. A filmed case, "The Bob Knowlton Story," role playing, and a lecturette reviewing factors that create a climate in which personal effectiveness is fostered are used. The concept is advanced that both personal and team effectiveness are functions of the situation as it is perceived by the person, of the skills of the participants both technically and in interpersonal relating, of the level of motivation of those involved, of the goals set, and of the environment in which the event occurs.

On the second day, module three offers a self-assessment exercise designed to stimulate the executive (who is still working with strangers) to examine his/her behavior in a variety of ways.

For example, we ask:

1. Looking back on your life, what additional skills would you have particularly wished to have?
2. What three things about yourself (characteristics) would you like to reinforce?
3. If you knew you had only six months to live, what would you change about the way you go about your life?

After responding to twenty questions in the 45 minutes allowed, executives are asked to join two colleagues and discuss their answers. Here too, the exercise is designed to make explicit skill training in listening, in presenting one's self, and in observing dialogue between others.

Subsequent modules focus on technologies of OD stressing other than interpersonal aspects. For example, elements of the work of Lawrence and Lorsch on organizational differentiation and integration are presented and participants are asked to assess themselves as change agents. Team Building Confronting Conflict (Sheldon Davis) films depicting a consultant working with a team are shown and discussed. On the third evening, in the module prior to moving to the work teams, the executives do a group decision making exercise. This is used to focus on the events in the decision making process in the stranger group as a prelude to convening the work group. At the close of this exercise, the Executive Learning Teams are asked to put on flip chart paper the concerns each has about starting with his/her work team the following day. One purpose is to provide an opportunity for the executives to learn from each other that there are few unique concerns!

Design for Second 2½ Days

On Wednesday morning, a consultant introduces the general design for the rest of the week to a meeting of all of the teams. The teams are requested to develop an agenda of things with which they wish to deal, indicating which will probably require more work back home. The team is divided into clusters of three or four to do this, and one member from each cluster reports to the team. The director or supervisor of the team works separately with the team consultant to develop his/her list. Questions are designed to elicit data, for example:

What happens when this team works on a task that helps you to perform effectively?

What, or who hinders you from performing effectively?

Prepare a "wish list" completing the sentence "When I think about this team, I wish that _____."

The purpose of these is to assemble a variety of responses aimed at the organizational level, at the interpersonal level, and at the personal level. When each sub-group has its data posted, the representatives and the director present the items and answer questions of understanding that may arise. Then, there is a general discussion in order to combine items to develop a working agenda for the group. All items in the data bank are, however, left on the wall to avoid squeezing the interest from them as they are combined. The team is asked to estimate how much they can realistically accomplish by the end of the week. Expectations of the director, the team members, and the consultant are exchanged in an effort to assure maximum understanding of expectations about what may be accomplished.

Early in the team discussion, the consultant suggests a look at what sort of teamwork is expected or required of the group. Where there are distinct differences, by analogy, where some team members see the team performing as a swimming team might and others see it performing in the mode of a basketball team, these differences and their implications are explored. It is observed that many individuals and teams are expected to perform differently in different circumstances and that misinterpretation of the roles to be played may cause serious difficulty. One obvious contrast occurs when the leader of an operational division plays multiple roles including helping to make the corporate decisions with his boss's team, acting as a leader of his work team, and collaborating with his peers as the work moves through his team to the next work activity.

When these matters have had an ititial exposure, the consultant helps the group to begin working on some of the problems or challenges arrayed in the data bank before them. As one of these moves toward resolution, the consultant asks the group to STOP ACTION and examine how they went about dealing with the issue raised. The steps are re-traced and, to the extent the team is ready, a team analysis is made of the process used. A tentative model for problem solving is put on the wall and the group may continue to use and revise this as it works on additional issues.

After the work team has been meeting for several hours and usually after several of the items in the "data bank" have been fully discussed, the consultant offers a format for an action agenda. The purpose of this agenda is to capture the agreements made in the team concerning action to be taken back home. At the end of the week, each member is given a copy which serves as a handy checklist when the team meets again for a few hours six weeks to two months after the workshop. A suggested format indicates who is going to take what action, with whom, to assure meeting what ends or goals, on what time schedule, and how the team will know that it has achieved the things it proposed doing. Thus, by the end of the workshop, the teams have been through a number of problems they have identified as important and, hopefully, have developed a working model for decision making. Essentially, this technique provides a self designed management by objectives procedure with related skill development. On the last day, the heterogeneous groups meet again to share experiences from their work teams. Finally, they are asked to evaluate the experience both as an individual and as a team member.

Nature and Merits of Multi-Team Building

Much of what happens in Multi-Team Building is similar to what happens in conventional team building. The experience, however, is different in a number of ways—in the media as well as in the messages. These findings have been clinically arrived at through working with a large number of teams (over 40).

The diversity of these teams is note worthy for they range in size from four to twenty-two and from agencies as various in mission as the Federal Communications Commission, the Internal Revenue Service, the Agency for International Development, each of the military departments, and the Central Intelligence Agency. Functional representation included teams from a Comptroller Office, an ad hoc team brought together to design an executive development program for a large agency, a small group charged with preparing a special budget submission, and a group of highly specialized professionals who administer components of a major national program.

The announcement of the workshop encouraged the manager to bring those central to the decision making process and some teams included administrative officers, secretaries, and related staff personnel. In a few cases, an in-house consultant came as part of the team and this strategy seemed to have a desired payoff. Each of these consultants has reported opportunities for additional work arising directly from the Multi-Team Building week.

Six of the distinctive qualities of Multi-Team are reported.

1. The experience at the Institute was characterized by a learning or educationally oriented climate rather than by a predominantly work climate. Though off-site conventional team building often captures some of this, it proved richer when several teams met in a residential educational setting. There were reports of teams that had an especially good referring to the "Spirit of Charlottesville."

2. The mixing of executives for the first two-and-a-half or three days had many advantages for both team leaders and members. It provided a

period for pre-work in which the participant could think through some of his own problems while he heard others talk of theirs. This recognition that others in very different settings have related concerns was the basis for a relaxation of tensions prior to the start of team building.

3. Diversity was characteristic of the teams that came to Multi-Team. Most apparent were great differences in the experience in group problem solving. It was surprising and encouraging to observe that as individuals with wide differences grow in self confidence in this development process, so, too, do teams. Beyond the positive effects of a week together away from the job, the opportunity to see other teams working to attain new levels of group understanding and effectiveness appears to reinforce or elevate team concept.

4. Teams that have in-house consultants working with them are encouraged to include them in the training. Where this happened, results were uniformly positive. It has allowed the consultant to develop a much closer relationship with the team and has resulted in a variety of new opportunities once back at the work. The opportunity offered other managers to see the role of the in-house consultant was especially useful.

5. Multi-Team is designed as an initial intervention; most teams come with no pre-work. One view is that the pre-work takes place both during the first two-and-a-half days and in the period when the work teams are engaged in developing data.

6. For some of the reasons stated above (see items 1 & 2), and others that are speculative, team building in conjunction with other teams seems to be far less threatening to the team leaders. Simply stated, this has resulted in many more teams participating than we could have hoped for in a single team setting.

There has been no research on Multi-Team Building Workshops. What is known is the product of clinical observations and subjective comparison of teams working in this setting and working singly in many other contexts. We do know that at least ten teams have done additional work on organization development as a consequence of a Multi-Team session. Several leaders have given accounts of their satisfaction through personal testimony and by supporting the attendance of additional teams through contact with colleagues both in their own organizations and outside. At a minimum, the experience has provided a basis for an improved team-concept. That is, team members were able to see themselves and their team as more effective after the meetings than they had before. Further, team members were made more aware of both problems to be faced and new opportunities available for facing them effectively.

Finally, we note with satisfaction the absence of the negative reactions that have sometimes characterized single or conventional team building. These factors are credited: consultants made a special effort to help team members deal with task-related behaviors that were getting in the way of effective performance; members were encouraged to develop a climate where threat was minimized and chances to take small risks were provided; and participants and team leaders alike could and did talk with others in the community of 60 about their experiences, both pleasant and otherwise, in the mixed or stranger teams and in the work teams, thus working out tensions while they were still manageable.

CAREER DEVELOPMENT FOR WOMEN
An Affirmative Action First*

Janice Kay

Corporations doing business with government agencies have been thrust into the forefront of the women's movement by necessity. . . . When the Affirmative Action Act was revised in 1972, not only did it require equal opportunity, training, pay and work conditions for men and women, but it stipulated that employers must develop career counseling and remedial training programs for employees. Some of the programs that resulted were thorough and effective, and some were thrown together with the hope of meeting the legal requirements.

One of the most exciting programs I've seen is outside the private sector. The State of Washington has embarked on a pilot project of career development for women that may well become a model program. The first state government to initiate such a program, Washington's far-sighted Civil Service Commission began planning the effort in 1973. The project, expected to take two years to complete, will involve 1,000 women Civil Service employees in all and 50 women trainers. Now past its half-way point, some 400 women have gone through the program and results are already being realized.

To date, evaluation of the program by participants has averaged 9.3 (9 = upper good and 10 = excellent). Minor modifications have taken place and each

*Reproduced by special permission from the May 1976 TRAINING AND DEVELOPMENT JOURNAL. Copyright © 1976 by the American Society for Training and Development, Inc.

trainer is developing her own professional style. We've had such responses as "full of new ideas and hopes . . . organized, practical, yet allowing for individual needs . . . inspired to work toward a career goal that has been a vague dream. . . . I feel important to the system now and feel Washington State cares about its employees, wants us to improve. . . ."

There is some talk that *"Career Development for Women in Washington State Government"* may be modified to include male Civil Service employees as well.

As a result of this program with Washington, I am now working on the creation of a data bank on career information with Mark Johnson, executive director of Washington's Occupational Information Service.

Setting Up the Program

Seminar groups are made up of approximately 25 women, with care taken to mix agencies, departments, salary levels, etc. The women spend two and a half days together in intensive session meant to give each member a new appreciation of her own skills and objectives as well as insight into finding the opportunities within her field. Sessions are held in a conference center live-in setting. It's important to have rooms with comfortable furniture, areas for writing and moving about, with coffee and soft drinks available to create a relaxing atmosphere.

Participation in the seminars is voluntary and requires a sense of commitment on the part of each participant. I believe the value is lessened if women are required to attend by their supervisors. Therefore, when the Civil Service Commission began planning for the seminars, information was circulated to 3,000-4,000 women employees and those interested were urged to apply.

Obviously, career growth for either men or women requires an organizational climate where individual growth is valued. Without a supportive atmosphere, the kind of training being given is of little value. In Washington, even those employees who did not actively participate benefited from an awareness of the State's concern and its desire to implement such a program. Training officers already on the State staff were selected and put through the course in two groups. Annotated copies of the workbook, complete with trainer notes, were given to the group leaders.

No other state has committed its time and resources in this manner to meet vocational counseling requirements of its affirmative action plan. Long hours, midnight brainstorms, writing and rewriting yielded not only the program, but an awareness that women can become a team, find unity of purpose, be committed to other women and work together to achieve parity.

Benefits and Objectives

What's the benefit of such a program to an employer? The enlightened company recognizes its responsibility for career development of employees. Modern behavioral research indicates the need for more than just imparting critical job skills. Employee satisfaction and productivity levels relate to both job challenge and to perceptions of career and development opportunities.

The employer who feels that today's labor is an investment in tomorrow, will develop employees who produce more, have greater loyalty and work harder than employees who consider their jobs only a series of finite tasks and processes or as stepping stones from one life status to another.

Today, more women are voicing concern over discrimination by sex and asking for affirmative action programs that provide:

1. Seminars to aid women with professional growth
2. Vocational counseling
3. Placement of women in positions of responsibility
4. Programs designed to motivate women toward career development
5. Management awareness of these needs.

Course Content

The program design for the State includes a two-day live-in session for participants and a four-day live-in course for trainers plus the manuals for each group. Its objectives are to help the working woman (1) focus on her unused professional strengths; (2) make conscious need-fulfilling decisions about her professional development and (3) see how she can effect career growth and affect others in the process. Those involved were asked to read *Women's Place; Options and Limitations in Professional Careers for Women* by C. Epstein in advance of the seminar.

The program presumes that growth occurs through the process of career goal setting, vocational self-assessment, the use and knowledge of resources for those changes and implementation of the change. To be successful, the participant must direct her own growth, so she begins by actively defining short-term and long-term goals.

To do that, the participant needs to understand her professional self as separate from her private self and to balance and evaluate the factors within herself, other people and institutions which are involved in realizing her career goals.

The exercises in the course material introduce the possibility of self-change and career goal-setting. The techniques used can be applied throughout the participant's life and should help each woman use the resources available within her own experiences for continued professional change and growth. The degree of success depends on her ability to learn to value herself accurately, to acknowledge strengths and weaknesses, to communicate with others, to give as well as receive help as part of a team, to set real goals, make decisions about them and evaluate results.

Each session of the program modules begins with a short introductory presentation by the trainer, one or more directed experiential exercises involving all the group, a discussion period and sometimes a written handout relevant to the exercise. The workbook filled in by each woman provides tangible proof of the experience as well as a do-it-yourself refresher for future use.

The modules covered include:

An Historical Perspective of Women

Exploration of Personal Self-Identity

The Career Planning Process

Washington State Government and Career Opportunities

A secondary objective was to develop a commitment and communication system among the women. "Solidarity" was stressed during class time and members of the group sat together during meals and spend evening hours in conversation over wine and cheese. As the days were long and sessions mentally exhausting, physical activity—from Ping-Pong and catch to frisbee-tossing, swimming and hiking— was planned to provide a needed break.

Trainers' Sessions

The program places a large responsibility on the participant. What of the trainer? Her role is to establish conditions for professional self-development and serve as a resource for participants. She should not determine goals, assess the participants or tell them what to do. On the other hand, she should not be a *laissez faire* leader who explains the exercises and leaves the group to its own devices. The trainer must be explicit in giving directions and must discuss seminar objectives, making sure that each person understands them.

The course for trainers lasted four days and each of the groups covered the basic material and spent two days on a module stressing trainer skills (1) learning objectives (2) the role of the trainer (3) introduction to group dynamics (4) the teacher and group processes and (5) effective use of the instructor's guide. Two additional books suggested for advance reading were *Group Process* by J. Luft and *Everyone Was Brave* by W. O'Neill.

The handbook containing trainers' notes, which supplemented the participants' workbook, was designed to:

I. Enable the instructor to develop a logical and complete teaching plan that leads to achievement of instructional goals.

Establish "extent" and "limits" of instruction

State goals/objectives

Outline the required continuity and organization

II. Provide a reference framework that will:

Establish the instructor as a guiding authority for her class

Provide rapid access to additional depth understanding.

Results To Come

With one more year to go, it's too soon to sum up the effect of the program on the career development of Washington's women civil servants. However, it has become increasingly clear that the program is relevant to any woman regardless of age, race, handicap or cultural background—and should work equally well for men.

The final results will be determined by the number of women in government who go on to managerial positions once considered only a "male" province.

MONITORING THE PROCESS AND
EVALUATING THE RESULTS OF ORGANIZATION DEVELOPMENT*

Donald C. King and John J. Sherwood

"How are we doing?" is a question often asked amid the uncertainties, ambiguities, anxieties, and newness that accompany many attempts at improving organizational effectiveness. While the people involved in these activities are raising this question, their supervisors and other interested onlookers on the outside are raising the question of accountability. Those supplying resources or those onlookers who see themselves being affected by any outcomes of an OD project are likely to be interested in measuring the product or evaluating the outcomes. Their question is: "What are you doing?" So, two questions are frequently raised, often by different parties carrying different perspectives: "How are *we* doing?" and "What are *you* doing?" This paper provides some ways of thinking about these questions and some alternative models for evaluating organization development efforts.

Our interest in writing this paper stems from three concerns or beliefs. The first is the frustration we have experienced in trying to induce organizations to devote time, money, and other resources to evaluating OD efforts. The second is our belief that evaluation has too often been viewed in a non-differentiated, all-or-noting way. We reject the idea that there is *one best way* to evaluate organization development. We see instead several kinds of appropriate evaluational

*Reprinted from Institute for Research in the Behavioral, Economic, and Management Sciences, Krannert School of Industrial Administration, Purdue University, West Lafayette, Indiana, Paper No. 452 (April, 1974).

activities ranging on a continuum from careful documentation of what occurs in an OD project, through process feedback, to evaluation of outcomes, and finally to field research where specific hypotheses or alternative approaches are rigorously tested using the skills and safeguards of the research scientist. All these approaches address themselves to the questions, "How are we doing?" and "What are you doing?"

This paper does *not* focus on how to conduct evaluation studies. Hopefully, it lays out considerations and raises issues which will enable the reader to make better decisions about how his own OD projects can most effectively be evaluated.

We begin by offering five alternative approaches to evaluation and give advantages and disadvantages of each approach. Next, these five models are put into an organizational context by a survey of some of the persistent obstacles to effective evaluation. Finally, two major issues in the design and execution of any evaluation scheme are outlined.

We hope the reader becomes more aware of the alternatives available to him in evaluating OD activities, and recognizes that there is not a single best approach to evaluation. We also hope to increase appreciation for the barriers that exist to evaluation and to increase understanding about why they exist. In our judgment, people have frequently deplored the lack of evaluation studies and have tried to cajole one another into doing more and better evaluation of OD projects without a thorough understanding of the reasons for lack of a history of sound studies evaluating organization development.

Five Models

Let's begin with a committee working on a task. How does a committee know how it's doing on its task and how do the members know how they are performing as parts of the problem-solving process? How does the organization know what contribution the committee makes to the goals of the organization? There are several ways to evaluate the performance of a committee and its members. Each provides us with a different model by which we can approach the evaluation of organization development projects.

Here are five models: (1) Ask the expert; (2) What's the target?; (3) Did we hit the target?; (4) Mid-course correction; and (5) Continuous monitoring. Each of these approaches provides a different perspective and each carries certain advantages and disadvantages (Weiss & Rein, 1970).

1. Ask the Expert

A consultant is asked to provide an independent evaluation of an OD program. The question is, "Tell us how we're doing or how they're doing!" The answer is given by an expert. This model usually calls for evaluation following the completion of OD activities, but expert assistance can take place at any point in the life of a developmental project. While expert evaluation is often given by an outside consultant in the form of a research contract, an internal consultant can also offer an expert evaluation. However, the closer the evaluator is to the organization and its project, the more likely he is to take the project's basic assumptions and organizational arrangements as given and conduct his evaluation within the existing framework. An outsider may be able, on the other hand, to exercise more autonomy in his questioning and take an independent perspective simply because he is not part of the culture. "The implications he draws from evaluation data may be oriented less to tinkering and more to fundamental restructuring of the program" (Weiss, 1972a, p. 21).

One dilemma in asking the expert is that the credibility of his response may differ depending on the audience. Those outside the OD activity, who are asking for accountability, are less likely to view his assessment as biased or self-serving than if the same information were to come from people involved in the change process. Whereas for the latter, unless the expert is able to establish that he has an empathic understanding of the people who are participating in the change process, his credibility with them may be low or suspect.

Advantages:

(a) The use of experts helps us avoid continuously reinventing the wheel. An expert provides competence in research design, data collection, and data analysis techniques. He also prepares and presents reports that are both technically sound and readable.

(b) When the evaluation is assigned to an uninvolved expert, it is not likely to get lost or compromised as the "suction" of the OD project increases.

(c) Where evaluation is conducted by an expert, the comparability of studies is greater, and therefore, just as expert evaluation builds on prior learning it also adds to the accumulation of an OD literature which may be useful to others.

Disadvantages:

(a) Relying on an expert may foster dependence on the competencies of others. Internal resources are then not developed with competencies to monitor their own projects.

(b) While an outside expert is likely to come with a theory or model to guide his evaluation, and this is often an advantage, because of his lack of involvement in the particular OD enterprise, he may impose an inappropriate model for evaluation.

(c) The expert's evaluation may be out of step with the needs of the change process itself. The expert's report is often too late to become incorporated within the OD activity. There is difficulty in synchronizing both the collection of relevant data and the expert's feedback with the progress of the OD project itself (Weiss, 1972b).

(d) It is the expert, not the client organization, that "owns" the evaluation data. This magnifies the problem of acceptance of the data.

(e) What if you rely on an expert, and he is not really an expert at all? Some people are experts in organization development without understanding evaluation research very well.

2. What's the Target?

Just as the progress of a committee meeting can be compared against a clearly specified and agreed upon agenda, so an OD effort can be compared with what it started out to accomplish. The process of establishing a target is part of what is often called, "clarifying the contract." Is the target (or targets) clear? Are we agreed on our objectives? Are we all headed in the same direction? If there are multiple objectives, do they complement one another, are they independent of one another, or are they antithetical to one another?

Sometimes objectives, roles, and procedures are established because they appear both reasonable and necessary for approval of an OD project by top management or funding sources or granting agencies. Yet, once the project is launched these "public" objectives may seem unrealistic and inappropriate to the new situation. An organization continually changes, as do time frames, priorities, urgencies, personnel, etc. Therefore, a useful first step is the translation of these public objectives into obtainable and measurable targets.

Advantages:

(a) A major goal of OD projects is often to achieve clarity in problem-definition and goal-setting, and then to link up organizational resources toward achieving these agreed upon objectives. To establish a clear and agreed upon target therefore represents an accomplishment in itself (Beck & Hilmar, 1972).

(b) The earlier evaluation is agreed upon, the less likely evaluation will be lost in ensuing activities.

Disadvantages:

(a) Where there is a press for early convergence, this may lead to conformity, and thereby to solutions which are satisficing rather than optimizing.

(b) While clear and early attention to goals represents in itself a contribution to organizational effectiveness, action must follow otherwise people may experience confusion between *stating* objectives and *obtaining* results.

3. Did We Hit the Target?

It is sometimes thought that the progress of a meeting can be side-tracked by evaluating its effectiveness while it is still in progress. It is also sometimes thought that organizational change is best measured after the change effort has been completed. Thus, some evaluation schemes urge, "wait until we're finished and then we'll see if we hit our target." In contrast to the second approach, this strategy assumes the objectives, resources, and the people involved as given, not as factors whidh themselves are subject to change. The Question is, therefore, "Given this combination of objectives, procedures, resources, and people, what did we accomplish?"

Advantages:

(a) By focusing on the extent to which the desired outcomes have been achieved, as opposed to examining the means used to reach the target, people are more free to choose their own instrumental actions to reach their objectives.

(b) Just as managers often appear to be "process blind," so OD consultants are sometimes "task blind." It is easy to become so enamored with the dynamics of process, that one's evaluation of an OD effort may become sidetracked in considering process variables at the expense of end results.

(c) The evaluation of an end product meets the needs of onlookers or others concerned with accountability.

Disadvantages:

(a) This evaluation assumes that the target is the most important thing to evaluate. Had this perspective been applied in the Hawthorne studies, we might have learned that illumination levels are, in fact, associated with higher productivity (Roethlisberger & Dickson, 1939).

(b) At the termination of a project, energy is likely to be diffuse and interest turned elsewhere, so evaluation is often difficult.

(c) If the target is achieved and that's all one learns, the key features in understanding how or why the enterprise was successful may be missed. If the target is missed, it may be precisely because earlier opportunities for modification were bypassed and the collection of data was delayed until the project was completed.

Both of the problems in (c) are greater if an OD event is a one-shot occurrence, rather than the first in a sequential series of programmed developmental activities.

4. Mid-Course Correction

One item towards the middle of the agenda of a meeting might be, "How are we doing so far?" At the onset there is agreement to evaluate the progress of the meeting at a predetermined point (or points) with the clear intention that the meeting can be modified should the new information call for such action. A similar plan can be used to evaluate the progress of an OD project.

Advantages:

(a) It provides opportunity for change based on new information or new circumstances. An opportunity is also provided to assess the original goals. This is particularly appropriate where the project is of long duration or occupies a small percentage of people's time and attention on the job.

(b) The clear expectation is established that the focus is to shift to evaluation at a given point in time, thereby avoiding the seduction of the task to the exclusion of measuring progress.

Disadvantages:

(a) It provides a conflict for participants. Are they to be "good soldiers" by being loyal and optimistic supporters of the program or can they be open to contrary information. This conflict is particularly sharp where onlookers are skeptical. If dubious viewers question the value of the activity in which one is involved, it is difficult to admit publicly that there are some real drawbacks to the activity.

(b) One may overreact to point-in-time information, if the project is assessed at the top of an upswing or at the bottom of a downturn.

5. Continuous Monitoring

An integral and continuous part of any OD effort is the expectation that we'll check on how we're doing by continuously generating relevant information. At the very heart of the concept of organization development is the belief in the organization's capacity to generate relevant information and its ability to act on such information in ways that both expand and utilize resources effectively (Argyris, 1970). Thus, it is easy to see an evaluation process which continually monitors progress as *the* super-solution. It is therefore important to recognize that there are limitations and disadvantages to this method, and also to remember that the other four models are respectable alternatives, each with its own strengths.

Advantages:

(a) Cycling new information through the organization to check progress, expectations, and resources is itself central to the developmental process. Such an evaluation cycle builds competencies and linkages between action—new information—feedback—action.

(b) Evaluation is most timely if it is initiated by new information entering the system, rather than by a prearranged time or by the termination of the project.

(c) Sometimes environmental imperatives require us to begin an OD project without a programmatic model of change or a clearly specified target. In this case, a continuous process of evaluation provides data about the self-consistency of our approach to problems and also about the emerging goals of the OD project.

Disadvantages:

(a) This model calls for a high level of sophistication and skill by all parties involved. It requires the ability to move in highly disciplined and flexible ways from the demands of the task to fruitful examinations of the process by which people are working together. In choosing this model, the difficulties in achieving these skills and developing the required discipline should not be underestimated.

(b) The language developed, techniques employed, and the data utilized may become quite idiosyncratic to the parties involved, and therefore perhaps, less understandable and persuasive to others. It may be difficult for others to learn from this approach to evaluation.

What is learned from this evaluation model is more likely to be a set of skills geared to monitoring behavior within the system, and is less likely to provide data for accountability outside the project. This model is, therefore, probably not very persuasive to persons who are not themselves involved in the OD project.

(c) Due to the constancy of the evaluation cycle whenever new information is available, the focus of attention is probably on small units and one may be unable to see "the forest for the trees." Learnings and insights may be lost and must be rediscovered in subsequent projects, because the perspective is limited to short-term events.

(d) For small task forces this may be the model of choice, because the smaller the unit the more appropriate and possible are frequent review, and evaluation. Due to the constraints of time, location, and competing tasks, it is difficult for large units or systems to continuously evaluate their progress.

While all five models have their strengths and their problems, they all suffer in varying degrees from defining the question of evaluation too narrowly. Three of the models focus on point-in-time measures (what's the target; did we hit the target; and mid-course correction). One of the other two models relies heavily on outside evaluation (i.e., ask the expert), whereas the continuous monitoring model relies heavily on internal resources. To provide information to onlookers and those concerned with accountability, asking did we hit the target probably perform better. As contributions to the development of resources internal to the project itself, early work on the target, mid-course corrections, and continuous monitoring probably offer more advantages.

Obstacles to Effective Evaluation

To many persons actively engaged in organization development, the need for more frequent and effective efforts at evaluation are clear; yet, there is widespread embarrassment due to our persistent lack of attention to evaluation and due to the lack of enduring credibility of our own folklore. Why isn't there a more sterling record of evaluating the results of OD efforts? We see three sources of the problem. There are obstacles to effective evaluation (a) in the client, (b) in the OD practitioner himself or herself, as well as (c) within the OD activity itself.

Obstacles in the Client

As stated at the beginning of this paper the questions—"How are we doing?" and "What are you doing?"—are likely to arise in any OD effort. Since both questions place pressure on the client to evaluate what he is doing, it is strange that there is such a paucity of well-regarded documentation and research on organization development. One way to understand the lack of evaluation studies, is to assume that there must *also* exist within the client strong countervailing forces serving as obstacles to evaluation. In addition to the time and cost concerns which are inherent in any decision to commit an organization to action, other more specific forces include (a) a belief that evaluation may disrupt the flow of the OD project; (b) a belief that the client system has already made its evaluation when it decided to launch the OD project; (c) a distrust that an evaluation study can adequately measure and report the real benefits of the project; and (d) a fear of negative or embarrassing data. These four forces are now discussed in more detail.

Evaluation as Disruption

In most organizations research and development activities are typically separated from operations. When viewed as an institution, the research function has also been separated from the work-a-day world. Research is seen as the province of universities or special institutes and think tanks. One result of this separation is that many people see engaging in research as being at variance with the business of getting things done. The researcher or evaluator is seen as a foreigner, who thinks and writes a different "language." Since research is outside the day-to-day world of work, when one enters that world it is often seen as an interruption. In fact, in many ways research is a disruption.

Decisions Already Made

When an organization has identified a problem, searched for alternative responses, evaluated its alternatives, and decided to move ahead with a particular organization development scheme, it has in fact invested heavily in evaluation activities. Many of us who are concerned with evaluation research tend to overlook this heavy, early investment by the client. To later suggest that the project be evaluated might understandably appear to the client as redundant or as second-guessing his decisions. The potential value of evaluation research after a change project is launched may not be self-evident to the client. He may need to be convinced of the utility in evaluating a commitment already made. One way to accomplish this is through the client's involvement in designing the process of evaluation (Campbell, 1969).

Distrust of the Adequacy of Attempts at Evaluation

All complex organizations have elaborate monitoring, evaluation, and control systems which attempt to measure the quantitative and qualitative nature of ongoing activities. Management information systems, production control systems, inventory control systems, etc. become more and more sophisticated each year. However, our direct experiences with such systems of measurement teach us that often these systems do not adequately mirror the "real" state of affairs within our organizations. We see these inadequacies even where the activities being measured appear to be readily quantified. Our experience further tells us that when we try to measure complex and soft variables—such as how people are behaving—it is difficult to achieve valid results. The client's experience therefore leads to a scepticism (which in many ways is quite healthy) as to what can and cannot be evaluated or assessed.

Fear of Results

A fourth obstacle within the client is the apprehension most of us have about evaluation. Namely, what is learned may be disturbing or embarrassing. It may call for action he doesn't want to take. The frequent reluctance of many poeple to see a physician when they find a lump has developed someplace in their body illustrates this concern. In fact, this example from the field of public health suggests a paradox: It may be that those organizations which most need the inspection provided by evaluation research are those least interested in seeking such information.

Obstacles in the OD Practitioner

The obstacles found in the client organization are often mirrored within the OD practitioner. The OD professional may be apprehensive about the results of any evaluation, he may distrust the validity of evaluation processes, he may see evaluation as disruptive, and he may already be convinced that the decision to embark on an OD project is right. In addition, there may be even more obstacles within the professional. Anyone who has been an active producer or a consumer of field research studies knows of the myriad of problems, traps, and difficulties in conducting respectable research in an organisational setting. In a recent survey of members of the National OD Network, Armenakis (1973) reports that the selection and quantitative measurement of criteria was the problem most frequently mentioned by professionals in this field. The second and third ranking problems were difficulties in using comparison groups and in controlling for extraneous influences.

The complexities of these problems can give rise to one or both of the following questions within the OD practitioner:

(1) Do I (or do available colleagues) have the required competence in evaluation research to conduct a sound evaluation of the OD project given the enormous difficulties?

(2) Will the results of an evaluation be sufficiently valid (and convincing) to justify the time and resources involved? Will I be able to professionally support the results?

Obstacles in the OD Activity Itself

There are two obvious obstacles within the OD activity itself. First, the method of evaluation or documentation which has been chosen may not fit. It may not prove useful as the project unfolds. Where evaluation is seen as an intrusion, or as something which is beside-the-point but will have to be endured, then people are likely to find lots of reasons for not getting involved in evaluation. A second factor within the OD activity is that often such activities are seductive and people become ego-involved in ways that reduce their ability to step back and view the project with dispassion and objectivity. There are sometimes moments in OD projects which generate affect similar to the intense emotional experiences found in T-groups. Where such a climate pervades the OD project, evaluation is easily viewed as irrelevant, if not profane. Recently, after a team building session in Chicago with an industrial client one of the authors walked more than six miles to cool himself out (a very uncharacteristic behavior for him).

Two Issues to Be Addressed

Whenever a cost-benefit analysis yields a "go" signal to evaluate an OD change effort, several important issues remain to be considered no matter what model of evaluation one chooses. We have chosen to address two issues because they are not treated·in the same manner elsewhere and because a more exhaustive survey of issues is beyond the scope of this paper. Two issues which must be faced in any effort at evaluation are clarity of the role of evaluation and the audience to which the evaluation is addressed.

Clarity of the Role of Evaluation

Two decisions assist in clarifying the role of evaluation within the framework of the OD project. First, are the action functions to be separated from the evaluation research functions, in terms of (1) who does each, (2) are they to be separated in time during the project, and (3) are they to be integrated together into the fabric of the project? As we noted earlier, each of these approaches to evaluation has its own advantages and disadvantages. Here we are simply raising the issue of clarity. It is very helpful if there is clarity and shared agreement early in the life of the project about when and how evaluation is to take place. Similarly, there must also be clarity about who is to assume responsibility for evaluation. Where responsibility is unclear, given the other demands mentioned above, it is easy for evaluation to "fall through a crack" and be overlooked by default rather than by decision.

Second, closely associated with any discussion of the role of evaluation, is the question, "What is the purpose of evaluation?" It is not enough for one to attempt to evaluate an OD project because one thinks he should, or because others appear to expect it. If an evaluation is to be worthwhile, it is well to examine its purposes. What will an evaluation permit us to say or do that we could not say or do otherwise? Documentation is often used to help others understand what you are doing when you yourself have little doubt of a project's present and future value. Whereas, research may raise questions about the value or usefulness of what you are doing or the way you are doing it. Therefore, questions about the purposes of evaluation raise their heads. Is the purpose to provide data for "believers?" Sometimes this increases their conficence in what they are doing. Is the purpose to attempt to persuade nonbelievers? If they are skeptics, sometimes a new set of carefully collected information can be persuasive. If they are confirmed disbelievers with emotional attachment to their position, there is little chance that an evaluation study will change their views. "Fully 35% boasts the promoter; only 35% sighs the detracter" (Weiss, 1972a, p. 32). Is the purpose to critically examine what's happening in the OD project and what its consequences seem to be? One must be prepared to face both positive and negative outcomes from research of this nature.

The Audience

There are three obvious consumers of the results of any evaluation of an OD project: the client organization, the OD consultant himself, and external audiences,

including those who are members of the client organization but who are external
to the OD project. Attention should be given to the relative importance of each
of these three audiences. Several decisions are contingent upon determining the
audience for the evaluation data what evaluation model to employ, what data to
collect, when the feedback of data takes place, and in what form these data are
fedback. An evaluation study which might be judged to be an outstanding article
by editors of the *Journal of Applied Behavioral Science* could be worth little as
input into the client system—the timing might be too late, the wording too technical, and the tone too general and impersonal. Conversely, evaluation results
which the client may find intriguing and useful might be viewed with little interest by outsiders, because documentation is seen as inadequate or evidence of
change as ambiguous.

Of these three potential audiences, the one we suspect is most easily overlooked or underweighted is the OD consultant. Documentation and evaluation
of our efforts can serve both to increase our understanding of the complex, long-
term, change activities in which we become involved, as well as to enhance our
skills in subsequent efforts. Fritz Roethlisberger once said that one problem
with managers is that they just don't learn from their experience. Experience
per se in organization development is no guarantee that we are becoming more
professionally competent. Evaluation data can provide opportunities to learn
from experience—opportunities that the experiences themselves do not provide.
Recently, Clark stated, "The need for codification was driven home to me when,
at a conference, I was asked by a young graduate student in psychology, 'How
do you know what to do when you intervene in the life of an organization?' I
bluffed, bumbled, and fumbled. Later I tried to analyze why my response was so
inadequate. I came up with the reason that, as yet, there has been little codification of our experience as practitioners and little connection made between theory
and practice" (1973, p. 640). Friedlander and Brown (1974) contend that "the
more sophisticated our efforts at evaluation and validation become the more
likely we will be able to develop research methods and competencies. . . . so that
our change efforts will become more and more research directed and data based,
as opposed to being based on the exploration of good intentions."

Finally, evaluation studies can increase the visibility of the OD professional
both within and outside his or her organization. Such visibility sometimes provides opportunities for opening minds that are skeptical or opening doors which
otherwise would remain closed.

Once evaluation data are collected, our interest is likely to turn to the question of how widely this information can be disseminated. Who are the appropriate audiences? Every organization has proprietary interests and some concerns
about confidentiality. These matters need to be clarified and understood by the
client and the researcher before the study begins. Both authors have been impressed with the great differences between organizations about how open they

are with data collected internally. Often the policies and expectations of an organization cannot be inferred either from its commitment to experiment and change or in the face-to-face behavior of members of that organization.

As in previous sections of this paper, we have left hundreds of questions unstated. In addition, we have not addressed two major issues which are sure to arise whenever a decision to evaluate an OD project is under consideration: (1) relevant data—who provides the data, who provides the criteria, when are data gathered, who collects the data, and are explicit linkages made between the data collected and the expressed goals of the organization? (2) Appropriate research procedures—what is the design of the evaluation study, is an action research model to be employed, is the study to use a clinical approach or is it to be based on statistical analyses, are control or comparison groups to be used? Carol Weiss addresses these issues of relevant data and choosing research procedures in her book *Evaluation Research* (1972a).

Summary

Models of five alternative ways to approach the evaluation of OD projects were sketched: (1) Ask the expert; (2) What's the target?; (3) Did we hit the target?; (4) Mid-course correction; and (5) Continuous monitoring. Each model provides a different perspective on the problem of evaluation and each contains certain advantages and disadvantages. The five approaches were next put into organizational context by a survey of some major obstacles to effective evaluation studies. Persistent obstacles were found in the client, in the OD consultant, and within the OD activity itself. In the final section, two issues were addressed which must be faced in any effort to evaluate an OD program—clarity of the role of evaluation and the audience of the evaluation.

References

Argyris, C. *Intervention Theory and Method.* Reading, Mass.: Addison-Wesley, 1970.

Armenakis, A. A. Practices and Problems of OD Practitioners in Conducting Evaluations of OD Efforts. Unpublished paper, Auburn University, June, 1973.

Beck, A. C. Jr. & Hilmar, E. D. (Eds.) *A Practical Approach to Organization Development Through MBO.* Reading, Mass.: Addison-Wesley, 1972.

Campbell, D. T. Reforms as experiments. *American Psychologist,* 1969, *24,* 209-249.

Clark, A. W. From sound intuition to better theory. *Journal of Applied Behavioral Science,* 1973, *9,* 638-641.

Friedlander, F. & Brown, L. D. Organization development. *Annual Review of Psychology*, 1974, *25*, 313-342.

Roethlisberger, F. J. & Dickson, W. J. *Management and the Worker.* Cambridge, Mass.: Harvard University Press, 1939.

Weiss, C. *Evaluation Research: Methods of Assessing Program Effectiveness.* New York: Prentick-Hall, 1972(a).

Weiss, C. W. A treeful of owls. In C. W. Weiss (Ed.), *Evaluating Action Programs: Reading in Social Action and Education.* Boston: Allyn and Bacon, 1972(b).

Weiss, R. S. & Rein, M. The evaluation of broad-aim programs: Experimental design, its difficulties, and an alternative. *Administrative Sciences Quarterly,* 1970, *15*, 97-109.

TASK FORCE MANAGEMENT IN DAYTON, OHIO*

James Kunde

Background

Dayton, Ohio was the first large city in the United States to adopt a city manager form of government. From the early days of its adoption, Dayton, with its plan of businesslike government, was widely heralded as the way a local government ought to be run. Dayton's charter became the model for the National Municipal League, and Dayton's city managers were widely recognized for their professional expertise.

After World War II, the council-manager plan of government accelerated its popularity in the United States. As cities grew and sprawled, the cost of government shot up. The businesslike approach of the non-partisan council-manager system seemed to be the answer to a need for greater efficiency.

In its fifty years of city manager efficiency, Dayton had been a prosperous town. The home of the National Cash Register Company and four divisions of General Motors, Dayton had been a bright example of the abundance of manufacturing. Always among the top cities in the country in per capita earnings, Dayton consistently occupied a favorable position among Ohio communities in employment.

By the mid-1960's, however, things began to take a turn for the worse for Dayton. Annexations began to come harder and a suburban ring began to form tightly around the City. In the mid-60's, Dayton's smoldering racial tensions blew

*Reprinted with permission from the author

up into riots. A responsive model cities program alienated the white working class and—for the first time in its history—Dayton's population began to decline. At the same time, the old reliable manufacturing base began to move out and shrink. Careful but slow urban renewal plans had captured little of the new service industry which also began to move to suburban locations. Income tax issues sorely needed to buttress a sagging property tax base began to fail repeatedly at the polls. By 1970, Dayton was a city in serious trouble.

Dayton had had plenty of warning. In fact, Dayton's city manager from 1967 to 1970 began strongly forging new approaches. Terms like Team Policing, Conflict Management, Pilot Cities, P.B.B.S. Budgeting began to appear around city hall. A one-stop job center was created and Dayton's model cities program soon boasted the nation's only "equal partnership agreement" between government and citizens.

The real shock to Dayton's smooth running professional public service was in recognizing that somehow the city had slipped away from them. The streets were clean and smooth. Traffic signals were coordinated and scientifically placed. Water quality was the highest in the state—but it all seemed for naught in the face of ever increasing human problems.

The problem, of course, was that Dayton's government had never been much more than a high quality and complex public utility. There was no need for social and economic planning because those decisions had always been made in a benevolent and prosperous private sector. As home-based industries became national and multi-national and as manufacturing became a sporadic benefactor, Dayton's economic and social planning fell to a corps of new professionals. Generally, these professionals were spread out into a myriad of single purpose agencies. Even with a dynamic and responsive regional planning commission, Dayton's ability to govern itself was questionable.

The Approach

Early in 1971, top appointed officials of Dayton's city government met in a retreat setting to try to figure out a new strategy. The meeting had been precipitated by the frustration of having new programs constantly started in new agencies, budget cuts in old agencies and generally collapsing morale within the ranks of the professional corps. Communication was poor in spite of numerous staff meetings and the availability of a new house organ.

A decision was made to request the assistance of organization development consultants in planning and conducting the retreat. While serving in Kansas City, previous to returning to Dayton as City Manager, the author had participated in organization development programs which emphasized interdepartmental collaboration and team building. The programs, which utilized university faculty members with training in OD, had been helpful in developing clearer focuses on prob-lem-solving in both the city and county governments. It was felt that consultants with skills in problem diagnosis, conference methods and team development could help the organization undertake a successful change effort.

At the initial city management retreat in March, 1971, approximately 35 top city bureaucrats were called together to assess why the city was in trouble, and what could be done. Attention was focused on the organization itself and its ability to identify real problems and work on them. Efforts were made to ex-pose trust issues and to isolate causes of frustration. At the end of the retreat, a consensus had been reached to attempt a dramatic change in doing business. Sev-eral interim task groups were set up to examine internal issues such as the conduct of the manager's staff meeting. It was understood that experience in these task groups would be weighed for validity as a process for dealing with the much big-ger issues that had surfaced in the discussion—issues like racism and housing.

After six months, the interim task groups had completed their work. A critical "task force on task forces" had been created to review and evaluate the work of the interim task groups and another retreat was called. After considerable discussion and review, it was decided that Dayton's city administration should make an all-out effort to attack basic problems in a team model—leaving the oper-ation of current functions to survive the best it could.

Shortly afterward, Dayton City Commissioners were asked to rank top city problems in order of priority. They were provided a lengthy list of problems that had been developed at the two retreats of city administrators. It was decided that nine topics were the maximum that could be handled by existing staff. After two sessions, a list had been created and agreed to. It included: racism, downtown development, employment, housing, youth, crime, Dayton's future, and organiza-tion improvement. Later on, transportation was added to the list when it was concluded appropriate manpower could be assigned.

It was decided that each problem should be addressed by a team of admin-istrators with no more than nine members. There was concern that this not be another committee system with the chairmen taking the responsibility and doing all the work. A chairman for each team was chosen who had little background in the subject area. The chairman of the Youth Task Force was the Director of Finance. Racism was headed by the Chief Engineer of the Bureau of Structures. Employment was headed by the Assistant Law Director; Crime, by the Fire Chief —and so it went.

Each team was provided a "balance" of people. Young and old, black and white, men and women (to the degree possible). Skills were chosen to include key contributors to the problem area as well as persons who had likely never given the problem area a moment's thought.

Team members were advised that the task forces should develop goals and a work plan to achieve them. There was no direct staff applied to the teams and it would be up to each team to determine the time to be devoted, when to meet and how to work. Each team was requested to use a "process observer" in its work to facilitate time effectiveness. It was further advised that management reward (compensation) would be based equally upon a person's performance in his regularly assigned job and upon the performance of his team. Poor cooperation of a team member was the team's responsibility to correct, with the assurance that reasonable action would be backed up by the manager.

The Work

The commitment to team management significantly altered the structure of the Dayton City organization. The structure that emerged was properly described as a matrix organization, with top management assuming responsibility for two dimensions of concern at the same time (See Figure 1).

The task forces were also expected to achieve an effective interface with citizens and other planning bodies outside the city organization that would effect their work. Dayton had already developed a unique system of citizen participation called "Neighborhood Priority Boards." These boards had the power to allocate funds and were administered under the City's model cities program—a so called "planned variation" of the Federal Model Cities Program. Planned Variation staff members were distributed among the task groups as were staff members of the City Plan Board. Several task forces put "outsiders" such as businessmen or professional staff of private agencies on their team. Several task forces also asked for specific new members. Several talented young persons in the organiza-

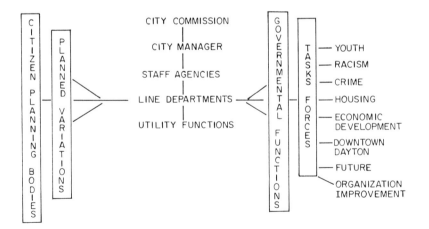

Figure 1   Functional organization of city government.

tion were requested by the task force to serve as members. In each case, assignments were made only after careful scrutiny to assure appropriate balance.

As work proceeded, several problems were discovered and dealt with. The task forces operated at top priority for nearly two years. Since virtually all top city administrators were involved, there soon was created a severe time problem for day-to-day administrative tasks. The city had been under an austerity program, having in 1971 cut over 25% of all its forces. Supervisory ranks had been trimmed as well, and all department and division managers had been complaining of the strain. Now the strain became nearly intolerable. However, an interesting thing happened. Somehow adjustments occurred. Problems were settled deeper in the organization without top management review. The organization discovered it had a greater capacity for delegation than it had supposed. Not all problems were dealt with simply, nor did the strain disappear in all cases. But as a general rule, most problems were handled without severe stress.

Another problem that appeared was the staff logistics of a working group. Who would do the minutes, type reports, do log work research? Some groups requested staff aides or secretarial assistance—all were denied. Most groups decided to handle staff and secretarial requirements among their existing agencies. This soon became the model for everyone—with few problems.

Another problem that arose was much harder to deal with. The task assignments were chosen because they represented problems that no one in City Hall took comprehensive responsibility for. However, the problems were all interrelated. Clearly there was a need for some mechanism of communication between task forces. A former City Commissioner who had headed up a multiagency attempt to coordinate services in a racially changing area of the city was chosen to be "task force coordinator." He worked full-time identifying common problems, facilitating communication, and organizing monthly sessions of the task force chairmen with the Manager.

Training and development techniques played a significant part in the task force effort. Many members were used to playing rather narrow professional roles. Some viewed attending meetings as a waste of time. Others had never acquired skills for participating in team efforts. A few expressed skepticism about the practicality of such a venture.

A kick-off training session was held for all task force members. Team building as an approach to organization development was described. Procedures were clarified, techniques for effective teamwork were explored in exercises and simulations, and task forces held their initial meetings with assistance by consultants. Adequate time was allowed for the expression of concerns and answering of questions. Top management's expectations for the program were openly aired.

Consultants worked with the Task Force coordinator to assess the progress of the groups. After a few weeks it became apparent that additional skills in group work were needed by chairmen and members. "Process problems" (difficulties in communication, decision-making, dealing with conflict, role definition, etc.) hampered the full utilization of the skills, experience and ideas of the members. Additional training sessions were suggested and were provided involving faculty members of a local university. As the coordinator, chairmen and members developed a baseline of experience and procedures they learned to work together more efficiently.

The Results

The two years of concentrated team management produced a number of concrete achievements. The Task Force on Racism developed an affirmative action program that dramatically altered the presence of minorities in city hall job classifications. By the end of two years, the city's employment of minorities approached overall city balance, and aggressive plans to integrate the all-white policy command structure had been initiated (although partially blocked in the courts). Most important, the actions of the Task Force turned around Black opinion toward City Hall. Instead of regarding city management as anti-black, most Black leadership decided that a genuine commitment had been made to right past wrongs.

The Task Force on Crime, rather than concentrating on demands for more police, focused attention on the need to improve the criminal rehabilitation system—even going so far as to offer the City's correctional farm as a reentry for persons to be discharged from state felon institutions.

The Task Force on Downtown Dayton helped spawn a new organization of public and private citizens dedicated to putting life in downtown. Their activity coupled with the unique economic planning developed by the Economic Development Task Force created a rebirth for Dayton's downtown. The Economic Development Task Force is perhaps the best example of exciting commitment. Through their work, Dayton was able to formulate and pass through state law an Impacted Cities Bill. This bill permitted the use of tax abatement to finance urban renewal activity, and made economic development a public purpose. Armed with this new tool, a commitment from the Mead Corporation to build a downtown tower spawned the Courthouse Square urban renewal project. The project represents over $60,000,000 in private funding of new office space, and the park designed into the project is already the focal point of new city life. Courthouse Square was the product of many agencies besides the City. The City, however, had to be the executor. To design, buy, level and rebuild virtually an entire central city block in a little over three years is an achievement unmatched anywhere. The work done by the Task Force in preparing City Hall for such an achievement was critical. The tools developed by the Task Force eventually formed the Citywide Development Corporation, a non-profit public private agency which uses city funds (mostly revenue sharing) to leverage private investment to achieve public purposes. This group has enabled the construction of a new downtown luxury hotel, with a local bank caused the redevelopment of the City's Oregon District, and has now made some major moves into revitalizing other neighborhoods.

The Task Force on Housing developed a unique neighborhood planning system which relied on different levels of housing code enforcement to assist local planning efforts. No major city has solved its housing problem and Dayton hasn't either; but Dayton's housing task force provided critical support and liaison to the housing dispersal plan of the Regional Planning Commission. It also provided support for the activities of Neighborhood Priority Boards—some of which have had marked impact on neighborhood stabilization. A remarkable start. The Housing Task Force also formulated a remarkable comprehensive strategy, developed in a report entitled: "Operation—Recycle the City." Their labor laid the foundation for Dayton's unique community development strategy, the results of which (Courthouse Square and Oregon Historical District) are receiving national attention.

The Youth Services Task Force created liaison with private agencies and with the City's Board of Education. As a result of their work, city police and school officials jointly worked out plans that significantly cooled racially tense city high schools. Detached youth workers and the city's conflict management trained police group performed remarkable feats in disfusing potential outbreaks which would have destroyed effort to revitalize downtown.

Dayton Future Task Force precipitated the City's first true annexation plan—permitting the city to leverage an annexation into a planned new town that might have spelled disaster for a good part of the remaining middle class housing of the city, had a coordinated plan not been developed. The group also caused the City to reexamine area transportation priorities and to exert city influence on the priority of a bypass highway that would have had immense negative racial overtones in the way it has been planned.

The accomplishments of the task forces can generally be summed into two categories. First, they precipitated city policy in critical governance areas—making it clear what City Hall intended to do and why. Second, they communicated overall purposes down into the ranks of the organization. When Courthouse Square came along, execution was quick and delays were minimal. No one misunderstood its importance or its relevance.

There is a negative side to Dayton's task force experience. Administrative initiative into policy was not received with full support by the City Commission. The Commissioners' need to question and to obtain ownership of the commitments often put a damper on the spirit of team members. Unaccustomed to dealing with policy issues in open public forum, many thought their ideas were not as respectfully treated as they might have been. Clearly policy coordination with elected leadership had not been well worked out for either the elected officials or the administrators.

Then came the problem—when is the task completed? Does the task force become a permanent institution? Without clear end states, the question of "sunset" was ambiguous. It may be possible some day to develop a matrix organization on a permanent basis. Such was not the case in Dayton. Shortly after a new city manager came on the scene in early 1974, the task forces were discontinued. A major reorganization occurred about a year later and most task force concerns are now handled within a newly designed city bureaucracy structured along an awareness of the cross-disciplinary reality which the Task Force groups had revealed.

The Legacy

The task force experience in Dayton has left a legacy. The organization formed an entirely new system of communication during the task force period—and much of that has been retained. Also, a great number of new faces rose to the top of the new bureaucracy. In many cases, these were the people who were "discovered" during the Task Forces' search for talent and skills. The task force process itself has been maintained to some extent—always on a temporary assignment basis. Dayton's program on Community Development Revenue Sharing was developed by a city task force that included "outsiders." It even included a member of the City Commission. Dayton's City Commission today is developing a program of policy leadership. In their work, they are going back and mining some of the ideas that the administrative task forces had developed a few years earlier.

A great deal of objective data could have been gained from the Dayton task force experience. In retrospect, it is too bad that more wasn't done to document attitudes and experiences throughout the period. The effort, however, was not done as a social experiment. It was done as a matter of urgent response to a very pressing problems of change. Through the experience, it showed the promise of being an effective tool that cities previously did not have. Whatever negative side effects it may have had, it was part of a response that most Daytonians would agree had a deep effect on the future of their city.

Of greater difficulty to measure are the attitudinal changes of those, both elected and non-elected, involved with Dayton government. The innovative experience with task force management opened up new avenues for creative government. Aided by a long history of good municipal management, the Task Force experience further reinforced the quest for increased "policy capacity" in Dayton government. In retrospect, the Task Forces functioned well in terms of measureable pragmatic output, and what may be more important, those years sowed the seeds for a more citizen-responsive, insightful governing process.

SURVEY FEEDBACK AND THE MILITARY*

Gerald C. Leader and Michael Brimm

This paper describes the first set of data that will be drawn from a major experiment to test the viability of an Organizational Development survey feedback system in a military organization.[1] As of April 1975, all of the statistical data has not been analyzed. Some of the clinical findings from the year-long study, however, have been collected and are the subject of this paper. The views expressed in this paper are those of the authors without any necessary institutional sanction. They should be viewed as tentative hypotheses which will be confirmed or disconfirmed as further data analysis progresses.

The survey feedback project as a total OD system is something more than just a statistical technique to feedback to superiors the attitudes of their subordinates. The project is essentially one of culture change. An attempt is being made to change the interpersonal and problem-solving behavior of 60 unit company commanders. This assault in many respects is squarely contrapuntal to 200 years of American military tradition. But the clash of two alien cultures can be instructive, particularly for ferreting out the major points of conflict between OD and military bureaucracies.

It will not be the intent of this paper to damn the military and raise the banner of OD. Most bureaucratic behavior has a simple functional explanation—it is the most effective method of coping with the situation known to the parti-

*Reprinted with permission from the author. Paper presented to *Academy of Management,* August, 1975. Additional copies can be obtained from the senior author: Boston University, 212 Bay State Road, Boston, Massachusetts, 02215.

pants. The behaviors prescribed by OD, in this instance the survey feedback project, will have to prove themselves a better alternative in order to advocate the latter over the former. As yet, all the data is not in.

The military bureaucracy has proved to be a formidable resister to change. Even at this early stage of analyzing the test results, it is clear that if survey feedback is to become a functioning part of a military system, specific "tension points" between OD and military practices must be confronted and resolved.

Survey Feedback System

On a quarterly basis over a period of a year enlisted personnel in fifteen battalions have been administered a survey questionnaire. Five companies (60-100 enlisted personnel, 5-12 non-commissioned officers, and 2-3 officers in each, headed by a company commander) comprise each battalion and represent the focal units of the study.

The survey instrument contains 13 demographic items and 63 questions asking for evaluation on a 5-point Likert type scale of the respondent's army experience and his unit leadership. This data is compiled for the company unit and "fed back" to the company commander. Neither superiors, peers, nor subordinates directly receive the aggregated data and can obtain this information only if the company commander shares it.

Computer print-out of the aggregated data takes two forms. Frequency distributions and summary statistics for the 76 questionnaire items provide one view of the data set. A second format collects data into 34 subject indices, providing summary statistics for these factors and comparative data from the total sample.

Two sets of data are offered for establishing comparisons. Battalion averages for each index provide a relative valuation vis-a-vis the company commanders' immediate peers who share a common command and task environment. As the five companies do not perform the same tasks, a second comparison is offered to so-called "similar companies." These summary statistics are compiled from companies in the sample performing the same task, though in a different situational context.

Organizational Development Meeting Sequence

The survey feedback statistics are but the grist for the sequence of OD processes that are used to analyze and subsequently act upon the data. It is initiated by the five company commanders meeting together upon receipt of each "feedback." They are encouraged to act as a supportive, problem-solving forum, working together to draw initial diagnostic meaning from the array of statistics and numerical data. Then each commander meets with groups or individuals from his own unit. These discussions further the diagnostic task, establishing a group to elaborate and/or act upon problems illuminated by the survey data. A second meeting of the company commanders then provides a locus of support and technical assistance in drawing together the outcomes of unit discussion with previously recognized issues. Another agenda for this meeting is the identification of common problems which suggest concerted action or require battalion-level changes.

A final prescribed meeting in this sequence brings the company commanders' immediate superior, the battalion commander, into discussion of problems recognized to be battalion-wide. While the company commander is the owner of all data, he is encouraged to selectively disclose the survey results during this sequence of meetings, both as measures of current situations or as problems for group concentration; but the dissemination of data remains his prerogative.

The survey feedback project was presented to company commanders in a formal briefing prior to the first data collection and in an intensive two-day training workshop which coincided with the first "feedback" of results. The latter occasion permitted trainers to present theoretical rationale for the system, provide personal support during the first iteration of the meeting sequence and promote commitment to the experimental system. Three months later, on the occasion of the second quarterly return of results, trainers were present for a half-day to encourage the participants to follow the meeting sequence.

Points of Conflict

One of the cornerstones of OD culture is open and intentionally honest communication. It is hypothesized that without this, effective problem-solving and resolution of conflicting objectives are impossible. These ideals, however, fly in the face of what bureaucrats learn very early in their careers—ritualistic compliance. Relations with superiors are facilitated by "Yes, Sir" 's even when the degree of actual compliance will be at some variance with the enthusiasm expressed in the verbal acceptance. This motivation is not laziness but protection.

Daily the company commander is inundated with a bewildering number of orders, some of them inconsistent with each other, if not totally illogical. The military usually does not rationalize the why of a directive and it would be out of place to ask. In a sense, there is no alternative but to verbally accede. The commander's discretion comes, however, in the degree of his actual follow through. For example, alert commanders recognize an implicit pact between their superiors and themselves with respect to many orders; nothing really has to be done unless there is check-up by a higher command. Commanders accept what is told them with little verbal parry, saving their true evaluations for private contemplation.

The implementation of OD procedures within industry has not been without resistance, some of it quite strong. This head-on confrontation is a welcome adversary, however, compared to the military's ritualistic pleasing patterns. You can deal with a committed player, but if he turns the other cheek, you are left punching the proverbial paper bag. Other kinds of change efforts may resort to the "clout" of superiors in the chain of command in resolving problems of marginal compliance. Survey feedback's commitment to development of more open communications between hierarchical levels would be contradicted by such actions.

The OD consultant has to develop a new set of skills to cope with the acquiescent posture of his client. He finds himself playing devil's advocate with himself in conversations with the military to provoke identification of potential areas of resistance. He tries to temporarily isolate the target participants of the OD effort (in this instance, the company commanders) from the military culture and establish with them a rapport that allows dissension, resistance and even apathy. None of these practices is as powerful an antidote to bureaucratic pleasing habits as the battalion commander's willingness to have his commanders discuss and argue with his directives. The next two sections explain this.

Required Buffer

The battalion commander is a critical element in the survey feedback system, despite his peripheral involvement with the data. Survey feedback's various facets are intended to combine to create a new and supportive management culture in the battalion. During the early development of this new culture, a continuing stream of reinforcements for previous practices and orientations is forthcoming from existing, unchanged organizational elements. As the battalion has a "horizontal" independence from other units, the critical interface concerns interaction with superior line and staff entities in the hierarchy. As these inputs enter at the battalion level, the battalion commander assumes an important role in determining their translation to and impact upon the company commanders.

In cases where a battalion commander has parried a part of this torrent of demands from above (usually reflecting a continuation of his preferred management style rather than a specific response to the survey feedback program), the infant culture of OD has evolved and can soon assume much of the buffering role for itself. In other cases, battalion commanders have passed along the entire flood of requirements and reinforcements emanating from superiors, adding their own whims to the already unmanageable flow. Such situations have greatly retarded systematic development of the new culture.

These findings are consistent with the rule of thumb of OD practice within industry that it is difficult, if not impossible, to establish a viable OD culture without the active participation of those higher in the hierarchy. The experience with the military would affirm with the following caveat: an OD system can function at the company level without the whole hierarchy giving assent, but the buffering role of the battalion commander is absolutely essential.

Positive Model

The company commander needs some evidence that it is possible to positively influence the solution of problems identified by the survey feedback data. A great deal of his work life is spent in executing directives from above. The daily routine of his working environment can promote a perspective that he is not in control. Dissonance is generated when the survey feedback project suggests a pro-active posture in shaping his command. Calling upon personal resources, a few commanders can "bootstrap" themselves out of the dilemma. The majority require some cue from their battalion commander that it's O. K. to do something more than passively acquiesce to these demands; problems can be sorted out and placed at their respective doorsteps, even those, and particularly those, originating at battalion and higher levels. Company commanders gain a sense of power to influence events, when their commander at least demonstrates a willingness to listen to suggestions. If he does something about them, even more power is accrued.

Many elements of the military system as described above are hostile to the development of an OD culture. Indeed, these forces left unchecked can easily purge the delicate web of relationships and ways of communicating that OD advocates. It is clear that the battalion commander is key to seeing to it that the culture is protected and nurtured.

Professionalism

Professionalism is an ethic which normatively prescribes and proscribes patterns of behavior. Combining mystical directives and emulation of mythical heroes, its power derives from the internalization of these dictates to create a self-monitoring system of behavior control. As operationalized in the Army, professionalism to a large degree is the antithesis of cultural dictates proposed in a system of survey feedback. Broad cultural notions of individualism, strength, and leadership form the foundations of the myth of professionalism.

A professional company commander should "sink or swim" on his own, avoiding the weakness of relying upon others for help and assistance. He also aids his fellow "professionals" by electing not to offer them his ideas or experiences, thereby helping them to discover strength in themselves. Looking to "battlefield heroes," the company commander should act decisively, directing his subordinates in a firm manner. Orders from superiors are accepted and passed along to the commander's subordinates as his own directives; it is highly "unprofessional" to note that an apparently meaningless order was given because "I had to." These factors combine to yield an image of the company commander —a leader of men at the first line of command and a major locus of power and decision-making.

The major tenets of OD, as prescribed in the survey feedback project, are in some contradiction to the professionalism ethic. Survey data become the gripes of subordinates. Group meetings with peers can violate maxims of individual effort, while meetings with subordinates can be manifestations of weakness and indecisiveness. Open discussion of unit problems would threaten existing command relationships and create situations which press for the source of directives in searching alternatives for action.

The "professional" company commander in the midst of the survey feedback project is in a bind. Caught between his soldierly tradition and the good feelings of sharing with others, he searches for reinforcement to resolve his ambivalence. Unless the OD culture has developed to the point where it is self-reinforcing, the professional ethic wins out. There are too many agents outside the study's spheres of influence—wives, friends and peers—who reinforce the military tradition to make an equal contest with OD.

Payoffs

The OD survey feedback project is a system to improve company effectiveness. It is designed to aid the company commander in his quest for organizational improvement. Unfortunately, the military, like most bureaucratic organizations, lacks precise operational measures of unit performance. Military readiness and high unit morale are sufficiently nebulous to defy accurate assessment. As a consequence, a variety of surrogate measures emerge to fill the void: scores on unit inspections, numerical training exercise results, percentage of paperwork submitted by a prescribed date, number of training classes conducted, etc.

As the military strives to improve unit performance and assess commander performance, it focuses on these short-term quantitative measures. It is forgotten that they are but surrogates, poor ones at that, for assessing long-term unit viability. The company commander, looking out for his own career, is forced into a never-ending game of marshalling his and his unit's efforts to passing the series of short run oriented quantitative hurdles. When one training test is completed, another inspection awaits preparation next week, with little time for viewing the whole.

This measurement system holds important implications for the success of implementing survey feedback in the military. The OD effort is not a part of the formal evaluation system. Indeed, it was consciously designed so as to preserve the confidentiality of the survey feedback data and make available to the commander information which may be critical of his performance, but not threatening to his formal evaluation within the military system. But time devoted to survey feedback activities receives no external recognition. More saliently, failure to conduct these activities or even look at the data is not considered a deficiency in the organization's reward system. In an environment where priorities are assessed by the existence of external measurement or the potential for being noticeably deficient, it may not be appropriate to subject a commander to the risk of jeopardizing his career in order to devote time to survey feedback.

Tentative Results

The foregoing has undoubtedly painted a rather pessimistic prognosis for the successful use of survey feedback within the military. The paper was intentionally focused on the friction points between the two in order to encourage a discussion of these issues. A more balanced assessment of the total survey feedback system awaits a comprehensive statistical and clinical analysis. Some positive results, however, have already been observed. Whether they are generalizable and replicable remains to be seen. Some company commanders have completely embraced the survey feedback system and are implementing it within their units.

A few groups of company commanders, meeting together for the first time on the occasion of the survey feedback training, have found this peer group to be an effective problem-solving forum and a basis for deriving personal support in their isolated tasks. Some have reported that the group meetings permitted a recognition of the commonality of their experiences with the other company commanders and have been able to give and receive help for the first time.

Data from the survey questionnaires has been broadly agreed to have face validity in describing unit situations. Individuals who had been initially skeptical of the data have found it to be valid after researching problems highlighted by the data.

Some individuals have used the survey feedback system to generate unit goals. This frees these commanders from the control to which they submitted in the ambiguity of goallessness.

Company commanders who have attempted to experiment with change strategies derived from diagnosis of the data have been rewarded in the iteration of the survey results, leading them to further their experimentation.

During the implementation of this program, numerous commanders have seen what they consider to be limitations on the power which they allegedly have. Those who have become disheartened now find the project meaningless, as they see themselves impotent to effect changes which emerge from data analysis. Others have responded to this sense of powerlessness by attempting to obtain power. Often in groups these individuals have confronted their immediate superiors with specific plans for correcting battalion-wide problems. In so doing, they have laid a claim to a role in the larger decision-making structure of which they are a part.

NEW PERSPECTIVES TOWARD MORE EFFECTIVE LOCAL ELECTED COUNCILS AND BOARDS*

Melvin J. LeBaron

> *You cannot teach a man anything.*
> *You can only help him discover it within himself.*
>
> Galileo

The Frustration

There is a new age emerging in the processes and politics of local government. It is an age removed from the industrial revolution, the land of plenty, and the great American dream. It is an age of unaccustomed limitations and uncertainty. An age without the familiar trappings of political patronage and predictable cause and effect. This new age is causing more and more local elected officials to second-guess their motives for running for public office. The world of local government today—unlike any era of the past—is a contradiction between knowledge and insecurity, enlightenment and despair, progress and depression, opportunity and stress, achievement and remorse, capability and frustration. These contradictions are having a profound effect on the social environment of local elected councils and boards.

Like never before in our history, local elected officials are finding that the multiplicity of unlimited potential is being bombarded by such overwhelming problems that solutions are beyond their mortal grip. There is a new complexity

---

*Reproduced with the permission of the author.

in the social environment of doing business in local government which requires
new awareness and skills on the part of those in charge of the business.

This new complexity is requiring elected council/board members to give
unprecedented consideration to their ability for being conscious of the organizational and social nature of their role. Too often, their only sensing of a situation
is "I don't like this," "I am uncomfortable with this," "I am frustrated . . . no,
angry." More and more, elected council/board members are recognizing these
feelings as only symptoms and are looking beyond the surface-level situation toward the source of the problem. This is requiring elected local officials to figura-
tively obtain a new set of glasses and begin to see their world from a new perspective. First, to see what is "really" there in the form of social interaction; and
second, to see new alternatives amidst the unprecedented complexities.

The Response

We, at the University of Southern California, School of Public Administration,
Center for Training and Development have been involved in creating greater
awareness amongst local elected officials, and in helping them to build the skills
necessary to handle the new complexities of their social environment. Back in
April, 1973, we conducted the first team building program for mayors and
councilmembers. Since that time, we have conducted numerous team development activities for members of local councils and boards in California and throughout the country. The feedback from participants in these programs has been so
positive, some of us in the University are re-arranging some priorities and commitments to give more time and attention to working with local elected councils and
boards. One reason for this shift in activity is that it serves a long-standing interest on our part toward helping local elected officials as part of our commitment
to government in general. The other reason we are making this commitment is
that working with local elected officials in the workshops has been a profitable
learning experience for us. As Galileo would say: "We didn't teach elected local
officials anything. We only helped them discover it within themselves." We each
provided the climate for each other's learning.

What follows is an effort toward capturing the learning we have received
from elected council/board members. It is being shared as a means toward building a stronger bridge across the chasm of complexity, and into the world of local
elected officials' development needs.

Power-Trust Dichotomy

Our initial approach toward helping elected local officials through this new age of
complexity has been to dissarm them. The workshops have been designed to

foster informal and open behavior. We put structure in the program, not in personalities. The staff exhibits a model of trust, not power. Our agenda is designed to create openness, not guardedness. The result of this approach is usually an "unfreezing" on the part of participants and a demonstrated willingness to remove some of their "facade" so we are all better able to "see" each other.

As a result of experiencing, and reflecting upon, this process we have learned that local elected officials live within a dichotomy of power and trust; but they are more familiar with—and therefore, more capable of handling—power than trust. Power is inevitable to someone elected to a local office and its appearance cannot be avoided. Politics is the struggle for power. Therefore, power becomes the objective of an election as a means to an end, which is sought in order to further the political process. This power is dependent upon its recognition, and it being given to someone from someone. People elected to local councils and boards know their power does not exist in a vacuum. They know there is always a grantor-grantee relationship.

As we look more carefully at both the power requirements, and power source of local elected officials we see a power base that is having some problems. First, power becomes a source of benefits and rewards, but these benefits and rewards usually don't materialize as they were envisioned prior to election. Second, much of the power is accumulated due to a fear of being disadvantaged, but too often, the harder a council/board member works in order to keep from being disadvantaged, the greater the likelihood of him/her being socially ostracized, which is loss of power. Third, a critical source of power is through respect for people and/or institutions, in which the accomplishment of the group goal is more important than individual gains and fears. This power source is the most desirable and useful but the hardest to generate because of the dynamics involved. Power in this context requires the council/board member to be more conscious of the principles of group dynamics which require him/her to: 1) be aware of the group (council/board) goals, 2) give visible evidence that he/she can make a contribution toward the accomplishment of these goals, 3) make a significant contribution toward maintaining the cohesiveness of the group, and 4) provide some kind of rewards for the other individuals in the group. Non-involvement or inappropriate involvement in this group process will cost the council/board member loss of power.

The group dynamic process cannot be maintained and strengthened using power alone. Power, in a group situation, often blocks as much process as it creates. It also tends to prevent council/board members from seeing their own humanness, and blinds them from the human qualities in others. We have found that council/board members recognize, once their attention is diverted away from a strict power orientation, that trust is the cosmic glue which holds a relationship together. The foundation may be power, but the support structure is trust.

Furthermore, the shift from a council/board member being elected, to a council/board providing service to its community, is the shift from an emphasis on personal power to an emphasis on group power. This process requires that the council/board member not subjugate his/her own power/influence, but that he/she use personal power to help the group become powerful. Again, the navigating device is trust.

Exposure-Feedback Process

The movement from power to trust is accomplished through communications. Particularly, communications which releases some of the unnecessary unknowns in the relationships of council/board members. In most of our programs we have used the "Johari Window" (originally developed by Joseph Luft and Harry Ingham), as a working model designed to assist council/board groups raise the trust level through communicating more effectively. The "Johari Window" presents the concept that all the information in the world can be divided into basically two categories: things that I know and things that are unknown to me. Of course, when you look at other people, the world can be divided into the same two sections: things that are known to them and are unknown to them. A quadrant can therefore, be set up which resembles a window illuminating four sections: 1) things that are known to me, that are also known to others—the Arena or Open Area, 2) things that are not known to me but are known to others—Blindspot Area, 3) things that are known to me, but are not known to others—the Facade or Hidden Area, and 4) things that are not known to me, and are not known to others—the Unknown Area. Trust is developed between and among council/board members through exposure of unnecessarily hidden information and through providing feedback to each other on observed behavior of each other. Exposure usually consists of council/board members expressing some of their own feelings and their expectations of fellow council/board members. This procedure shrinks some of the facade and enlarges the arena. The blindspot area decreases in size as the council/board members share feedback with each other related to their particular perceptions and observations of each other's behavior.

Council/board members regularly see their colleagues as having "blindspots" around such behaviors as pontificating, not listening, making emotional outbursts, flip remarks, jumping to premature conclusions, being insensitive, and carrying hidden agendas. Perhaps the most notable blindspot that council/board members regularly identify, is that some are "blind" to each other's areas of strengths and weaknesses for making contributions toward problem solving.

All of this exchange of perception and feedback allows council/board members to "up periscope" and look at themselves and their relationship in a new way. This approach is not easy; quite the contrary, it is a very difficult one. It forces the council/board members to be honest with themselves and each other—

something they may not have done before. It forces them to confront issues which they may have shunted aside. The requirement, of course, is that this feedback exchange be done in a kind, humanistic atmosphere.

Some typical items which council/board members frequently reveal as things they have a tendency to keep hidden from other council/board members are the need for more approval, appreciation, respect and recognition. Individual council/board members often express a previously unrevealed lack of knowledge and understanding of his/her particular function. Feelings also become a major issue when council/board members share some of their "hidden areas." It is not unusual for them to be reluctant to share their feelings and to begin a process of openness by indicating that they tend to hold back feelings. Once the environment becomes safe enough they identify previously hidden feelings of insecurity, inadequacy, frustration, and concern.

This exposure, although usually done in an anonymous fashion, to spare personal embarrassment, is handled on the assumption that a working relationship among and between councils and boards requires collaboration and valid knowledge. This collaboration and valid knowledge is produced as the council/board members as a group begin to unfreeze and deal with themselves in terms of what they really mean to each other.

Awareness

Socrates said: "The unexamined life isn't worth living," which, if applied to council/board relationships would become: "The unexamined council/board relationship isn't worth being part of." In order to establish a framework for an examination of their relationship and as means to awareness and building skills for change, it is customary to ask council/board members a critical awareness question: "What characteristics best describe us as council/board members?" Characteristics which council/board members are most willing to ascribe to themselves usually break-out into categories of *ego concerns, personal feelings, personal strengths,* and *hang-ups.*

Typical *ego concerns* the council/board members see in themselves are: needing ego satisfaction, self centered, protective of power base, wanting to be appreciated, seeking recognition, desire to excel, and egotistical.

Personal strengths which most council/board members identify as being characteristic of themselves are: hard working, goal oriented, leaders, responsive, loyal, knowledgeable and concerned, gregarious, problem identifiers, desire to serve, political realist, polished, and ambitious.

The most prevalent *personal feelings* which council/board members reveal are: dissatisfied, frustrated, confident, impatient, sincere, and fragmented.

Frequently mentioned council/board member perceptions of their own *hang-ups* are: opinionated, reactionary, provincial/parochial, shallow, unsophisticated, hidden agendas, unkindness, lack of sensitivity, tunnel thinking, prejudicial, bullets or marshmallows, vested interests, non communicative, lack openness, isolated part of the team, and uninformed on real issues.

This awareness process reveals a tremendous number of driving and restraining forces which council/board members have among themselves; and the data therefore, becomes a foundation for solving some of their problems, and building their particular team. The development and anaylysis of these data also affects a sense of "ownership" on the part of council/board members toward the problems and the process.

An interesting by-product of this activity is a greater realization on the part of individual council/board members that he/she and every other member is a many faceted and complex being; and that the individual make-up of colleagues does not consist of mechanically fitted parts, well lubricated, and designed to follow the predictable rules of physics and mathematics. This awareness becomes the launching pad for moving into personal space connected to basic needs, styles, and patterns of fulfillment.

Interpersonal Behavior

It has been said that people and ships both toot the loudest when they are in a fog. Another comparable saying is that imagination was given a man to compensate for what he is not, and a sense of humor was provided to console him for what he is. These comments being the case, and being applicable to council/board relationships, it must be time for them to get out of the fog or laugh at themselves for being so bewildered. Actually, we have found, neither is easy to do, and sometimes council/board members are not up to doing it.

Many council/board members are aware of their interpersonal world, and its impact on the process of council/board business, only in a general, vague and undifferentiated manner. Symptoms of some problems abound, but causes and ways of coping are elusive. Obviously, there are many factors at work in council/board member interpersonal relationships which are impossible to comprehend or simplify. There are some factors however, where only lack of knowledge prevents a more positive outlook. Bringing to consciousness the nature of a council/board members interpersonal situation is the first step in assisting them to cope with it. We have found in our council/board member team building programs that interpersonal awareness and evaluation liberates energies and confidence necessary for council/board members to more appropriately deal with interpersonal issues facing them.

The feedback from participants in council/board member team building activities regularly suggests that the process of self-discovery and interpersonal awareness is enjoyable as well as valuable. We receive continuous documentation that the openness heightens mutual support, common understanding, comprehensible conversations, shared opportunities, conclusive negotiations, and new directions toward change. The responses tend to validate our programmatic assumptions, which are that whenever council/board members can soothe areas of conflict and/or ambiguity related to interpersonal communication and behavior, the decision making and policy commitment will be easier, quicker, and more effective.

The following summary of discoveries and reactions as made by council/ board members in recent council/board member team building sessions, tends to support the need for greater clarity and openness in the relationship between and among council/board members:

> The most helpful part of this experience was the skillful building of an atmosphere within which we could communicate meaningfully.

> This experience was important because the improvement of interpersonal relationships to help in problem solving is desirable expecially with council members who seldom have the time, or in some cases, the interest, to sit down and discuss roles, personal strengths, and weaknesses.

> I highly recommend this experience, because human beings need to learn to lower their differences, to be honest, and to be more viable, effective persons.

> The greatest impact of this session was that it helped by self-awareness. It gave me tools to use in changing some things I don't like.

> The most helpful aspect of this program was finding out what the mayor really thinks, and my being completely trustful about my feelings.

> This experience particularly enabled me to become more true to myself; enabled us as a team to be honest.

> The greatest impact of this session was that I feel I have a better concept and grasp of some of my characteristics which tend to cause misunderstanding in others.

> The greatest impact of this session was that it indicates a need for me to make adjustments in the manner in which I function as a mayor—and as a person.

> The impact of this session was the identification and reinforcement of strengths. It provided opportunity for 'time out' to review where we stand and what can be done to improve.

> This session was most important because it gave us an opportunity to become better acquainted with the most 'silent' council member.

In most council/board member team building programs, greater interpersonal awareness was achieved through the use of the FIRO-B instrument. This instrument is designed to measure several areas of social behavior and attitudes which persons hold. It intends to measure the individual.'s preferences for involving himself/herself with others and his/her acceptance level of the social function he/she performs.

The FIRO-B, which stands for Fundamental Interpersonal Relations Orientation—Behavior, (originally developed by William Schutz), measures the individual's need in three social areas: The needs for Inclusion, Control, and Affection. The instrument measures an individual's needs system in terms of both "expressed" need, which is the actions an individual initiates toward others; and "want" need, which is what the individual wants to receive from others.

Based on a sample of FIRO-B scores from 35 participants in recent council/ board member team building workshop, some behavioral implications are:

1. The council/board members on the average, have a strong need for self-preservation. It is important for them to be in control of their relationships. They do not look too kindly upon efforts of others to control them. It is likely they will take charge of things when with people, and try to get most people to respond to them.

2. These council/board members, on the average, thrive on giving and receiving affection. They have a high need for others to give them expressions of warmth, compliments, and appreciation. Quite likely they will be sensitive to criticism, yet critical of others. To a lesser degree, but still at a significantly high level, they also express intimacy, closeness, and warmth to others. They would have difficulty if anyone acted cool and distant toward them.

3. These council/board members on the average, have a strong desire to be in contact with people. They like to mingle and be in the company of others. Their preference is to initiate contacts with others rather than to be asked to join. The situations they get involved in are those situations that will help them feel more important. The typical council/ board member is not particularly selective about groups he/she joins and would have difficulty being alone over long periods of time. The attention of being included by someone else is something these people would like to receive. They like to be listened to, but usually as a means to an end—a means of securing greater control of a situation and, or receiving greater appreciation from others.

Council/Board Member Prototypes

After numerous days and nights interacting with council/board members, and watching them perform in groups and in council/board meetings, certain prototypes begin to emerge. These prototypes may provide another lens through which to see more clearly the human qualities of council/board behavior.

A. Dominant-Prominent

This person is often the real leader of the council/board. He/she is strong-willed and powerful. It is not uncommon for this person to be a prominent doctor or lawyer, and/or to come from one of the oldest families in town. If a male, this individual may appear as a compassionate father-figure, or come on as a ruthless S.O.B.—but he is strong as a leader, and has power.

The *Dominant-Prominent* is selective about involvements. He/she chooses carefully where his/her time is spent, and with whom. *Dominant-Prominent* has learned how to say "no," and how to set priorities which are based on satisfying a need for self-importance, control, and recognition. He/she is the most willing of all the council/board members to have his/her ego needs openly recognized and responded to. Although *Dominant-Prominent* has money, he/she doesn't use it to get things done. He/she is too smart to indulge in dollar diplomacy. In fact, *Dominant-Prominent* is so smart he/she doesn't need money as a motivator. He/she is probably the nearest to the natural leader type on the council/board, and therefore, has a variety of options, and a reliable impluse, to guide him/her through interpersonal relationships and political movements.

Appearance is critical to *Dominant-Prominent*. How things look is more important than how things really are. Events and situations are planned and evaluated in terms of their prestige value. Public relations is given far more emphasis than human relations. It is by the power of having the votes that you get things done according to the *Dominant-Prominent*.

The *Dominant-Prominent* motto is: "Have I told you lately how important I am?"

B. Game-Fame

Game-Fame is the undisputed political animal. He/she believes that: "All the world's a game—you play, or get played." *Game–Fame* is openly power-mad, but generates more "mad" than "power." He/she does not have much power or influence but lots of "mad." *Game-Fame* is quick/short tempered with a need to have his/her own way. As a result this person is usually trying to get by with something—something which is often a little bit shady. He/she is quite willing to exploit the elected office for personal gain if he/she can get away with it.

It is unlikely that *Game-Fame* has any motivation except that which comes from self-interest. He/she is constantly trying to get something "on" staff people so he/she can use them. He/she plays (in transactional analysis terms) a game of "gotcha," not to mention his/her artistic touches at "ain't it awful," "if it weren't for you," and "see what you made me do." *Game-Fame's* general orientation to life (again, in Eric Berne's transactional analysis terms) is: "I'm OK, you're so, so."

Those who fit the *Game-Fame* prototype are often people who haven't made it in their own fields so are out to "make it" in government. He/she has a basic contempt for public servants but is "available" for any of the "benefits" of public office. He/she plays the stereotype political role of the extroverted personality, including such characteristics as: loud-mouth, glad-hand, and outward-appeal. But, what he/she does is obvious.

Game-Fame is so unsubtle about what he/she does that everyone recognizes what he/she is. In fact, *Game-Fame* is not considered dangerous because you can predict what he/she will do.

Game-Fame is most noticeable as a "pompous ass." This "high and mighty" appearance usually covers up an alley cat morality and reprehensible personal life. This is particularly true in the case of male council/board members.

Game-Fame spends most of his/her time in council/board business. He/she often has little else to do. His/her "business" of course, is to fool the public and search for people who will work for him/her. Eventually, he/she ends up frustrated because he/she can't do the anticipated damage or get the desired rewards. Consequently *Game-Fame* usually ends up working behind the scenes with dissident groups.

C. Fog-Bog

Fog-Bog is fogged-in and bogged-down. He/she is simple, naive, unaware and overwhelmed.

"*Fog-Bog*" are two short words which are carefully selected as the name for this prototype as a symbolic suggestion that this person is short on imagination, creativity, ideas, innovation, intuition, initiative, drive, leadership, and perhaps, I.Q.

Although *Fog-Bog* is lacking in some critical qualities, he/she is "nice people." It is easy for him/her to get elected because he/she doesn't make enemies, and he/she is not a fool with friends. He/she will usually have roots deep in the community, and is often elected and controlled by a *Dominant-Prominent.* One thing *Fog-Bog* does know is how to vote, and how to count!

Fog-Bog is vulnerable however, and can be easily intimidated and used by a smart city manager or chief administrative officer. He/she is easily manipulated by flattery.

If there were such a thing as a motto for *Fog-Bog,* it would be "Let's just all get along and do our best—whatever that means."

D. Viable-Reliable

Viable-Reliable is true blue and dedicated too. He/she is not involved for personal glory but is totally convinced he/she has something to contribute. The theme for *Viable-Reliable* is "I believe in you—and me."

This prototype evaluates everything. He/she is sure before leaping, and is constantly picking up new ideas. This person knows he/she is smart and can get things done.

Viable-Reliable is basically altruistic and is not stimulated or motivated to run for higher office. He/she is fully convinced he/she has something to contribute to the community and will put up with a lot of distractions to get the job ·done.

Viable-Reliable is well respected and liked by the administrative staff. This is primarily because he/she: 1) has high principles and a belief in people, 2) has a near perfect attendance record at meetings, 3) is supportive of staff, and 4) comes to meetings prepared with "homework" done.

Although *Viable-Reliable* is often somewhat reserved and doesn't push himslef/herself on others, he/she is actively involved in many things. He/she also has a well balanced sense which helps him/her regulate and select the most appropriate involvement.

Viable-Reliable is often an energetic crusader and spends many hours pursuing causes, and gathering data on cases of inappropriate use of funds and personnel. He/she is particularly sensitive toward the need for good manners when dealing with the public, and sometimes considers himself/herself as a self-appointed ombudsman.

In looking at council/board prototypes it is important to keep three things in mind:

1. Election to a local council/board is an open process and we will continue to have individuals with varying degrees of talent and commitment as members of local elected councils and boards because they get our vote and we elect them.

2. No one council or board member is likely to totally fit any one prototype. He/she may have a predominent number of characteristics that fit a particular description but most council/board members are likely to be mixtures of two or more prototypes. These prototypes are not meant to be a pure form of describing any single council/board member.

3. Council/board members have particular reasons for seeking elected office, and these reasons will condition their behavior toward one or more particular features of a given prototype. The acting-out of prototype behavior is often affected by one or more of these original motivations:

Being elected to council board is a stepping stone to higher office.

He/she was paid to run and told to stay until the next opportunity comes along.

He/she has an extremely strong ego and feels being elected is a personal necessity.

The salary is attractive and he/she needs the money.

Becoming an elected council/board member is an opportune and automatic way out of the dead-end of being a commissioner.

He/she represents a group and has a cause.

He/she is a true believer and is convinced that he/she is right about everything and has been "annointed" for the office.

Being local elected official would be good for business.

He/she cares about the community and perceives himself/herself as knowing the right things to be done.

Learnings

Among our learnings from the work with local elected council/board members are several perceptions, which, if shared may contribute to a greater effectiveness within elected councils and boards throughout the country. Some of these perceptions are:

A. The Wrong Wall Syndrome

This is the first issue that needs to be raised when spotting problems within an elected council/board. Many council/board members spend much of their life climbing up the community ladder only to find that it is leaning against the wrong wall. They spend years of their life "jumping through the hoops," only to find, after they are elected, that being a council/board member is not the "prize" they anticipated. The by-product of this misplaced pursuit is unnecessary stress, tension, conflict and unhappiness which impacts both the individual and council/board. The end-product is often heart-attack, divorce, "dropping out," and other forms of personal-potential waste.

Too many council/board members are fatally overcommitted to what they are not. Few of them who find themselves caught in an elected role which they can't handle, are able to liberate themselves from the foreign expectations and lack of inner sense of meaning. Too often, council/members give in to the system, or give up on themselves because they fail to make an identity with their real self and the real role of council/board member.

Dealing with their own self and facing the uncertainties surrounding this identity crisis is a most important, but often neglected part of being a council/board member. The easier course is to let others make critical decisions for them, and this is usually what happens. Council/board members who are unprepared to live out their elected terms subjected to the unmanageable results of placing themselves in others' care and running the risk of leaning on the wrong wall, need to call a moratorium and take a pilgrimage through the gateway of self development.

Self development puts a heavy emphasis upon "self" in the development process and requires a council/board member to take ownership of his/her own particular needs, wants, feelings, and expectations. This is a diagnosis of self which extends into a personal inventory of personal goals, leadership abilities, work habits, value systems, life-style preferences, accomplishments and failures, and attitudes and behaviors. Many drives operate within council/board members, and each drive has its own degree of intensity. More attention needs to be given to measuring and communicating a council/board member's needs for recognition, authority, freedom, personal growth, prestige, influence, self-realization, uniqueness, and money. With information on all these subjects assembled and consolidated, a council/board member can organize the basis for a workable plan designed to put him/her on the right wall.

B. Cue Tips

Many council/board members are hung-up over the disparity between expressing how they feel about something and their concern that they always exhibit the "right personality." As a result true feelings are suppressed and outward expressions are closely "managed," and they do not say what they really mean or feel.

To understand and work with each other, council/board members need to handle their communications with the aid of cues. Communication cues give a council/board member added communication skills and a better handle on relationships. Without cues in communication they are often unable to come to the point in an argument; unable to show appreciation; unable to let another council/board member know they are upset.

Council/board members don't pick up more cues in communication because they suffer from process or psychological blindness. That is, they don't see or hear what is to be seen or heard. They aren't adequately aware of group process; they are too often subjected to feelings that are being "acted out:" they don't decipher the double-level messages, power plays, and hidden agendas. They often pick up less relevant cues and pay too much attention to words when actions in the form of body language and facial expression speak louder than words. Or, they often misinterpret cues by drawing up their own self-made assumptions as to why other council/board members are doing what they are doing rather than checking out impressions and getting some validation from the person or persons in question.

There are several things a council/board member can do to make greater use of cues in communication:

1) Develop greater insights into themselves and the impact they have upon other council/board members.

2) Develop a better understanding of the characteristic ways in which other council/board members behave, and the cues with which they feel most comfortable.

3) Gain a better understanding of group process; that is, those forces and roles that can be recognized as fellow council/board members relate to each other in formal and informal groups.

4) Create a better awareness of the culture within which the council/board functions as a group; that is, the organizational facts of life in which their communication takes place.

5) Realize that understanding is not enough. Council/board members also need skills to better assess people and situations. They need skills in active listening, giving appropriate responses according to the situation, dealing with meaning and feelings, and sharing their expectations of others.

C. Team Building Process

Local elected council/boards are social institutions. As such, there is a direct relationship between how well the members get along with each other and the effectiveness with which they get things done. They cannot function effectively and productively if they as individual members do not understand each other as people and do not realize how their interaction affects their own function and that of their jurisdiction. Council/board members must be able to communicate and act effectively in groups. To really perform effectively they need to become a team.

Council/boards, however, even in social settings, do not automatically become a team. They must first involve themselves in team building activity.

Team building with councils/boards is directed toward making the unit a better place for individual members to achieve goals. It focuses on goal setting procedures, task accomplishment, role clarification, communication processes, and interpersonal relationships. It is not a panecea to council/board members problems—but an opportunity for them to look at their function in a new way.

Very often council/board members consider working on group process to be a waste of time. They also, sometimes fear that attention to group involvement will destroy some of their own individuality. Indeed, the products of group activity, are often inefficient and costly. The issue is not whether councils/boards can afford to do team building but whether their win-lose decisions, low-level achievements, and ineffective interactions has brought them as a group to a condition in which they cannot afford *not* to engage in a process of team development. The lack of involvement in a real team process by many of our council/ boards is costing us dearly in duplication of effort, loss of achievement, and wasted time. To verify this statement just take some notes on the process of interaction next time you attend a council/board meeting.

The team building process is an awareness and skill building process. Team building we have done with local elected councils and boards focuses on "5-L's": Listening, Learning, Linking, Leveling, and Lauding.

Listening

It is a well worn cliche to say we need to listen more. It is not a cliche to say we need new tools and skills to perform active listening adequately. Listening is not just talking. Active listening is a process of clarifying the ambiguity or confusion in a message and achieving a common understanding as to it meaning.

Council/board members, because of their diverse backgrounds give out diverse meanings to the same words. They get hooked on words rather than engaging the meaning of the words. They need to realize that they each speak to one another in code and there needs to be a decoding process. This is listening!

Listening between and among council/board members is an active process utilizing primarily the techniques of paraphrase. Statements by one council/ board member needs to be followed by questions from another. Questions like: "I'm not sure I understand, will you say that again?" "Let me be sure I have your point, you feel we waste too much time, right?" "Are you asking us to drop the project?"

Unfortunately, much of a council/board member's education toward public office misleads him/her into thinking that communication is easier than it is. This is because much of their communicating to the point of election has been in the form of giving speeches and presentations—generally a one-way process. As a result, when the reality of a two-way communication really hits, there is a tendency for the council/board member to become discouraged and give up by either avoiding the situation or blaming the communication inadequacy on someone else. Communication among and between council/board members is like an iceberg, it has its vast hidden areas—what appears on the surface is but a small part of what is really involved. Listening is the bigger part of communication but people at the pinnacle of local government too often are conditioned against listening.

Learning

Despite Galileo's 16th Century philosophical value toward learning, which is quoted in the beginning of this article—the direction giving method of learning prevails today. Ever since the ancient and wise tribal elder told the young hunters how to stalk their prey, we have continued to employ a learning process in which the teacher or expert is in charge of how things are done and what is taught. This approach has been built on the value of authority being placed on the person directing and teaching, and a stigma of dependency on the individuals listening to directions. Council/board members are well conditioned to such traditional learning methods, as are most adults. As a result of being so conditioned, council/board members reinforce behaviors, among themselves and with others, such as dependency, lack of imagination, low motivation, and inappropriate involvement —which they could do without.

Council/board members need to be more conscious of the contribution each can make to any given situation, recognizing that the role of the informed and the ignorant is a constantly revolving thing. One of the first issues council/board members deal with in team building is re-learning how to learn, which requires that they become more conscious of their own and each other's capabilities, feelings and motivations, and potential contributions toward a consensus process.

Linking

Linking between and among council/board members is what the team building process is all about. A council/board team is not unlike a football team. It needs an occasional time-out and huddle to maintain itself, and to determine if all members are linked together on the goals, purposes, positions, game plan, score, talents, capabilities, roles, responsibilities, strategies, oppositions, strengths and weaknesses. It is not enough for a council/board to just call itself a team without giving time and effort to its own maintenance and linking, any more than it is for a football or basketball team to call itself a team and not recognize the need for time-outs.

The two variables in council/board member team building are differentiation and integration. Where there is a high degree of differentiation between and among council/board members, and a high need for integration of effort; there is a high requirement that their efforts be linked together.

The problem of linkage within most council/boards is that members have well-developed competitive skills but generally lack collaborative skills, which often gets in the way of the quality and quantity of accomplishments. The process of becoming a team and working as a team often requires a new orientation toward the rewards of elective leadership on the part of the council/board member. Support and guidance for the linkage time-out must be provided by a third-party consultant who must be well trained in team building processes, organizational behaviors, and the nature of council/board relationships. The time-out for linkage must also be viewed by the council/board members as a process and not an event. It requires preparation for readiness and follow-up for continuity.

Leveling

Council/board members are taught to be "polite," to have the "right personality" —in essence: to play roles. As a result they put lots of energy into "managing" their communications by not saying what they really mean or feel. This creates an incongruence in their communications in which much communication comes in the form of misled messages and leads to frustration and uncertainty. A council member of one of our major cities recently said: "The biggest problem in this relationship is to bridge the gap between each of our needs and the acceptable expression of these needs. This requires new tools and skills."

Leveling is saying the things that one thinks are most significant to say in any relationship, with the intention of helping the person with whom one is leveling to learn from the experience in which both are involved. Leveling is an extremely powerful technique. The reason more council/board members don't level is that leveling is feared as capable of destroying a person, whereas it can be used to help him/her—depending upon the skill used. The consequences of leveling are a function of, a) the intention, b) the skill, and c) the interdependence and trust in the relationships. Leveling requires council/board members to develop courage, skill, understanding, and respect for self and others.

Without the use of leveling techniques, councils and boards waste large amounts of time with circuitous communications, hidden agendas, double-level messages, insinuations, put-downs, and game playing—all of which divert attention and energy away from problem solving.

Lauding

Council/board members are often strangers from each other, and in state of loneliness when it comes to a transfer of human kindness. They often complain that they don't know if they are appreciated or not, and they don't know what they can do to please other members.

Despite recognition of the importance of praise as a motivator, council/board members among themselves are too often miserly about lauding one another. Their conversations having to do with each others' performance are too often superficial and inane. They have a tendency to refuse to express their deepest feelings of appreciation and deepest fulfillment because of being afraid they might expose themselves unduly and give someone ammunition against them.

Council/board members are frequently stricken with paralysis of self-expression. It is common to see council/board members working together who are afraid to share—to be truly charitable—because someone may take advantage of them.

The council/board member relationships requires all the "stroking" it can get. All members have recognition available from various outside sources, but this availability is not enough. There needs to be an intensity to the "stroking" which only they as peers can provide to each other. One of the most valued experiences for council/board members in our team building programs has been when they list the things they like about what the other is doing. It is noteworthy, that in so many cases, they had not previously taken time to do this, and yet they enjoyed it so much.

There is a tremendous need for council/board members to take time and use time to let each other know more about how they are appreciated and what they would like to be appreciated for.

Summary

This is a frustrating, yet dramatic, period in our history. A period in which we must leave the industrial age because we have been so successful at reaching its goals. A period when the scourges of an industrialized society creates problems and puzzles that must be solved. Many things are occurring in the lives of all of us, but particularly in the lives of elected local officials, that are difficult to understand. The appearance of so much opportunity amidst so much uncertainty is the source of a major conflict between and among elected councils and boards. They need new competencies to increase their abilities to more effectively cope with the pressures of leaderships and stability. Some of these new competencies can be achieved from:

1) The provision of process skills, knowledge, awareness, and facilitation on the part of council/board members.

2) The establishment of an internal climate within the council/board that will insure continuity in the development and training experiences so that results of particular learning opportunities are continually reinforced.

3) The provision of learning experiences for council/board members which will increase their ability to resolve conflict generated by the many forces confronting them.

4) The provision of the opportunity for council/board members to analyze, assess, and improve their personal style of functioning, their decision-making skills, and their ability for working through interpersonal behaviors toward setting council/board goals and maintaining commitment toward those goals.

5) The provision of fundamental skills to facilitate feedback from and to each other as council/board members, and from and to the elements of organization life surrounding them.

6) The provision of a program designed to develop them as a council/board into a better working team, increasing their ability to delineate and

attack problems, and improving their utilization of resources within the team.

7) The utilization of a qualified outside consultant to facilitate learning processes and help with change.

8) The recognition that it is unnecessary and harmful for one council/board member to be embarrassed by the behavior of another council/board member.

This paper has been an attempt to assess and share the experiences of outsiders working within local elected councils and boards. The work, which was designed toward helping council/board members improve their effectiveness, has produced results. The results have come in the form of learnings and discoveries, which should establish a new promise for council/board members to see through some of their ambiguity and value displacement. The sometime agonizing process of changing behaviors and exposing conflicts has proven a step in the right direction for those local elected council/boards that have been involved. It would be wrong however, to conclude that nirvana is created in any one learning experience.

Inevitably, the process of council/board member team development shows that any "phoenix" which might "rise from the ashes" does not happen by luck or nature; rather, the "phoenix" is created by doing and committing to newer and riskier ways of doing things.

A STRUCTURAL APPROACH TO ORGANIZATIONAL CHANGE*

Robert A. Luke, Jr., Peter Block, Jack M. Davey, and Vernon R. Averch†

This is a report of an OD program which resulted in significant delegation of
authority and changed the attitudes of several key executives from a belief in
close, continuous supervision to the view that most lower management will
work productively without close supervision if given the opportunity and training. The innovative features of this case are twofold: First, the change was accomplished by structural alterations; and, secondly, the consultants were more
architects than trainer-intervenors. The real change agents in this case were line
executives. The consultants worked closely with these executives to shape and
mold a new structure, but it was the latter who were actually responsible for the
changes.

OD consultants often define their role as conducting events, training programs, and personal consultation in order to change a client's attitude about
people and his relationships with them:

> Organization Development is a response to change, a complex edu-
> cational strategy intended to change the beliefs, attitudes, values and
> structures of organizations so they can better adapt to the dizzying

*Reproduced by special permission from *The Journal of Applied Behavioral Science.* "A
Structural Approach to Organization Change," by Robert A. Luke, Jr., Peter Block, Jack
M. Davey, and Vernon R. Averch. Volume 9, Number 5, pp. 611-635. Copyright © 1973
NTL Institute.

†The authors would like to acknowledge the effort and contribution made to the program
by Charles Johnson, Alan Steiger, and Edward Weiss, the Management Development Team.

rate of change. Whatever the strategy, organization development almost always concentrates on the values, attitudes, relations and organizational climate—the "people" variables—as the point of entry rather than on the goals, structure and technologies of the organization (Bennis, 1969, p. 2).

By way of contrast, the OD effort reported here focused on changing the structure of the organization, i.e., the role responsibilities and relationships of organizational members and their centers of accountability, from which behavioral changes and, finally, attitudinal changes flowed. The program significantly altered the chain of command by creating new roles, modifying existing roles, and changing the managerial style of middle and top management. The project proved an effective means of developing managerial personnel and enabling personnel at several levels of management to gain more control over their jobs and environments.

Lawrence (1958) and Dalton, Barnes, and Zaleznik (1968) report on similar structural change programs, which were completely designed and carried out by top management of the organizations under study. Their reports are a researcher's description and analysis of structural change efforts and, as such, provided useful guidelines to the consultants involved in this case. Beer, Pieters, Marcus, and Hundert (1971) report on a program initiated at Corning Glass Works, which resulted in a new organizational role—an integrator—that greatly facilitated the problem-solving capabilities of multifunctional task forces. Beer and Huse (1972) demonstrate that structural and interpersonal changes can support and reinforce each other in a systems approach to organizational change.

Background

The client organization is a large retail food chain with annual sales of $800 million and a work force of about 18,000. In 1969, a new top management team initiated an OD program to improve employee training. For two years, the program emphasized training events designed to effect attitudinal and behavioral changes (Averch & Luke, 1971). This effort aroused the interest of several top executives, who believed OD would make a contribution to the company. These executives allowed the OD staff to attend, as members, key meetings.

The senior author's participation in one of these meetings, the Store Operations Meeting, led to the development of the project described here. A monthly Store Operations Meeting is chaired by the Corporate Vice President of Store Operations, his staff, and the person (Store Operations Manager) charged with overall store performance and second in authority to the Divisional Vice Presidents. These meetings, attended by the four Divisional Store Operations Managers, test ideas for new work systems and design methods for implementing them in the stores.

During the September 1970 meeting, concern was expressed about the slowness with which a grocery management system for ordering and stocking merchandise was being implemented in stores. In an earlier field test it had proved to be an efficient management system. Training Store Managers to use this system was delegated to the District Manager (DM), the direct supervisor of 10-15 stores. A lengthy discussion of his role revealed that though he was supposed to be a trainer and resource person, as well as supervisor of the Store Manager, a DM actually devoted his time to inspecting stores and personnel to make sure that company standards were met. DMs did not view training as a priority. They merely outlined the new system and told Store Managers to implement it. Results were therefore sporadic.

During the October meeting, the group considered ways of helping the DM implement the grocery system. Three alternatives were proposed. One was to create a new job, that of a grocery specialist who would work for the DM and put in the system. This was a typical method of introducing new procedures: create a specialist in that area and charge him with implementation. The second suggestion was to assign a current store manager to spend half his time training other managers in the system. The third alternative, suggested by the OD staff, was to change the role of the DM from a line executive to a consultant without line authority, and make him available to managers in all areas of store operations, including system implementation. The rationale for this suggestion was that the close, inspection-like supervision of Store Managers by the DM and Specialists resulted in an overload for the Store Manager, who was often in a position of trying to please his many bosses. He therefore had minimal control over his store and little time for training or implementing new work methods. With less direct supervision and more training available from a consultant, it was hypothesized that Store Managers could more effectively manage their stores.

Historically, the company had relied on close supervision at all levels. The idea that Store Managers could manage their units effectively without direct supervision seemed absurd to several members. However, the chairman and one Store Operations Manager (the third author), who volunteered a district of 15 stores, felt the consultant concept might be a way of developing more competent Store Managers. The OD staff was asked to develop a proposal for a consultant structure, which is outlined in Figure 2. Figure 1 depicts the traditional DM-Specialist structure.

The basic functions in running a store are twofold. Merchandising consists of developing sales programs that yield an acceptable profit, attract customers, and ensure product variety. Store Operations, as the name implies, is concerned with the mechanics of getting work done—scheduling employees, stocking shelves, ringing registers—in a way that is economical but still attractive

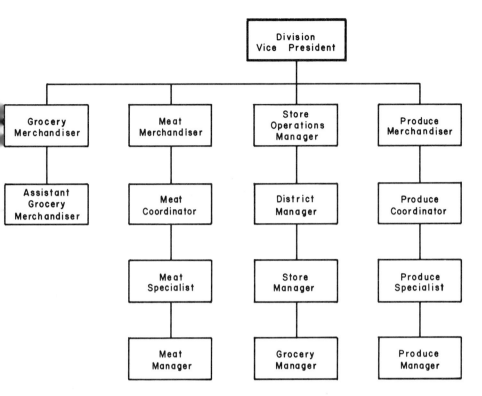

Figure 1 Traditional district manager–specialist structure.

to customers. Under the traditional structure, three lines of authority reach the store. Merchandisers develop the sales program, which is passed by their assistant, the Coordinator, to Specialists, and then to department heads. Operational responsibilities are initiated by the Store Operations Manager and transmitted to the Store Managers by the District Manager, who is also responsible for overseeing the grocery merchandising program. The Store Manager therefore left the perishable department of his store to his department heads and their Specialists, and restricted his activities primarily to the grocery and front-end departments. This limited his ability to manage the entire store. In addition, his boss, the District Manager, when visiting the store, would inspect for problems—dirty floors, poor appearance of personnel, inadequate check-out service, incorrect prices, and so on. With the traditional structure and DM role, a Store Manager was primarily concerned with maintaining standards and overseeing the grocery department; he had little time or sense of priority for training, management, and new systems in the organization.

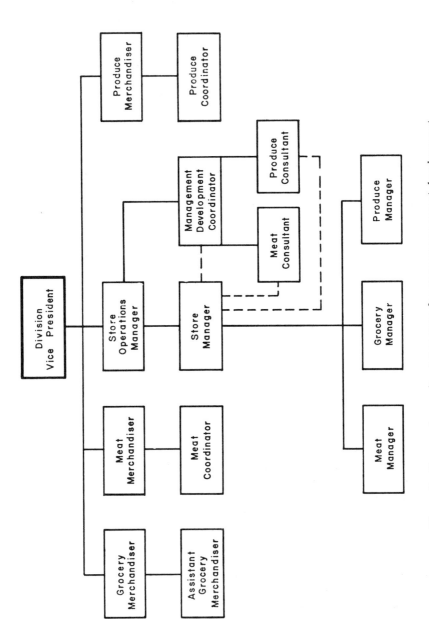

Figure 2 Proposed consultant structure for store management development.

In the consultant structure, the roles of District Manager and Specialists were changed from supervisory to consultant to the Store Manager. Department heads were to report to the Store Manager, while the managers reported directly to the Store Operations Manager. The Management Development Coordinator (MDC)—the title dreamed up for the ex-DM—and the meat and produce specialists, now called consultants, were to function as a team, under the leadership of the MDC, to consult with and train managers in all areas of store management. Within the limits of overall company policy, the manager now had the final say about in-store priorities. The consultants had no line authority; the Store Operations Manager now supervised and evaluated in-store performance.

Method

This structural change is similar in type and intent to that described by Lawrence (1958). In that case, top management designed the change without behavioral science consultation. In this case, however, the first, second, and fourth authors served as OD consultants to the project. The third author was the major client and change agent. He frequently referred to "our view from the cat bird seat," and that is an accurate description of our relationship to the project. Our primary roles were as consultants to him, the MDC team, and Merchandisers.

Following the November 1970 Operations Meetings, the four authors developed the consultant model and a method of implementation, which was presented for approval at the January 1971 Division Managers' Meeting—a monthly meeting of the top 25 executives. The Division Vice President and the President agreed to try it on an experimental basis and to review the results in six months.

To test the new structure's effectiveness in developing a range of managers, we selected an average district composed of managers with varying competencies. To have chosen only the best managers obviously would have stacked the deck. We also selected a current DM for the MDC role, to see if a DM could in fact operate effectively as a consultant. The Operations Manager and senior author jointly interviewed four DMs (selected by the Operations Manager as most promising) and independently selected the same man. The new consultant was the youngest DM, with the least amount of time "on the road," but was the only one of the four who asked some hard questions about the merit of the whole idea. He had been with the company for 12 years, having worked his way up to DM from clerk.

We felt that the selection of the MDC was critical to the project. Lawrence (1958), in describing the management-initiated program at Food World, concluded that the ability of DMs to adapt their managerial style to the new rules was largely responsible for the success of the program in several districts.

Training Needs

The next step was to select meat and produce specialists to serve on the MDC team as consultants for perishables. This selection was left to the MDC because it was important that he have confidence in his assistants.

All three new consultants were highly competent in store operating methods, but we felt they needed training in human relations and consultation skills to perform their new roles effectively. Their training in management had been solely a function of their experience: When a person is promoted to District Manager, he is simply given the keys to a company car and told to supervise his stores.

In February 1971, the new consultants attended a week-long sensitivity training program to accelerate their team building and to increase their awareness of the impact of their behavior on others. In their new roles, they would have no line authority for influencing managers and would therefore be more dependent on their own interpersonal competencies. In addition, the new structure would facilitate their use of interpersonal skills and awarenesses gained at the program. By definition the consultant role meant that the MDC members would not be as subject to hierarchical constraints of organizations, which typically discourage the use of interpersonal skills learned at T Groups.

The consultant skill training for the MDC members was done on the job, following their return from the T Group, while they were still a District Manager and Specialists with line authority. The OD staff rode with each man on his visits to a store, observing his style and method of working with store personnel. Between stores, at lunch, and over end-of-the-day cocktails, we analyzed with them why they handled situations as they did, what their objectives were in particular stores and whether or not they were accomplished, and what impact they had on the people with whom they worked. We would occasionally suggest different forms of behavior for them to try out the next day and we would then analyze the results. At the end of this month-long process, all three knew, in terms of their own behavior and recent experience in the stores, what it meant to be a consultant rather than a boss.

While the consultant training was taking place, the OD staff, under the leadership of the Operations Manager, held meetings with divisional executives to map guidelines and establish evaluation measures (to be reported later). A week before implementation of the experimental consultant structure, the OD staff conducted a two-day team development workshop for the MDC team, the managers in their new district (we felt the MDC team should work with a new group of managers rather than having to undo relationships with their current managers), and the division management. The purpose of the workshop was to establish the MDC's credibility and accelerate the relationship building between

Ground Rules for Consultant District	Ground Rules for DM District
1. Consultants will make appointments for store visits and develop a quarterly contract with each manager.	DM visits stores unannounced to inspect for adherence to company standards.
2. Store managers' performance will be evaluated by the Store Operations Manager. MDC team will have no evaluation responsibilities for managers.	DM evaluates a manager's performance and conveys his evaluation to the Store Operations Manager.
3. Store Managers are responsible for total store results.	Store Manager responsible for results in grocery and front-end departments only. Perishable specialists responsible for results in meat and produce departments.
4. Consultants' performance would be evaluated by Store Operations Manager on the basis of their ability to perform as consultants and on the basis of managers' opinion of their helpfulness.	District Manager and Specialists' performance evaluated by Store Operations on the basis of results in the stores.

Figure 3   Differences in ground rules for consultant vs. traditional district store management.

MDC team members and their new store managers, who did not believe the company was actually committed to allowing them to manage their stores with the consultant resources of the MDC team. The workshop included typical relationship-building activities and role plays designed to demonstrate how the MDC team and division management would respond to problems in the experimental district. Figure 3 shows the ground rules for the consultant district and those for traditional districts. The differences were major and called for new behavior at all levels of the division.

One change not explicitly reflected in Figure 3 is the Divisional Perishable Merchandisers' loss of control over the specialists (see Figures 1 and 2). Formerly, the merchandiser or coordinator closely directed the activity of specialists; under the consultant structure, the consultants on perishables reported to the MDC. Much of the resistance to the consultant structure came from Divisional and Corporate Merchandisers, and one reason was a loss of staff from their organization.

The Consultant Structure

Start-Up

The consultant structure, thoroughly planned and written out, went into effect in April 1971, the beginning of the June quarter. It was immediately beset with major problems.

Two weeks later, the Division decided on a major sales promotion for these stores and felt the managers were not capable of handling the promotion without supervision. It sent teams of people from the office into the stores for three weeks to oversee the promotion. The MDC team was taken off the road and put to work in a store being remodeled. In the Division's eyes, the business needs were more critical than the experiment, though they did protect the status of the MDC team by avoiding asking them to play a supervisory role during the promotion. Nevertheless, this reintroduction of supervision of the stores was a clear message to all that the Division felt uncomfortable about the managerial competencies of the store managers. Although that was probably an accurate judgment, the promotion plan considerably heightened the managers' skepticism about company commitment to the consultant structure. The first and third authors had their first real confrontation over the issue of the company's commitment to developing managers. This episode marked the beginning of a productive discussion about how managers can be developed on the job without causing serious damage to the business. Following the promotional effort, which lasted four weeks, the MDC team really began its consultant role.

The team members had to establish their credibility with the managers all over again, and it is to their credit that they were able to do so. At this point, the success or failure of the project was very much in their hands. Rather than ignoring or pooh-poohing the managers' feelings, as would be typical, the MDC team dealt directly with them while beginning to develop working contracts.

Problems began to occur in the meat and produce departments and store-wide payroll, a predicted consequence of the learning curve experienced by the managers as they take over management of their stores. Store Operations responded by holding weekly group meetings in which the managers were told of the problems and exhorted to improve. Store Operations described them as "hammer and tong" meetings. After several such meetings, little improvement was noted, and Store Operations was becoming increasingly frustrated in not being able to get the managers to improve. The OD staff suggested that Store Operations instead perform their control and management role through individual performance appraisal sessions with the managers. The Operations Manager agreed to try this approach. He discontinued the weekly meetings and conducted an hour-long review with each manager at the manager's store. (He felt he would get better results by going to the store instead of calling the managers into the office.) During the first half of each review, the Operations Manager went over the figures, identifying areas that needed improvement and complimenting managers on areas that were doing well. The second half of the review was the manager's time to talk about his problems. These reviews represented the first time an Operations Manager had ever spent an hour with each manager in a district on his performance, and the experience was highly satisfactory for both. The managers were ecstatic at being able to talk nose-to-nose with their Operations Manager, and the Operations Manager reported he developed a much better understanding of the managers and conditions in their stores. The performance reviews remain as the primary control vehicle for Operations and represent one example of management's loosening up its supervisory control patterns.

The district received an inordinate number of visits from corporate executives, many of whom came "not to praise Caesar but to bury him." The consultant approach was viewed very skeptically by many, who would report problems and apparent examples of the structure's failings to the Divisional Vice President and the company's Executive Vice President. The OD staff's response was to ask these people to chart the results—sales, gross profits, payroll per cent, and so on—in the consultant district and in the control district[1] rather than relying on periodic "eyeballing" to evaluate the effectiveness of the consultant district. With the exception of the meat department, which everyone, including the managers, acknowledged would take the longest to learn to manage, there were no differences in financial and performance results between the two districts. As the second author was fond of saying, "At least we're up to the level of no difference." This was considered a success of sorts, in view of the fact that the betting around parts of the company was that the consultant stores would simply go under.

At this time the MDC members were encountering two major problems. The managers were not asking for help. In the early stages, the opportunity to manage their own stores went to their heads, and they would call the consultants only on minor problems or to bail them out of serious situations that usually could have been prevented by earlier planning with their consultants. In addition, the Merchandisers continued to see the produce and meat consultants as their staff and would ask them to go to stores to resolve particular problems. This put pressure on the consultants: to be consultants rather than bosses, they could not carry out the orders of the Merchandisers. Merchandisers and Coordinators were supposed to communicate directly with the Store Managers within the new structure, but this was inconvenient for the Merchandisers—and old habits die hard.

A major review meeting involving the Division Management, Corporate Merchandisers, the MDC team, and the OD staff, was held in July. All the above problems were thoroughly discussed and the following modifications made:

1. The MDC members, still acting as consultants and not supervisors, could take more initiative in pointing out problems and suggesting solutions, but it was still the manager's decision to act on the consultant's recommendations. A consultant was given the option of not working with a manager if he felt a particular manager was avoiding him.

2. The Corporate Meat Merchandiser agreed to design a management training program for the managers. This represented the first such training program for Store Managers by a Merchandising office.

3. The ground rule was established that when a representative of Divisional and/or Corporate management visits a store, he will inform the manager of his observations and can suggest that the manager call his consultant. Previously, top-echelon visitors would order the manager to make changes on the spot or inform Store Operations but not the manager.

The meeting also cleared the air, and the consultant structure operated more according to plan for the remainder of the six-month period, with one major problem still unresolved. Division management, and particularly Store Operations, continued to feel uneasy about the managers' developing competencies. They therefore retained many of the former functions of the DM, such as calling stores weekly to adjust their labor budget or sales projections and inspecting the stores for appearance and adherence to standards. During the transition period, while the managers were developing, Store Operations still had to meet their responsibilities; as a result, the Operations Manager became a "high-priced DM" for about six months. This put an enormous workload on Operations, for they still had five other districts to manage; and they had to be convinced, through the efforts of the Store Managers, that the latter could adequately manage their stores. The managers' positive response to the performance reviews was the first indication Operations had that this might be possible; and toward the end of the six months, Operations saw more and more improvement in the stores. Hence, at the end of the six months, Operations people were on the verge of becoming believers.

Six Months Later

At the end of the six-month trial period, the consultant structure was operating according to plan. Operations continued to retain the controls the DM previously exercised and there continued to be no difference in the performance between the two structures. The consultant structure was designed to replace close supervision with training, on the hypothesis that this would develop the capabilities of Store Managers. As we have seen, the "hard" measures demonstrated no difference between consulted managers and supervised managers, though it is important to remember that the Divisional office still maintained a high degree of control over the managers' budgets. Hence, at this point, the performance data are inconclusive.

To assess the impact of the experiment on the Store Managers, the OD staff administered a nine-item questionnaire to managers in the experimental and control districts. The questions were intended to assess the managers' feeling of support from management, the degree to which their abilities were being used, and the degree to which they felt involved in decisions. The baseline data were collected in April 1971, two weeks before the start of the experiment (Table 1). The postmeasure was taken in October 1972 (Table 2).

Table 1 shows that, prior to the experiment, the supervised managers gave higher than average responses to six of the nine items. In comparison to the soon-to-be consulted managers, supervised managers felt their boss (DM) complimented them more on a good job, they were more knowledgeable about DM standards for evaluation, received more help in problem solving ans support with higher management from this DM, felt problems were being more confronted, and that their skills and abilities were being used better. Consulted managers felt they were slightly more consulted on decisions, received slightly more encouragement from their DM to exercise judgment and initiative, and saw a career with the company as somewhat more attractive.

Table 2 shows the amount of change in the two groups' average responses to the same items six months later. At T_2, "boss" was interpreted to mean MDC team by the consulted managers. Table 2 shows rather clearly that, from the managers' perspective, the consultant structure had accomplished its primary developmental goal of increasing the utilization of managers' skills. The consulted managers' show a noticeable positive increase on all but one item while the supervised managers show a decrease on six items and slight gains on three.

It is important to mention that during these six months, the Division encountered a severe decline in sales, experienced a large union wage settlement, and underwent a rather traditional cost-cutting program. In all districts except the consultant district, this meant that supervisors were exercising much closer control over managers. Managers in the consultant district were given guidelines for reducing costs but had more leeway in their execution than did the supervised managers. The closer supervision of the supervised managers may well explain the decreases on those items measuring support from management, career attractiveness, and the degree to which they were consulted on decisions.

The OD staff also conducted open-ended interviews with the MDC team and consulted managers, which demonstrated that the managers neither wanted nor appreciated the traditional DM function. In response to the question, "What do you miss under this style of working that you had when you had a District Manager?" 13 said they missed "nothing"—and that's their word. Many volunteered that they did not *miss* "the aggravation of do-it-my-way," "being treated

Table 1

Average of Consulted and Supervised Managers' Responses to Project Evaluation Questions at T_1

Items	Consulted Managers ($N = 15$)	Supervised Managers ($N = 15$)	Difference
1. How often does your immediate boss encourage you to show initiative and exercise judgment? (never/always)	4.57	4.44	+.13
2. To what extent does your boss compliment you when you have done a good job? (never/always)	3.57	4.11	−.54
3. To what extent do you know the standards your immediate boss uses to evaluate your performance? (never know/always know)	3.72	4.00	−.28
4. How would you rate the help your immediate boss provides you in solving problems? (never helpful/always helpful)	3.86	4.34	−.48
5. To what extent do you feel your immediate boss backs you up with higher management? (never/always)	4.29	4.44	−.15
6. To what extent do you feel problems are being faced rather than ignored? (never faced/always faced)	3.72	4.22	−.50
7. How well do you feel your skills and abilities are being used? (not used/used very well)	3.57	4.23	−.66
8. How would you rate the extent to which you are consulted when decisions are made which affect your work? (never/always)	4.28	4.00	†.28
9. How attractive does a career with the company appear? (unattractive/quite attractive)	4.43	4.22	+.21

Table 2

Amount of Change in Consulted and Supervised Managers' Average Responses to Project Evaluation Questions—T_1 to T_2[a]

Items	Consulted Managers ($N = 15$)	Supervised Managers ($N = 15$)	Difference
1. How often does your immediate boss encourage you to show initiative and exercise judgment?	+.18	+.37	−.19
2. To what extent does your boss compliment you when you have done a good job?	+.76*	−.08	+.84
3. To what extent do you know the standards your immediate boss uses to evaluate your performance?	+.61*	+.01	+.60
4. How would you rate the help your immediate boss provides you in solving problems?	+.97*	−.14	+1.14
5. To what extent do you feel your immediate boss backs you up with higher management?	+.21*	−.64	+.85
6. To what extent do you feel problems are being faced rather than ignored?	+.63*	+.08	+.55
7. How well do you feel your skills and abilities are being used?	+.55	−.03	+.58
8. How would you rate the extent to which you are consulted when decisions are made that affect your work?	+.14	−.20	+.34
9. How attractive does a career with the company appear?	+.01	−.22	+.23

*Indicates items on which consulted managers scored lower than supervised managers at T_1 but higher at T_2.

[a]Parametric tests of statistical significance are not applicable to the data for reasons of sample composition; i.e., neither district respresents a probability sample. However, using the nonparametric sign test, the probability of the consultant managers' rate of change being higher, on 8 of 9 items, occurring by chance is .04.

like a child," "getting my ass kicked," "never knowing what he [the DM] is going to do when he comes around," "bone-crushing meetings," and more. Many consulted managers talked about a new-found sense of pride in their work and a new feeling of wanting to advance in the company. To a man, they expressed a great deal of respect and affection for the Operations Manager, whom many had previously spoken of in less glowing terms; and they felt that his performance appraisals were helpful in their development as store managers. In short, the consulted managers were "turned on."

Consequences

Reactions of the Consultants

All three continue to miss the authority and control they had as members of a DM team and some of the traditional prestige and status associated with authority. Nevertheless, they also feel they have gained in-depth experience in dealing with people and in effective problem solving. Members of a DM team have formal line authority—or a club, as it is more popularly known. Whether or not the club is used, its mere existence does make managers listen more carefully and respond more quickly. Without the club, the consultants have had to rely on their interpersonal skills to accomplish work. Evidence of their effectiveness is shown in Table 2, question 4. Consulted Store Managers perceive the consultants as more helpful on solving problems than control managers perceive their DM team to be, which suggests that the consultant structure has developed capabilities for interpersonal competence and problem-solving training through the new role and behavior of the MDC team.

The report itself was submitted to the Division management and to the President. This, and the fact that the consulted stores were at least holding their own in terms of performance, enabled management to agree to continue and expand the experiment. Within six months, two additional consultant structures were implemented.

Personnel Changes

One consequence of the initial consultant structure, which continued from October 1971 to February 1972, was that each manager's performance was much more visible to Operations since it was far more intimately involved in the stores and with the managers. It became apparent that two managers, who had the most years of service with the company, were unable to manage a store effectively without direct supervision. They made the least use of the consultants and found it most difficult to make decisions on their own. They were transferred out of the district and replaced by men who Operations felt could manage their stores independently of close supervision. Operations put two other managers who were having difficulty into each other's store. One went from a high to a low volume store, usually considered a demotion, and, with fewer responsibilities, performed quite well. The manager who went from a lower to a higher volume store, usually considered a promotion, surprised Operations by doing an outstanding job. Hence, 13 of the original 15 managers were still in the district a year later and were doing at least an adequate job.

Cutting the Umbilical Cord

By March 1, 1972, the Division management felt confident that this group of managers could manage their own stores. At their initiative, Operations decided to go the whole route. For the first time in the company's history, a group of managers were given sole responsibility for meeting their quarterly sales and labor budget. Usually, Operations, through the DM, would call managers weekly, asking them to increase or decrease hours or sales projections. Until now, Operations had used this approach with the consulted managers. For this quarter, however, the managers were to receive no instructions but would review their budgets with the Operations Manager at the end of the 4th, 8th, and 13th week. Sometime in the future, as managers acquire more competence—and Operations more confidence in their competence—managers may be able to run their budgets for a quarter or even a year.

Performance Results

A district's quarterly performance is measured by the percentage of increase or decrease in sales, its increase or decrease in sales per man hour (number of labor hours divided into sales), and its increase or decrease in labor per cent (labor dollars expended expressed as a percentage of sales), when compared to the same quarter in the previous year. Improvement, or lack thereof, is a major indicator for measurement of the value of new programs.

Applying these measures to the June 1972 quarter, we find the consultant district had the smallest decrease in sales (sales throughout the division declined 1971-1972), the smallest increase in labor per cent (all labor per cents increased), and was one of two showing an increase in sales per man hour (Table 3). As a district, the consultant district had the best showing for the June 1972 quarter. Table 3a shows the performance of the districts on the same measures for the June 1971 quarter. Table 3b compares the rank-order improvement position of each district for the two quarters. As a total district, it is interesting to note the consultant district was in fifth position in 1971 (clearly in the bottom half) but

Table 3

Rate of Change in Sales, Sales Per Man Hour, and Labor Per Cent in the
Consulted District and Supervised Districts During the June 1972 Quarter
Compared Against the June 1971 Quarter

District	Sales	Sales Per Man Hour	Labor Per Cent
1.	−19.7%	−$3.26	+1.5%
2.	− 4.3	−$1.19	+1.0
3.	−12.8	+$1.20	+1.2
4.	− 6.0	−$2.13	+1.1
5. (Consulted)	− 5.4	+$1.38	+ .4
6.	−11.6	−$ .20	+1.0
Division Average	−11.7	−$ .58	+ .9

Table 3a

Rate of Change in Sales, Sales Per Man Hour, and Labor Per Cent in the
Consulted District and Supervised Districts During the June 1971 Quarter
Compared Against the June 1970 Quarter

District	Sales	Sales Per Man Hour	Labor Per Cent
1.	+10.0%	+$1.32	+.9%
2.	− 8.6	+$4.12	+.4
3.	+ 7.9	+$2.94	+.3
4.	+25.0	+$2.28	+.4
5. (Consulted)	+ 9.8	+$ .49	+.9
6.	− 7.3	+$ .38	+.7

had attained the number one position by 1972. At the end of the first year of
the experiment, the consultant district had outperformed the other five from
1971 to 1972.

Table 4 compares districts' performances against their June quarter, 1972,
budget. The consultant district is the only district to meet or exceed its budget
in all three categories. This suggests that the consulted managers were better
able to manage their budgets than were their supervised colleagues.

On the basis of these results, Operations believes managers can assume
major responsibility for profit goals, and it has taken the necessary steps to implement that view. (Gross profit responsibility is usually tightly controlled by
the Merchandisers.)

Table 3b

Comparison of the Districts' Improvement Rank-Order Positions in June 1971
(Table 3a) and June 1972 Quarter (Table 3)

District	Sales 1971	Sales 1972	Sales Per Man Hour 1971	Sales Per Man Hour 1972	Labor Per Cent 1971	Labor Per Cent 1972	District Rankings* 1971	District Rankings* 1972	1971-1972 Difference
1.	2	6	4	6	5.5	6	4	6	−2
2.	6	1	1	4	2.5	2.5	3	2	+1
3.	4	5	2	2	1	5	2	4.5	−2.5
4.	1	3	3	5	2.5	4	1	4.5	−3.5
5. (Consulted)	3	2	5	1	5.5	1	5	1	+4.0
6.	5	4	6	3	4	2.5	6	3	+3.0

*Determined by ranking of sum of ranks for each year.

Table 4

Performances in Terms of Sales, Sales Per Man Hour and Labor Per Cent,
In Relation to June 1972 Quarterly Budgets of Consulted District and
Supervised Districts

District	Sales	Sales Per Man Hour	Labor Per Cent
1.	−5.0%	−$1.45	+.3%
2.	−6.5	−$ .52	+.3
3.	−3.7	−$ .13	+.1
4.	−2.9	−$ .69	+.1
5. (Consulted)	+ .1	+$ .49	−.2*
6.	−4.8	+$ .59	−.1

*A savings against the plan in labor dollars of $15.534.

Conclusions

Attitude Change

Perhaps the most significant change associated with the consultant structure is
not the change in behavior and performance of the managers, but the change in
attitudes about supervision. Not all executives are convinced, but the Operations
Manager, the Divisional Vice President, the Corporate Vice President of Store

Operations, and the President now believe that 75-80 per cent of current managers can contribute more to the company if they are supported and trained rather than merely closely supervised. The possible consequences of this attitude shift for the management philosophy and structure of the company are obvious. It is also important to underscore that this change in attitude occurred as a function of these executives' direct experience with a situation intimately familiar to them. It is unlikely they would have occurred as the result of a specific OD attitude-training intervention in this company.

Behavioral Changes

Changes in behavior took place at the level of Store Manager, who made more decisions, became more involved in perishable departments, and made regular requests for help; at the level of District Manager and Specialist, who identified problems, suggested solutions, and trained managers instead of simply inspecting their performance; at the level of Store Operations Manager, who now meets with his managers on a regular and individual basis to plan with them and discuss their performance instead of relying on a District Manager to convey his orders and giving managers no performance feedback; and at the level of Divisional Vice President, who took an obvious risk in allowing the project to start in the first place and supporting and developing it throughout the first year. Again, these behavioral changes did not occur solely out of a belief that individuals should gain more control over their lives or that training and feedback are inherently good things. They were required to support the change in structure, which was deemed necessary because the old structure was not helping the company move ad fast as it wanted in developing managers and implementing systems. One moral, therefore, for OD practitioners might be that form follows function, not vice versa.

Resistance, Risk, and Ethics

The executives most opposed to the consultant structure also tended to be those executives who (1) were the firmest believers that "everyone needs a boot in the ass," or (2) lost staff and therefore power under the consultant structure—the Merchandisers, or (3) both. Most executives had worked their way up from stock boy level under a management structure of close supervision. For many, the consultant approach disconfirmed the merit of a management style which they had skillfully learned and mastered over the years and on which a large measure of their positive self-concept undoubtedly rested. Similar discomfort was noticeable among other District Managers, who, seeing the amount of company interest in and support of the MDC team, began to wonder about the security of their positions. It was also evident among most Merchandisers, who, actively or passively, resisted the consultant project.

Although the Store Managers responded enthusiastically, the consultant structure meant new evaluation criteria for them. Just doing well what their bosses asked of them no longer sufficed. The two managers who could not manage without close supervision were demoted as a result. Hence, there was an element of risk in the project for managers, and the project was imposed on them; they really did not have the option to say no.

The risk was high for the MDC team as well. They too had risen through the ranks to their current positions of District Manager and Specialist, and one reward for their efforts was the authority and prestige of line positions. The consultant structure removed their line authority, a fact which we have seen they continue to lament, and thereby removed some prestige from them in the eyes of many. Had the project failed, the MDC members stood to lose the most. Though they were given the formal opportunity to decline, all three would have found it difficult to decline a new position for which they had been hand-picked. So, in reality, their freedom of choice was also limited. In their case, and in the case of the managers, the success of the project has enhanced their individual standing in the eyes of company executives. By virtue of their pioneering, visible positions, the MDC team and managers received far greater attention and positive evaluation by management than have their colleagues in other districts. In their case, the risk paid off. Nevertheless, the consultant project raises important ethical questions for both executives and the OD staff. For example, how much should others be asked to risk for the sake of change that executives and OD staff feel will benefit the company and contribute to people's development and autonomy? To spare the reader a long discourse on ethical dilemmas for which there are no definitive solutions, suffice it to say that the planning, design, experience, and evaluation were conducted in an open atmosphere which allowed all the opportunity to voice their views and exert influence. Of course, we did not realize a totally democratic situation: strands of vested interest and political pressures were evident (e.g., let's not speak out publicly about a program the President, Division Vice President, or Operations Manager—depending on what level one is in—endorses). We did fully share intentions and plans, and we asked critics to support their views with data and applied the same criteria to our enthusiasm. As a result, we like to think the project was conducted ethically, though we are fully aware that some coercion and imposition occurred.

Implications for the OD Consultant

Unlike many OD programs which use training interventions—T Groups, team building, workshops focusing on management by objectives, and others—the OD staff saw its role as that of an architect, i.e., one who makes himself familiar with the client's problems and needs and works with the client to design a structure to meet the need, but leaves the final acceptance decision to the client. We proposed a new structure, offered some training experiences (the off-site T Group and 2-day team building laboratory), recommended new behavior (that the MDC be a consultant, that the Operations Manager conduct performance appraisals), and continually evaluated results. In each case, the client made the final decision, and, as a result, our influence on the system was determined by the client's perceptions of how well our designs or recommendations met his needs.[2] This is not a model of subservience, for our recommendations and urgings are consistent with our beliefs in the value of training and of increased autonomy as well as authentic confrontation and evaluation; and they are clearly different from recommendations that most executives would have made to speed up the implementation of the grocery system. The architect style did seem to enable the client to own the changes rather than merely to rely on our expertise and recommendations.

The use of any OD strategy is a design question, and we present for the reader's consideration the model of architect to be included with other models of training and consultation for system change.

Future Directions

As this report is being written, June 1972, the Corporate Human Resources and Store Operations staff is preparing a proposal that will create a management division task force for each of the four divisions. The task forces will be composed of a vertical slice of current management and will plan the management structure and needed training supports—both interpersonal and technical skill development training—required in each division. If accepted, the task forces will represent the company's first commitment to involving in management planning those who will be affected. It will also represent its first commitment to using the Human Resources staff in management planning. Prior to this proposal, all such planning and decision making were done by a select few executives who met in private. Under the terms of the proposal, the task forces will be coordinated by members of the Human Resources and Store Operations departments.

Hence, though the initial consultant project proved successful, its contribution to the company does not rest only in its demonstration of the structure's effectiveness as a management development program. More importantly, the structure has had an impact on the attitudes of many organization members who now accept McGregor's (1960) theory that people in organizations seek challenge and responsibility to the benefit of themselves and the organization. If the consultant structure experience will also change the *process* of management, it will have been successful beyond our wildest expectations of October 1970.

Postscript[3]

The division management task forces met through the summer of 1972 and developed the following management structure: The role of Store Operations Manager would be deleted and two new *staff* roles created for each division—Sales Manager, charged with coordinating the division's sales program, and an Administrative Service Manager, charged with coordinating the quarterly budget-setting process. Each role reports to the Division Manager. In place of District Managers, a new role was created, that of a Zone Manager, who reports directly to the Division Manager and has line responsibility for sales, budget, profit, and personnel functions throughout 18 to 20 stores. The Zone Manager's role is clearly that of a line manager and as such can introduce the needs of his particular area into the Division's planning in the areas mentioned above. Working for the Zone Manager is a produce trainer, meat trainer, and grocery trainer, each of whom serves as consultant staff to the 18-20 Store Managers in the same way as did the Management Development Team in the consultant structure. In addition, face-to-face quarterly performance appraisals are now in effect between each two levels from Corporate Senior Vice President to Store Clerk; and an incentive bonus plan, based on performance and store conditions, has been introduced for Store Managers.

The changes made by the task forces have resulted in a more direct line relationship between stores and the division office, considerably reduced the number of people exercising line authority over the Store Manager, and retained the practice of training and development as a management strategy. Full implementation of the structure is one to two years away. A recent study indicates a 15 per cent improvement in productivity for those stores now operating under the structure and a generally high level of acceptance of the structure by those participating in it. The consultant structure, as described in this case study, has been eliminated as the new structure takes effect.

Notes

1. The Division Vice President identified a control district which he felt was most similar to the consultant district among the other five districts.
2. Not all our recommendations were accepted. Training the MDC team and manager to conduct in-store meetings, performance appraisals with employees, and a team development workshop for the Division management are examples of recommendations that were not accepted.
3. This article was completed in June 1972. The authors are pleased to report that during the intervening year the company has continued to make major changes in its management structure, building on the consultant experiment.

References

Averch, V., & Luke, R. Organization development: The view from within. *Training and Development Journal,* 1971, 25 (9), 38-42.

Beer, M., & Huse, E. A systems approach to organization development. *Journal of Applied Behavioral Science,* 1972, 8 (1), 79-101.

Beer, M., Pieters, G. R., Marcus, S. H., & Hundert, A. T. Improving integration between functional groups: A case in organization change and implications for theory and practice. Symposium presented at American Psychological Association Convention, Washington, D.C., September 1971.

Bennis, W. *Organization development.* Reading, Mass.: Addison-Wesley, 1969.

Dalton, G., Barnes, L., & Zaleznik, A. *The distribution of authority in formal organizations.* Boston: Division of Research, Harvard Business School, 1968.

Lawrence, P. *The changing of organizational behavior patterns.* Boston: Division of Research, Harvard Business School, 1958.

McGregor, D. *The human side of enterprise.* New York: McGraw-Hill, 1960.

MY ERRORS IN OD*

W. J. Reddin

This is an account of errors which I believe I have made. These errors have occurred in relationship to my role as change agent working as a process consultant.
For each error there is an illustrative case study in which I was directly involved.
Some of the case studies could be used to illustrate more than one error but I
avoided this in order to provide more examples. The errors include bottom up
change, creating change overload, raising expectations above delivery point, inappropriate attachment, trapped in one part, changing only a subsystem, inappropriate use of behavioral vs. structural interventions, losing professional detachment, assuming a change is needed, and not seeking help oneself.

There are many book-length case studies of OD interventions; and there
are many prescriptions concerning the consultant's role. In spite of this extensive literature, however, explicit discussion of actual errors does not represent
the thrust of OD writing. Some go as far as to suggest that if the client has only
itself to blame (Tilles, 1961; Woody & Woody, 1971). Examples of errors do
exist, however. These include failure to understand why a client relationship
deteriorated (Symposium, 1964, pp. 114-119); change overload and discrepant

*Presented on Friday, August 13, 1976, to the Organization Development Division at the
Academy of Management's thirty-sixth annual meeting, August 11-14, 1976, Kansas City,
Missouri.
Paper also was published as "Confessions of An Organizational Change Agent," *Group and
Organization Studies,* March 19, 1977, *2,* (1) 33-41. Copyright © 1977 by International
Authors. Used with permission of the publisher, University Associates, Inc., and the author.

values; changing only a subsystem, while the top man was not involved (Bennis, 1966, pp. 152-165); and Beckhard (1969, pp. 93-96) has produced a list of twelve reasons for OD failures.

Bottom Up Change

When change agents tell me of their plans for a bottom-up change attempt I remind them of the military dictum that the penalty of mutiny is death.

> In 1959 I was a consultant to a company team planning a change program for a 20,000 employee firm. The budget was enormous. We planned a series of ten month-long residential seminars, for 30 managers each. The entire top management was to attend, except the nine man top team. The first week of the seminar was a T-Group, the second was social issues at which prominent journalists and activists spoke, the third was planning and organizing, the fourth was objectives. The post-seminar reaction forms were the highest I have experienced. After running three of the ten seminars the top team cancelled the allocated budget and the program was abandoned. What had happened was that successive waves of managers with a radically changed idea on how the company should be run were causing a tremendous disturbance and we had made no preparation to enable the top team to deal with it.

I am frequently pressured by clients to make this error again but, recently at least, have not done so. The man who makes the representation to me usually explains that the top man is too busy, doesn't need it, could simply read the book, or if only I could speak to him for a couple of hours. I have my armament of counter-arguments and sometimes, shamelessly, even suggest that the top man should attend an unfreeze seminar for symbolic reasons. Beckhard (1969) touches on a related problem which top team commitment and participation can avoid: "a continued discrepancy between top management statements of values and styles and their actual managerial work behavior" (p. 93). Bennis (1966, pp. 157-160) gives an example of this error.

Creating Change Overload

It is often an easy matter to create more change than a system can conveniently cope with, thus creating change overload.

> I once held a four day team building meeting with the top team of a food processor employing about 1,000 people. The company had experienced no real change for the previous decade. The discussion

came to center on the organization chart and it was agreed to reorganize the top 100 positions in the company. This was easier said than done. The two most powerful men on the top team were highly rigid and in implementing the change grew more and more authoritarian. What was designed as a healthy program of evolutionary change descended into a program to write more detailed job descriptions.

The potential for creating change overload can be high, but it is difficult to predict its occurrence. The most rigid systems are ones most likely to experience it because they are the ones least equipped to handle change. The change agent who has a continuous interface with the client should be able to identify the possibility of change overload and help with adjustment to it. If, however, his relationship is "drop in again when you are in town and let's have another team meeting in a year or so," this potential problem is difficult to monitor. I tend to avoid change overload now by requiring a continuous association and avoiding single interventions. Bennis (1966, pp. 153-155) refers to a similar error.

Raising Expectations Above Delivery Point

Perhaps the easiest error to commit in organization development is raising expectations above delivery point.

The top man of a government department decided to introduce MBO by participative means. At my suggestion, we had a meeting to discuss it. At this point, several errors had been committed. MBO certainly in the traditional format, is not suitable for most government departments, as power is so diffuse. The top man's autocratic decision was hardly the way to introduce a participative approach and the launch would raise expectations above delivery point. There was great excitement at the meeting about the new management style. Everyone thought things would change completely and immediately. However, over the next few months budgets were done the old way and some key decisions were imposed autocratically. A program that might have been a success if introduced slowly, got a bad name in its opening months because of the raised expectations.

The best way to avoid this error is, from the start, to think and talk in terms of 3-4 years. Beckhard (1969) refers to "short time framework" (p. 94) as a condition for failure. Another way to avoid the error is to describe every OD intervention as an "experiment" but I have never done this as it can tend to lower the responsibility of everyone involved and allows failure to be explained away too easily in terms of "we agreed it was just an experiment."

Inappropriate Attachment

Many change agents would share the view that the nature of the attachment to the client is the key element in influence attempts.

> The chairman of a 10,000 employee subsidiary of a British industrial giant invited me to dinner with his board at their country house training centre. It was an epic meal and the vintage port flowed. The conversation was witty and I had to lean on my limited classical education to keep up with the literary allusions. In preparation for an MBO conference I had in fact recently re-read Thucydides' *History of the Peloponnesian War* and this gave me some good lines. My first error was accepting the first invitation and then my next was visiting in similar circumstances yet again. It was a superb, if unconscious, seduction job by the client. My relationship to this client became intellectual, witty companion. My attempts to change it were met with incredulity.

Versions of the error are failure to obtain multiple entry, attached too low down in the organization, interfacing with an individual, not a group, slavish dependency by the client, "We really need you," or client counterdependency, "You have served your purpose." At times I have been attached as servant, master, captive behavioral scientist, visiting professor, tame seal, and resident magician. Sometimes I have to remind clients that I have not walked on water recently. Sometimes I have to remind myself.

Obtaining the appropriate attachment can be one of the most difficult things to accomplish. It can be facilitated by having a few "ground rules" which the client accepts at the start. These might range all the way from not eating with the client, a rule Tavistock once used, to never talking to any one individual alone. The attachment issue is particularly difficult for the internal change-agent; and the ideal structural device is a three year guaranteed terminal assignment with all renumeration issues settled in advance. Beckhard (1969) refers to "overdependence on outside help" (p. 94) as a condition for OD failure. This is one face of the multifaceted problem of attachment.

Trapped in One Part

One element of good change strategy is multiple entry but it is all too easy to become trapped in or by one part of the organization.

> A brewery used my services to improve its marketing orientation. The change program was highly successful and over three years the profits moved from $500,000 to $1,000,000 and the sole competitor's profit fell from $500,000 to $70,000. During this same period

the position at the top of the marketing team increased in power greatly, moving from what was essentially public relations officer to sales manager and then to vice-president marketing. All this was very well, but was not seen that way by production who had seen its considerable power and prestige erode. The OD emphasis should have then, or earlier, shifted to such interfaces within the firm and I made several unsuccessful attempts to achieve this. In the mind of production, I was the wicked consultant who had hurt them. In the mind of marketing, I was their man to use in the fight against production. All this might not be too bad but twelve years later very low trust still exists between the two sub-systems to a degree that I even now discuss with the marketing vice-president whether he ought to move on.

The possible solution to this problem is in obtaining and maintaining multiple entry and in anticipating the consequences that might arise from current change efforts. A good signal of where one might be needed is who the client most talks about disparagingly.

Changing Only a Sub-system

Changing only a sub-system was a common error of mine especially when working with large systems.

In the early 1960's a 1,000 employee division of a 3,000-employee power commission engaged in a successful attempt to increase participation. Indications of this were that line crew foremen, not head office engineers, selected line tools, and meter readers wrote their own rule books and established their work norms. A major conflict boundary developed between this division and other divisions and the central systems unit. Fundamental disagreement arose over how many signatures there should be on expense accounts, what is an appropriate discretionary amount for truck drivers to spend on repairs on the road and, the biggest fight, where should computerized individual performance data be fed: to the individual, his superior, or to a staff unit? The issue is unresolved today and in this tightly-integrated technology two quite different climates exist where, presumably, any one type of climate might be better.

While the example refers to subsystems aligned vertically, the error applies equally well to systems aligned horizontally. The error then involves treatment of one level but not another. Beckhard (1969) states a particular case of this general error as "a large gap between the change effort at the top of the organization and efforts at the middle of the organization" (p. 95).

As every system is partial to every other system, and since the one predictable thing about OD is its unpredictable consequences, this error is likely to be continuously made. The best way to avoid it is to establish specific measurable objectives at the start and obtain agreement to them not only from the system assumed to be directly involved but adjacent systems such as head office, owners or politicians. If these adjacent systems, say essentially, "good, why don't you get on with it," this is at least one indication of subsystem autonomy to make the changes without impairing other relationships.

Inappropriate Use of Behavioral vs. Structural Interventions

The bread-and-butter of the psychologist is the random error of the sociologist. Those of us concerned with change in behavior in organizations can easily be biased too strongly to either side. Is the personality clash a function of poor role clarity or of low human-relations skills? Either of these may at times explain most of the variance. But what if one chooses the wrong one in a particular case?

> I was once asked to plan a change program for a Montreal production subsidiary of a U.S.A. firm which had fired four of the subsidiary's general managers in six years for failure to show a profit. The trust level was low and most managers had moved to a very low level of risk-taking. After I had started to unfreeze, team-build, develop candour, etc., an independent study by the parent company uncovered major errors in the transfer-price system within the subsidiary and from the subsidiary to the parent company. When changes in these prices were introduced, profits started to appear and the current general manager stayed eight years. The company needed a cost accountant, but initially got a change agent.

> A similar error was narrowly avoided when the president of a fish packing firm turned down my idea to start team-building sessions with his trawler fleet captains. The problem was that the competing Russian fleet all cooperated with each other while his own trawler fleet captains did not, leading to much lower productivity. He pointed out to me that under Canadian Maritime Law the trawler fleet captains and crew were not employees but merchant co-adventurers. Each was an independent businessman. Not only the legal system but the existing community structure and a long local history all supported this view. To imagine that much could be done by a seminar demonstrating that cooperation optimizes the system but not necessarily optimizes each individual in it was farcical. It would be rather like rearranging deckchairs on the Titanic. The clincher was when he told me about the first, and last, Christmas Eve party that the executive committee had arranged with the cap-

tains. It had to be on Christmas Eve because trawler captains used the occasion to announce their first strike. Their spokesman apologized for the timing, but explained it was the first time they had been together.

Beckhard (1969) refers to precisely this error as "no connection between behavioral-science oriented change efforts and management-services/operations-research-oriented change efforts" (p. 94). To avoid this error one must either oneself develop a wider range of conceptual tools or to somehow bring such tools to bear. Psychologically-oriented change agents could do well to read more systems theory, sociology and even MBO.

Losing Professional Detachment

A surgeon once told me that during operations it was not uncommon for him to tell dirty jokes to the nurses. He explained that such behavior served to maintain a psychological detachment from the patient, which might have affected the surgery.

> After working with one U.S.A. client intensively for two years, it became apparent to me that the client was talking change and had built a staff to implement it but that no change was taking place. For various reasons I was emotionally involved with this client and wanted the program to be a success. My style became abrupt and argumentative. Instead of trying to analyze resistance with the client I was berating it for not changing. At the time I put my change in style down to my innate style flexibility; after all, very few of us remain who are equally adept at Theory "X" and "Y" (McGregor, 1960), even when appropriate. Now I see it simply as emotional involvement leading to a lowering of effectiveness.

As a boy of 17 I was roaming Eastern Canada in the winter looking for work which was hard to find. I heard of a free two-day residential course conducted by the St. John Ambulance Brigade, meals provided. I decided that it was my public duty to learn first aid. Never will I forget one instructor's comment that went something like this:

> "Suppose you are the first on the scene of a two car collision. People and their legs are lying about and there is lots of screaming and blood. If you want to be helpful, first say to yourself it is their problem, not mine."

His intent was to shock us and of course he did. He was saying do not get too emotionally involved with the system you are trying to help. The implications of this aspect of the role relationship are many and contentious. Has the client really got the right not to get well? Is hoping the client will get well a poor professional posture? Is joining the client the ultimate defeat?

These days I pay more attention to my own feelings and watch for the danger signals. For me, at least, they include post-meeting depression, not understanding what is going on, making remarks that are a little too smooth or crude, liking the client, wanting the client to like me, wanting an intervention to lead to a terrific success, attempting to impress the client or obtaining much satisfaction from client praise.

Assuming a Change Is Needed

It is easy to get trapped by the belief that new is better than old or that a new label changes something.

Sometimes we attempt change when the system clearly does not need it. We never know when to give up. Two young Scouts whose younger brother had fallen into a shallow pond rush home to mother with tears in their eyes. "We're trying to give him artificial respiration," one of them sobbed, "but he keeps getting up and walking away."

Not Seeking Help Oneself

The long-standing problem of those in the helping professions is not to seek help themselves. It is hardly necessary to supply an example; the prior examples attest to it. The best way I know to avoid this error is to first admit one's failures to oneself and take a fair share of the blame. Then to identify others in a similar line of work who also know you as a person, and arrange for regular telephone chats concerning current clients. This is what I have done. I have not found it useful to seek such assistance from clients, or from external staff also working with the client, or those who work closely with me. They are as emotionally involved as I am and just as prone to distort, albeit in a different direction. Another more structured device has been proposed by Bennis (1966), who commented on the Clinical Pathology Conference where medical students and doctors find out why the patient really died. He believes it is a good teaching practice but, "No equivalent teaching device exists in the behavioral sciences, unfortunately, mainly because we are in a relatively early stage of developing a practice" (p. 152). In a footnote he continues, "There are other reasons as well, for example, the understandable desire for secrecy regarding failure or mixed successes and the difficulty of ascertaining precise causes in these complex social-change ventures" (p. 152).

This is clearly a highly personal account. I am not at all tempted to develop a paradigm of errors that change agents might make. This is simply my conceptualizing of part of my experience. I am sure that embedded in what I identify as errors are many of my assumptions about man, the role of change agent, and the change process.

References

Argyris, C. "Explorations in consulting-client relationships." *Human Organization*, 1961, *20*, 121-133.

Argyris, C. *Intervention Theory and Method.* Reading, Mass.: Addison-Wesley Publishing Company, 1970.

Argyris, C. *Management and Organizational Development: The Path from XA to YB.* New York: McGraw-Hill, 1971.

Beckhard, R. *Organization Development: Strategies and Models.* Reading, Mass.: Addison-Wesley, 1969.

Bennis, W. *Changing Organizations.* New York: McGraw-Hill, 1966.

Boehme, W. "The professional relationship between consultant and consultee." *American Journal of Orthopsychiatry*, 1956, *26*, 241-248.

Bowman, P. H. "The role of the consultant as a motivator of action." *Mental Hygiene*, 1959, *43*, 105-110.

Burke, R. J. "Psychologists consult with organizations: Alternative strategies of involvement." *The Canadian Psychologist*, October, 1971, *12*, 482-497.

Covner, B. J. "Principles for psychological consulting with client organizations." *Journal of Consulting Psychology*, 1947, 227-244.

Daumer, K. H. J. *Planned Organizational Development and Change: A Clinical Study.* Ph.D. dissertation, Case Western Reserve University, 1969.

Ferguson, C. K. "Concerning the nature of human systems and the consultant's role." *Journal of Applied Behavioral Science*, 1968, *4*, 179-193.

Gibb, J. R. and R. Lippitt (eds.). "Consulting with groups and organizations." *Journal of Social Issues*, 1959, *15*, 1-76.

Mann, F. C. and F. W. Neff. *Managing Major Change in Organizations.* Ann Arbor, Mich: Foundation for Research on Human Behavior, 1961.

Rice, A. K. *The Enterprise and Its Environment.* London: Tavistock Institute of Human Relations, 1963.

Schein, E. H. *Progress Consultation: Its Role in Organization Development.* Reading, Mass: Addison-Wesley, 1969.

Sofer, C. *The Organization from Within.* London: Tavistock Publications, 1961, and Chicago: Quadrangle Books, 1962.

Symposium, "Outside consultants to industry: strengths, problems and pitfalls." *Personnel Psychology*, 1964, *17*, 107-133.

Tilles, S. "Understanding the consultant's role." *Harvard Business Review,* 1961, *39,* 87-99.

Woody, R. H. and J. D. Woody. "Behavioral science consultation." *Personnel Journal,* 1971, *50,* 382-391.

JOB REDESIGN
A Contingency Approach to Implementation*

William E. Reif and Robert M. Monczka

A story about the late Thomas Watson of IBM is now part of management litera-ture. In the early 1940s he asked a woman on the assembly line what she did *not* like about her job, and she promptly replied that it was doing the same thing over and over. That, reportedly, is what gave him—and IBM—the idea of job en-largement, an experiment that is no longer an experiment, but a program widely recognized as a means of dealing with job-related problems of worker satisfaction and productivity. It is variously referred to as job enlargement, job enrichment, job redesign, but the last is probably the most accurate, since all these efforts center on designing, or redesigning, jobs to include a greater variety of content; require a higher level of knowledge and skills; give the worker more autonomy and responsibility for planning, directing, and controlling his job; and provide op-portunity for personal growth and meaningful work experiences.

In theory, job redesign makes performing the job more rewarding, or in-trinsically satisfying, and that, in turn, motivates the worker to be more produc-tive. In practice, though, the results of job redesign have been mixed, and both employers and employees in many cases have become disenchanted with the whole concept. A careful examination of projects that have failed has led these authors to conclude that the concept itself is sound, but that what was lacking was a sound strategy of implementing the programs.

*Reprinted by permission of the publisher from PERSONNEL, May/June 1974 © 1974 by AMACOM, a division of American Management Associations.

The strategy set forth here is based on a contingency approach to job re-design that can identify, analyze, and evaluate the organizational variables that determine the successful application of job enrichment. Jobs cannot be enriched in isolation if the expected results of increased job satisfaction and productivity are to be realized; rather, management must view the undertaking within the context of the total work environment. This calls for an understanding not only of the job and its requirements but of these broader aspects:

> The psychosocial environment, which shapes the attitudes, values, and be-liefs of individual workers and work groups.
>
> Technology, which places definite constraints on a job's potential for en-richment, particularly in terms of conversion costs, availability of equip-ment and systems, and technical expertise
>
> Management, which ultimately is responsible for the success or failure of any major organizational change
>
> The complex set of interrelationships between and among jobs, workers, technology, and management

The contingency approach to implementing job redesign places heavy em-phasis on diagnosis and the development of diagnostic skills that will direct the job designer to work situations where changes in task structure and processes will have the greatest effect on changing job attitudes (job satisfaction) and be-havior (performance).

A Contingency Model of Job Design

The contingency model of job design regards the organization as an open system and emphasizes the relationships between organizational components and between the organization and its environment that affect the performance of the whole. In other words, primary concern is with the overall effectiveness of the system, not individual subsystems, and with the interdependence of all system compo-nents. It follows that changes in job design will affect all other organizational variables and in turn will be affected by them. This means that if management wants to maximize its return on investment in job enrichment, it may have to adopt new policies and practices and make other appropriate organizational changes that will bring the whole system into phase with the newly designed job. The contingency approach forces the job designer to think in terms of the whole system, and to realize that he is dealing directly with just one part of a highly complex, dynamic organizational environment.

Let's examine the four basic components of the contingency model that the job redesigner must take into account, and see how each component influ-ences the direction and degree of change that result from a redesigned job and acts as a determinant of the success, or failure, of the job enrichment project.

Contingency Model Components: Job Design

There are ten key job dimensions or characteristics that are manageable—that is, are capable of being modified or changed—and therefore provide the basis for enrichment: variety, autonomy, interaction, knowledge and skill, responsibility, task identity, feedback, pay, working conditions, and cycle time.

> *Variety* refers to both object variety—the number of parts, tools, and controls to be manipulated—and motor variety—work pace, physical location of work, and prescribed physical operations of work.
>
> *Autonomy* refers to the degree of worker latitude in selecting work methods, work sequence, and work pace, and the degree of worker choice in accepting or rejecting the quality of materials, securing outside services, and obtaining other inputs to the job.
>
> *Interaction* refers to the amount (number of persons contacted and time spent) of required interaction with others and optional interaction for purposes other than direct assistance in performing the work.
>
> *Knowledge and skill* requirements concern the amount of time spent in becoming proficient at the job.
>
> *Responsibility* is determined by the degree of ambiguity of remedial action required to solve routine job problems, the time span of discretion allowed the worker before his performance is reviewed by superiors, and the probability of costly errors in work for which the individual is accountable.
>
> *Task identity* refers to the ability of the individual to relate to his work, in terms of factors such as clarity of cycle closure and visibility of transformation (seeing how his job contributes to the total work effort) and of the value added to the finished product by his contribution.
>
> *Feedback* refers to the quantity, quality, and timeliness of information the individual receives about his job performance.
>
> *Pay* refers to the economic rewards the worker receives for doing his job.
>
> *Working conditions* refers to the physical aspects of the job and the immediate work environment, such as lighting, temperature, and cleanliness in the work area.
>
> *Cycle time* refers to the length of time required to perform the major unit of work.

Contingency Model Components: Psychosocial Environment

This organizational variable is a composite of the psychological characteristics (self-concepts) of the individual workers; the perceived status (role concept) of the individual as a member of the formal and the informal organizations; and the sentiments, activities, interactions, and norms of the small work group. Although the worker can be characterized by many dimensions, this discussion will be limited to three that are most pertinent to the application of job enrichment: (1) position in the need hierarchy, (2) level of knowledge and skills, and (3) work attitudes, values, and beliefs.

Position in need hierarchy. The disposition of workers toward higher-order or lower-order need satisfaction is a key to how receptive they are to job enrichment. Those who are concerned with fulfilling lower-order physiological and security needs are likely to be strongly motivated by economic (extrinsic) rewards, and may have little interest in working on "enriched" jobs. In fact, they may react negatively to any suggested changes in job content, viewing such a move as another attempt by management to get more out of them for no mare pay. On the other hand, those who value the satisfaction of higher-order needs, such as esteem, autonomy, and self-actualization, will usually respond favorably to job enrichment. They more readily identify with the rationale for job enrichment and are positively motivated by increases in variety, interaction, and responsibility.

Level of knowledge and skills. The ability of workers to perform well on enriched jobs is, of course, critical to success; if they are not capable of handling the more demanding job requirements, the organization is not going to experience the expected increases in job satisfaction and job performance. Job enrichment by its very nature creates a situation in which the worker is faced with greater autonomy, which means less structure; more freedom of action and opportunity to use discretion; more responsibility, which means he will also be held accountable for results; more variety, which means more and different tasks to perform; and more complex interactions, which increase the need for communication skills and for understanding of human behavior.

Management must be willing to provide the training necessary to qualify workers to perform at the level required by the redesigned jobs; indeed, if management is not in a position to do so, it would be best not to consider job enrichment.

Work attitudes, values, and beliefs. If employees identify with the work ethic of occupational achievement, believe in the intrinsic value of hard work, and strive to attain responsible positions, job enrichment will be viewed as supportive of their needs and they will be receptive to it. Conversely, if workers have a negative attitude toward change, feel inadequate because of lack of knowledge, skills, and previous work experience, and do not subscribe to the Protestant work ethic, they will probably choose not to get involved. Management had better be sure that workers want job enrichment before giving much thought to extensive changes in job design. As a means of motivating workers and increasing productivity, job enrichment is effective only when the individuals involved are eager to make the transition to redesigned jobs.

Contingency Model Components: Technology

The success of job enrichment also depends on technology, of which we'll consider three aspects—dominance, cost, and application.

Dominance refers to the extent technology delimits the human aspects of the job and determines output. Most jobs are designed so that workers, within certain limits, are capable of setting the rate at which they will produce. One of the assumptions of job enrichment is that an increase in job satisfaction will result in some proportionate increase in job performance, but it is obvious that if the worker has little or no control over productivity, the expected benefits will not materialize. Consequently, the potential payoff from enrichment will be greater if it is applied to jobs that are free of technological dominance than if it is applied to jobs where the machine, process, system, or pace of the assembly line is the primary determinant.

Cost. How much will it cost to change the characteristics of the job? When major technological changes are introduced as part of an enriched job design, it is likely that conversion costs will be high. In situations where the cost considerations are overriding, job enrichment may not be a practical, cost-effective solution to problems of low morale and worker dissatisfaction.

Application. As we have said, changes in job design can be limited by the state of technology and the organization's ability to apply it. But one of the alternatives to enriching dull, repetitive, routine jobs is to automate them, thus relieving the worker of basic, meaningless tasks. Unfortunately, the existing state of technology may not permit that alternative to be chosen, or technology may be available but the organization may not have the managerial and/or technical expertise necessary to apply it.

Contingency Model Components: Management

The major considerations here are management philosophy, attitude toward change, leadership style, and superior-subordinate relationships.

Management philosophy is a composite of the attitudes, values, beliefs, and experiences of the management group. It is primarily responsible for molding and firmly maintaining the character of the organization. "Character" defines the purpose of the organization, decides the policies by which it will be governed, and determines the means it will employ to achieve its objectives. The underlying philosophy is behind management's general response to job enrichment, a response that will depend to a great extent on concern for improving the quality of life at work. A genuine interest in workers' needs and work-related objectives cannot be instilled by company memos, but must be a part of the moral fiber of the organization.

Attitude toward change. As has already been emphasized, the effects of changes in job content cannot be confined to the task structure; rather, they will serve as the catalyst for changes in the psychosocial environment, technology, and management. Job enrichment will be effective to the extent that management takes a corporate approach to change and is willing to weigh the possible systemwide consequences of redesigned jobs. For example, members of management should be ready to accept the fact that job enrichment may require the redesign of their own as well as their subordinates' jobs, because enriching the lowest-level job theoretically can start a chain reaction that, if allowed to run its course, will eventually result in the redesign of all jobs (though this pervasiveness is actually seldom seen).

Leadership style. The basic attitudes that management has about workers can color its reaction to job enrichment. If management holds to a basic Theory X set of assumptions about employees, and believes that the average worker is inherently lazy, has little ambition, and dislikes work and will avoid it if he can, there will be many problems associated with the implementation of job enrichment. If the opposite, Theory Y, view is held, the concept will be compatible with management's assumptions about the qualities, capabilities, and motivation of the workforce.

Superior-subordinate relationships. In turn, leadership style is reflected in a manager's relationship with subordinates. The autocratic manager finds it difficult to delegate responsibility, to give up some of the planning and control aspects of his job to his subordinates, and to give them the opportunity to use their own discretion in matters relating to job performance—all vital ingredients of enriched jobs. For the more democratic, employee-centered manager, accepting job enrichment may require little more than formalizing a program that he has been practicing informally, on an individual superior-subordinate basis, for some time.

Measurement and Monitoring

The feedback loop of the contingency model should be able to answer three basic questions:

> What is the present status of all key organizational variables and what is the level of outputs from the system?
>
> What are the specific results that management wants to achieve from job enrichment?
>
> What progress is being made toward the achievement of those objectives?

The answer to the first question will provide management with valuable information about the state of critical variables such as job characteristics, worker attitudes and work behavior, technological dominance and cost, and management receptiveness. The other two questions force management to define "success" for specific job enrichment projects and to establish the system for measuring progress toward the achievement of the agreed-upon objectives. Once the project is under way, a continual monitoring program should be established for periodic evaluations of how changes in job design are affecting job satisfaction and productivity.

Implementing Job Enrichment: Theory into Practice

The first step in the implementation process is an organizational audit to identify and critically evaluate the status of key organizational variables that affect the eventual outcome of any job enrichment project [see table]. The accompanying figure presents an audit format that can be used to evaluate the various dimensions of job design, worker characteristics, technological capabilities, and management philosophy. The 24 sets of bipolar statements describe conditions that are most and least favorable to job enrichment: applying them to a particular work situation provides a simple, yet useful, means of judging the organization's ability to support job enrichment projects.

If the situational analysis reveals a supportive organizational climate (and there are no particular circumstances warranting special consideration), management can proceed to design and implement enriched jobs with a high degree of confidence that the project will succeed. If, on the other hand, the analysis brings to light several seriously limiting factors or potential problem areas, management will want to deal with them before initiating changes in job design.

The organizational audit emphasizes again the importance of applying job enrichment contingently. No two organizations are alike in terms of job structure, worker characteristics, technological capabilities, and management; so the concept must always be tailored to fit the needs of a particular work environment. A thorough analysis of the situation will provide management with the information it needs to develop an approach to redesigning jobs that will most effectively meet its own unique requirements.

An Organizational Audit Format for Job Enrichment

	Most Favorable Conditions for Implementation	Least Favorable Conditions for Implementation
I. Job Design		
1. Variety	Little variety exists because of the way jobs are presently structured, but there is potential for variety because there are a large number of parts, tools, and controls that can be manipulated, and the work pace, physical location, and prescribed physical operation of work can be modified to meet individual requirements.	The work environment is such that little potential for increasing variety exists (for example, a toll booth attendant on a highway).
2. Autonomy	Inputs to the job and methods of doing the job (procedures, sequence, pace, etc.) do not have to be totally dictated to the worker by the production/operation system.	The production/operation system defines work flow, methods, pace, and sequence and changes cannot be made without seriously affecting scheduling, line balance, worker efficiency, and output levels.
3. Interaction	The opportunity exists for people to work together as a team—that is, the job naturally requires the coordination of tasks or activities among several workers.	The job can be performed best by an individual working alone.
4. Knowledge and Skill	The job can be made more challenging by adding additional or more complex tasks, and workers are capable of meeting more demanding job requirements.	It would be inefficient to incorporate new tasks into the existing job structure, and/or increasing worker proficiency would be difficult to achieve.
5. Responsibility	It is feasible to reduce reliance on the "only one way to do the job" approach to performing work and making work-related decisions.	It would be economically or technically unrealistic to allow variability in the way job situations are handled.

6. Task Identity	The job can be redesigned so that the worker can see the value of his work in terms of its contribution to the total work effort.	An increase in the scope of the job would reduce the likelihood that the individual could successfully complete his task efficiently.
7. Feedback	It would not be difficult to redesign the control system to provide workers on a regular basis with information about their job performance.	Information cannot be readily provided workers because of cost and data-collection problems.
8. Pay	The wage payment plan is not based solely on output.	Workers are paid under a straight piece-work wage plan.
9. Working Conditions	Working conditions, along with other hygiene factors, are perceived as satisfactory by most workers.	Working conditions are considered to be unsatisfactory by most workers.
10. Cycle Time	Short, with potential for expansion.	Longer cycle times would interfere with other, interrelated work activities.
II. Psychosocial Environment		
1. Personality	Workers are self-confident and achievement-oriented.	Workers lack self-confidence and have low achievement drives.
2. Work Attitudes, Values, and Beliefs	Workers are positively oriented toward the work ethic and willingly accept change.	Workers do not readily identify with the work ethic and fear change.
3. Position in Need Hierarchy	Workers are primarily concerned with fulfilling higher-level needs (esteem, autonomy, and self-actualization).	Workers are primarily concerned with fulfilling lower-level needs (physiological and security).
4. Knowledge and Skills	Workers are capable and motivated to develop their talents to the fullest.	Workers have little interest in developing new knowledge and skills, or lack capacity to do so.

(continued)

An Organizational Audit Format for Job Enrichment (continued)

	Most Favorable Conditions for Implementation	Least Favorable Conditions for Implementation
5. Work Group Characteristics	Younger, more highly educated.	Little education, unsatisfying work experiences.
III. Technology		
1. Dominance	Workers, not technology, are primarily responsible for output and quality levels.	Emphasis on equipment, machines, and systems in job design; technology primarily dictates the quantity and quality of work.
2. Cost	Low dollar investment in technology.	High dollar investment in technology.
3. State of Technology	Technology is available to improve the quality of working life	Technology is not capable of dealing with problems of worker dissatisfaction.
4. Organization's Ability to Apply Technology	High, in both a technical and managerial sense	Low.
IV. Management		
1. Management Philosophy	Concerned with the utilization of human resources to the mutual benefit of the individual and the organization.	Primarily concerned with production; view job enrichment only as a means of increasing output.
2. Attitude Toward Change	Positive.	Negative.
3. Leadership Style	Democratic, employee-centered.	Authoritarian, task-centered.
4. Superior-Subordinate Relationships	Built on Theory Y set of assumptions about work behavior.	Built on Theory X set of assumptions about work behavior.
5. Union Management Relationships	Open, supportive.	Closed, antagonistic.

OD AT THE GRASS ROOTS
First-Line Management Team-Building in a Public Housing Project*

W. Lynn Tanner and Muhyi A. Shakoor

Introduction

Public housing projects are critical and life-sustaining organizations in our social structure, attempting to cope with the extremely complex change of this turbulent era.

Hence the significance of this team-building effort, which grew out of a recognized need for continued training and creative utilization of project management personnel, in the face of rapid organizational decentralization. The effort grew out of a federal housing program which ostensibly was to develop a management information system, improve and beautify the physical plant, increase project security, and improve first line management processes through training. These activities were to occur in the local agency for Housing and Urban Development with one local housing project staff as a pilot project.

Statement of the Problem

The team-building effort began in Scott-Carver, a large and typical public housing project. The client was the Management and Maintenance staff collective, hereafter referred to as the project staff. The consultants found the project staff

*Reprinted with permission from the authors.

to be lacking in a project-wide or team perspective, which caused friction between the management and maintenance personnel. The friction became increasingly significant, given a new thrust toward decentralization in the agency.
Moreover, need for a team perspective was heightened by the intricate social
networks among the residents of the housing project who daily faced a wide
range of issues in their marginal struggle for survival. These residential issues
were widely diverse often from unit to unit.

Finally, there existed specific managerial skill-deficits among members of
the project staff. These deficits were in budget preparation, housing unit preparation and maintenance response time, rent delinquency and evictions, and managerial reporting.

The need for a team perspective and managerial skill development in technical as well as interpersonal areas combined to shape the development activity
with the project staff. Specific areas for work became staff to staff relationships
(i.e., project manager to housing aids, assistant manager to maintenance foreman,
painter to manager, ets.). Other areas included tenant-staff and police-tenant-
staff relationships. Such complex relationships demanded that the project staff
become skillful in problem-solving, decision-making, and conflict resolution.

The potential benefits were far-reaching. The development of the project
staff could bring them into a stronger, more productive relationship with residents. This development also might influence various peripheral staff and be particularly threatening to higher level administrators. In the face of a successful
renewal effort with the project staff, Central Office administrators might have
to relate to the emerging, and potentially more powerful, lower level leadership
not previously demonstrated in the project management staff.

Training and Team-Building Theory

This section provides some background on training and team-building and reveals
the thinking which partly motivated the method of the consultation effort. The
method grew out of what the consultants found valuable in existing research and
what the consultants were forced to find in themselves. That is, this research
and consultation brought into focus the abstract quality of much organization
development research. In this organization, the client system was composed of
a large, economically marginal-nonviable, population. This demanded of the
consultants, theoretically and actually, new personal and professional development. Just as an economic analysis of capital equipment makes apparent the
need for ongoing maintenance, analysis of the use of manpower and basic human
energy in social bureaucracies shows that such organizational structures must
also conduct ongoing maintenance programs consciously focused on the development and maintenance of human capital. Such human maintenance is a major

part of improved organizational functioning and movement toward the accomplishment of organizational tasks and objectives.

Traditionally, training interventions have grown out of the assumption that organizations are improved when there members are trained to perform their work proficiently. However, research evidence suggests that the degree of success depends on the *type* of training. Training programs designed to improve skills and motor activity frequently demonstrate positive effects (Crawford, 1962; Wolfe, 1951). There is also evidence that leadership training (Shartle, 1956) and laboratory education (Bunder and Knowles, 1967; Dunnetee, 1969; Hall and Williams, 1966; Rubin, 1967; Schein and Bennis, 1965) result in some behavioral and attitudinal change. Most additional studies (Campbell and Dunnette, 1968; Fleishman, Harris, and Burtt, 1955; and House, 1967) suggest that training may lead to individual change but still have little impact on the organization (Fleishman, 1955; Sykes, 1962).

These studies suggest that if training is to be an effective intervention, it *must* be coupled with a change in the organization's culture which will support and facilitate the objectives of the training effort. This notion is fundamental in organization development consultation and team-building theory as an integral part of such development models.

Although the group or department is the basic working unit of an organization, many organization members, particularly at administrative levels, consider work in groups to be a waste of time. The processes of problem-solving, decision-making, conflict resolution, and communication demand skills by members of work groups. Work groups with deficiencies in these areas may often be ineffective and pay high costs in terms of energy loss and anxiety. Even if the group is successful in achieving some goal, successful reaching of the goal does not justify an inefficient means. Unilateral decision making processes, for example, may sometimes result in resistance by employees, leading in turn to inefficiency and high costs.

Team-building is an ongoing process, directed toward the continual diagnosis of a group's work procedures and interpersonal relationships. The work group in this case being the local housing project management staff serving residents at Scott-Carver. Work procedures included such things, therefore, as follows:

1. *Team organization for task accomplishment.* Did the project staff remain together throughout the task or did it subdivide for certain segments of the work? Did the project manager function as an active member role or was he aloof?

2. *Team decision-making procedures.* Did the members vote or was consensual decision-making practiced? Did the project manager reserve the right to make the final decision, or did he "live" with staff decisions?

3. Were staff meetings designed for making a decision? If so were the
provisions made to identify which members would assume responsibility for various steps? How long did it take the team to accomplish
its purpose for a particular meeting, and was enough time allotted?
Did the staff waste time on discussion of irrelevant matters?

Team building is *not* sensitivity grouping for the sake of accomplishing personal growth or "group spirit," although these are desirable products. The real
aim of team-building was to build a staff group norm that encouraged examination and open discussion of the effects of staff members' relationships as related
to project effectiveness. For example if two team members' continual bickering
was adversely affecting the team's work, this matter should have been legitimate
team business. Members should have felt free to explore the reasons for the bickering and to take steps for resolving the problem. Feelings and attitudes would
be legitimate data.

One of the most important facets of team building was discerning how the
project team handles internal conflicts. The notion that an effective team is one
which "runs smoothly," with no conflict is a mistaken one. High quality decisions depend on the extent to which teams *surface* staff member conflicts and
attempt to resolve them. Hall and Watson (1970) have demonstrated that groups
that treat differences of opinion as a help rather than a hindrance while working
toward consensus on decisions tend to make higher quality decisions than groups
that ignore disagreements or decide by the traditional majority rule.

Team management, particularly in urban housing at the residential level, requires different skills from those needed in more commonplace patterns of management, such as one-to-one employer-employee relationships, or situations in
which all authority is vested in a leader. Blake and Mouton (1964) and McGregor
(1967) stress that skills of team management have to be learned. Therefore, effective team management, especially in housing projects having staff members
who relate directly to residents, requires a team leader or project manager to
delegate more expeditiously and trustingly. He/she must share power and learn
to manage shared power by becoming less of a director and more of a consultative manager, coordinator, and resource person.

During team meetings the distribution of authority and responsibility
was continually clarified. The project manager was encouraged to take a leading role in this clarification. He explored learning to deal with subordinates'
feelings about him as a superior and as a person. This same issue was also to
be explored later between project level management and Central Office management.

Training in team management skills constituted a major part of the consultation philosophy and effort.

Inter-Team Building and Conflict Management:
The Management, Maintenance, Resident Interface

Individuals who work together interdependently over a period of time inevitably experience conflict. So do work groups in an organization. Intergroup conflicts at interfaces such as management-maintenance, management-resident, maintenance-resident, or resident-central office were often destructive rather than constructive. They often have been a central factor in the blocking of progress of the local housing authority in its accomplishment of organizational objectives. Sherif (1951); Sherif and Sherif (1956) found that once initiated, competition between groups tends toward stability, but collaborative behavior often remains unstable. Collaborative relationships between groups, especially when there has been previous conflict, require considerable intergroup trust. The slightest sign that this trust is being violated is likely to lead to a rearousal of conflict. For two groups to work collaboratively, they must have a superordinate goal, i.e., a goal which one group alone cannot reach. Indeed, this was the case with most housing project staffs dealing with management, maintenance, and central office all delivering service to residents.

Most organizational units characteristically have interface with more than one other unit. Intergroup problems may therefore involve three or more groups as was the case in this consultation effort. Organization development specialists at TRW systems, for example, have extended the usual intergroup session to involve three or more units. In an organizational "mirroring" exercise, as they call it, one group receives feedback from two or more other groups concerning interface problems they have with the "central" group. If most of the problem areas exist between two of the groups, the third group may serve as a consultant or mediator—an objective third party which "mirrors" the conflicts between the other two groups.

In order to function, an organization must have groups which work together interdependently. Housing projects like other organizations must continually examine the effectiveness of relationships between its work groups, surface unproductive conflict, and search for ways to maintain collaboration.

Consultation Design

The design in this consultation effort had two primary points of focus. The first involved entry into the client system. Specifically, this meant the establishment of a relationship with the project staff. This entry would allow for the diagnosis of the management, supervisory, and related residential problems in the Scott-Carver project.

The second point, to be operationalized after entry, would be the establishment of action-steps and time frames for improvement. Integral to the improvement plan would be the establishment of routes to other opportunities for both the project management and paraprofessional staffs at Scott-Carver. These opportunities would be options for personal as well as professional competence and greater awareness of alternatives.

The consultants found that in the Scott-Carver project, the issues of social and economic survival were primary. The word alternatives is critical here, in the sense that many of the team members were residents who had never experienced ongoing or career employment. The consultants found that the staff would not permit acceptance feelings to surface, or allow psychological entry to *any* consultants, or central office administrators. Unless the alternatives presented by consultants were viable, immediated, and leading to visible improvement of the staff persons' quality of life, entry was in fact a mute question.

In addition to the issues of entry and psychological acceptance of the consultants with the project staff, the consultants also faced the issue of entry with the larger HUD agency. Because the consultants entered the consultation effort as part of a federal grant, special demands were made of them that they frame their effort in writing, in such a manner as to be acceptable by the HUD bureaucracy. Entry at the administrative level was accomplished with the support of a director of training within the HUD agency able to translate the needs of the larger organization to the consultants, and conversely the needs of the consultant to the administrators. This person therefore served as linking-pin and translator-advisor between the consultants and the organizational administrators. The product of this relationship at entry resulted in a series of ongoing planning meetings with the directors of management from the HUD agency central office. These meetings focused on the development of informal support structures by the consultation team, directed toward the project management staff and their relationship to the central administrative office. These planning meetings allowed for the planning of a critical position of future interface between the project staff and the central administrative office.

The proposed learning design focused on a staff-consultant relationship developed through a series of educational work sessions. These sessions focused on building an effective project management team, diagnosing its work procedures and its methods of handling relationships. These might be internal staff interpersonal relationships or relationships between the project staff and other persons external to the staff, but within the housing project. The educational work sessions with the project staff occurred approximately every 18 days over a period of six months. The program design attempted to allow the management staff time to experiment with learnings and make organizational applications within the housing project. Application was directly related to action steps developed by staff members within work sessions. The sessions [roman numerals] were as follows. Asterisks denote sessions which were followed by planning meetings with agency administrators.

I* Organizational entry and diagnosis

II Team Formation and Development

III* Building Team Skills

IV* Building Team Skills/Research Quest ionnaires

V* Management by Objectives and Action Planning

VI Conflict Management and Intergroup Skill building

VII* Communication Skills and Resident—Management Staff Issues

VIII* Collaborative Budget Planning

IX Integration of Team Building Concept and Behavior Change, Research Questionnaire, and Consultant transition out

At the project management staff level the educational work sessions above were presented in a manner almost completely opposite to that required by administrators. The administrators wanted to know what the content would be. The project staff wanted the content translated into process language, in other words, into a language and behavior by the consultants which expressed the benefit to them as a staff content of the educational work sessions. It was out of this expectation that a quality of interaction concept emerged between the project staff and the consultants. This concept was developed and operationalized in the sessions as an explicit effort to effectuate a conceptual and usable understanding of the terms *process* and *product*. Through this exploration throughout the work sessions, the consultants were able to effect within the staff some shifts in the conceptual understanding of the team members. The project staff's involvement as people all trying to survive took on an additional dimension as they saw in their own minds that their success and accomplishment personally and occupationally was directly related to the degree that they as a staff were conscious of the *quality of interactions* they had within the staff and with others. This awareness was further heightened as the project persons realized the relationship between this consciousness of the quality of interaction and the quality of product, namely their managerial effectiveness.

Some Recipes and Prescriptions

The following are brief summaries of the first four education work sessions. They should give the reader an insight into the nature and climate of the sessions as well as the cognitive/didactic content:

Team Development Session I

This session, the first in a proposed series of nine team development sessions, was directed toward the establishment of a psychological climate for work, with emphasis on the initial team building processes. The question of entry was central to this process. As organizational consultants, it was felt that successful entry into an organization for the purpose of organizational change activities does not mean getting into the organization at any cost. Rather it means establishing the ground rules, the expectations, and the kind of relationships that will give the entering team every opportunity necessary to accomplish change objectives and will ultimately permit those coming in to leave an organization that *owns* the changes and methods used for changing.

The following questions are reflective of the types of questions in the minds of the consultant as they engaged in this process. Each of these questions were operationalized into an event in the consultation effort: How do I "connect" with this client? Am I clear about why I was called in? How do I establish a personal and honest relationship with the client? How can I earn the client's trust and confidence? How do I establish a problem solving climate which is nonthreatening for the client? How do I avoid being seen as "the Great Healer"? How do I get the "hidden agendas" out on the table? Who do I tell the people in the organization I am?

Among the questions typically going through the client's head at entry are these: What are the consultant's motives? How much information can I divulge to an outsider? Is the consultant competent? Will the consultant attempt to change the organization in a way that is unfavorable to me? Does the consultant like me? Is the consultant the right person for our problem? Is the consultant interested? Will the consultant try to take over? Is the consultant honest and worth my trust?

The first session therefore focused on the entry stage of team development. The day's session was divided into the following parts:

    I. Introduction by Consultants

        A) Clarification of roles

        B) Clarification of relationships

        C) Agendas: Open and hidden

        D) Establishment of psychological climate through sharing

    II. Reaction by Client System Members

        A) Discussion

        B) Clarification of relationships

        C) Agendas: Open and hidden

III. Perspective Forming

    A) What is consciousness, perceptivity, and an organizational/personal reality?

    B) What are the components of institutional and personal racism relationships to reality, perceptivity?

    C) Film on institutional racism

    D) Process reactions

    E) Future meeting issues

    F) Conclusions

Team Development Session II

This session focused on team formation issues in Team Development. Team formation in the author's view was here concerned with initial events in the building of an effective working team and the gestation period of development generally not considered in work groups. Team-building was considered as a continuing process of diagnosing the effectiveness of a group's work procedures and interpersonal relationships. Integral to this process was the development of interpersonal and managerial skills for improved functioning. Session two was directed toward how these events occur. The session was presented in the following two parts:

Part one which consisted of didactic and experimential components as follows:

    a) Perception, consciousness and their relationship to organizational/managerial impact (a lecturette)

    b) Mini Experiments: How to look at groups and organizations

        Process content

        Cyclical models

        Behavioral descriptions

        Projections

Part one, then, though its didactic and experimental components, formed an informational base for part two, conducted in the afternoon of the meeting day. Part two consisted of the following events.

    A) Personal self inventory

    B) Developing climates for trust and sharing in small groups

    C) Surfacing intragroup issues

    D) Effectively working between groups and developing norms for collaboration

This session began to move away from issues of entry and set the stage for active participation in the growth process. the team could be characterized as highly willing to participate, self-confronting, and committed.

Team Development Session III

This part of the session was built on a major notion in organization theory which states that one of the most important facets of management or worker team building is discerning how the team handles internal conflicts. The old notion that often floats through organizational structures that says that an effective management or work team is one which "runs smoothly" with *no conflict* is a mistaken one. Our position, further elaborated, is that high quality decisions depend on the extent to which teams surface and attempt to resolve member conflicts. Hall and Watson (1970) substantiate this in their research showing how the idea of learning about self and organizational effectiveness fit together.

To build on these ideas the session then focused on helping the team members to explore their own skills through role plays. The role plays related to real life situation on the job. Some of these might be job conditions such as anger by a client. Superior/subordinate agreement i.e. the role of a painter and an angry resident concerning the painting of other apartments and not hers.

Experiential exercises were processed and constructive praise and criticism were given to each team member. This type of process worked on developing intergroup sommunication and identifying in individuals both the lack of skill and previously unknown skills. As a result, group resources were identified and examined.

The concept of management as a team was then developed further in the latter part of this session. A film, which explored the history of the research in this area and the present methods being used, demonstrated that groups which *treat differences of opinion as a help* rather than a hindrance and work toward consensus on decisions, tend to make higher quality decisions than groups which ignore disagreements or debate by the traditional majority rule. Team-building and team-management require that a new set of skills are needed from those used in the more commonplace patterns of management such as one-to-one boss/subordinate relationships, or in situations where all authority is invested in a leader.

Blacke and Mouton (1964) and McGregor (1967) have aptly stressed the point: *Skills of team management have to be learned!* Administrators in the future will need to give the same lead time for these types of learning activities since they now regularly grant 1-5 years lead time for planning and construction of facilities.

This session was particularly important for many members of the team because they were able to experiment with new parts of their own skill package. Insights were gained by both the person in the role play as well as the observer. It was the observer who was able to project himself into the situation and observe the talent or lack of talent of the persons in the role play situation. It was emphasized by the consultants to all group members that where people needed to work on their skills, *no negative evaluation would be made.* In this type of situation it was essential to maintain a supportive and constructive climate.

At the end of the session specific homework was assigned. The homework took the form of having the group/team design new patterns of behavior for themselves that would improve their own work effectiveness and enhance their work environment. A series of team meetings were scheduled to be held on the project site without the consultants, before the next formal team building session. It may be summarized that the following concerns for team development were explored during the session: organizational conditions of morale, motivation, conflict, and functional job assignments. Self-responsibility, responsibility to the team, and the relationship of these to team productivity was explored. Finally, the consultants investigated issues of organizational climate, and how positive climate can be maintained while simultaneously keeping basic honestly with colleagues and meeting organizational and personal goals in the work setting.

Team Development Session IV

The morning session got off to a very enthusiastic start with many team members speaking with considerable pride in themselves about work they had accomplished between Sessions III and IV.

The team-building process had developed faster than the consultants or the members of the team had anticipated. The theory being followed in this session centered around the idea that team maintenance and development is focused on the promissory aim of building a group norm which encourages examination and open discussion of the *effects* of team member's relationships and task accomplishments.

The first part of the morning was filled with some important discussion and descriptions of the team's activities, accomplishments and problems. They were centered on attendant parts of the general concept of organizational climate and its influence on individual motivation and team task effectiveness.

The afternoon session utilized a simulation exercise which required each team member to complete a specific outlined task within a specific time period. Secondly, the team was divided into two groups. Each group was given a task that had to be worked within a specific time frame. A group consenual decision was to be arrived at without a vote of majority rule. A process for tallying individual scores and group scores was devised. This enabled each person to compare their score against the group's score and pointed out the superior scores obtained through a collaborative effort as opposed to individual isolated efforts.

A very productive session followed this simulation. The primary content of the discussion involved the following varied and sundry (but significant nonetheless) organizational issues: communication skills, listening skills, compromise, how to identify people's unused resources in an organization, the dynamics of building a team, and how to fully use team talents in effectively doing work. Problems with hierarchy, delegation of power, competition, ego, and organization product were also deliberated during this session.

In summary, this session provided for the team the opportunity to see and work on the concept of organizational and team maintenance. It was re-emphasized that effective management and decision making processes are not had without conscious and regular organizational team maintenance.

The project staffs left with new energy and more homework for the next session.

The reader may note that later work sessions, listed but not described, focused on the integration and synthesis of personal and organizational competence with managerial skills and interpersonal process. The synthesis of the personal-interpersonal and managerial skill building were in fact common threads throughout the sessions and the consultation effort.

This article has not focused on the central office staff, the impact of the project staff on central office not the data collected through research instrumentation. The authors see this chapter focusing primarily on the integration of theory and practice in organization development as applied by practitioner-consultants.

In the early stages of the change effort the administrative staff worked to understand the need for strengthening the human management resources in the project staff. Crises more than any other factor shifted the heads of central office administrators. The authors assert, at this point, the necessity for more well trained first line management.

Without well trained and motivated project management teams the concepts of follow-through and change maintenance become empty bureaucratic rhetoric. The sad collapse of many change efforts an both national and local HUD can be traced to ineffective management and despair in Public Housing Projects.

This consultation effort seems to indicate that it is important for national level administrators to consider an alternative research emphasis. The shift in orientation might be to support the type of research that will build and expand first line management talent. The past emphasis on bricks, hardware and computors all seem rather mythological when time is spent in the projects. Without the training of first and second level management and their staffs, how can one realistically expect implementation of policy.

Summary and Conclusions

This organization development effort, from its inception to conclusion was seen in holistic terms as giving strong emphasis to the natural formation of both structure and process. It was assumed by the consultants that this organization would continue to need the macro aspects of organizational form. It would continue to need the rational, intentional, comprehensive layout which characterizes traditional "effectively" structured organizations. This would include classification, authority controls, job descriptions, and explicit power layouts for "effective" organizational operations.

These macro aspects of the organization provide the formal framework which allowed the sociopsychological dimensions of the client group to be specifically acknowledged and included in our consulting efforts. Areas of primary concern were informal patterns of authority communication, and decision-making phenomena, leadership, inter-personal relationships, group dynamics, personality theory, role concepts, authority and power notions, and environmental conditions.

The consultant efforts to develop an integration between the macro and micro aspects of this organization at the grass roots brought out strongly the contextual and situational dimensions faced by the Scott-Carver Staff. *The intracultural and nonverbal dynamics were of critical importance in this regard.* Effective change agents understand that organizational systems create informal and formal boundaries. Entry into any formalized work system and the credentials necessary for acceptance by the members of the system. This understanding was particularly crucial in this effort.

Entry by an outside consulting team into an all black public housing management group has its own unique entry criteria. The Social, economic, political and intra-cultural dynamics are framed by verbal and nonverbal boundary mechanisms. Organizational or group penetration by the consultant is seldom accomplished in minority settings in our society. Some important questions to be considered in relation to this entry process are as follows:

1. Has the consultant developed the nonverbal skills which allow cross cultural transfer in communication to take place?

2. Does the expectation exist that the client system must move to meet the outsiders (consultant's or higher management's) frameworks for meaning? Is there an expressed intention to understand the culture of the organizational milieu?

3. What outside interventions are presently taking place with the client community housing project?

4. What interventions have happened in the past? Were they accepted? Rejected? Is there a residue of negative or positive feelings in the client community related to past interventions?

5. What projects have creditability with the client community?

6. What individuals in the population have particular influence? Who is trusted? Individually or agency?

7. Demographic and statistical data check through census S.M.S.A.'s and M.R.C.'s.

8. Can the consultants relate emotionally to the client milieu with minimal evaluation and personal projection?

9. Do the consultants have an awareness of the behavioral check out they will experience throughout the consultation process?

10. Is the consultant clear that to be an advocate of change, implicitly assumes real change in him or herself?

These ten considerations represent significant areas for inquiry.

Further, management team-building is also linked with community development and social organization. Organizational change theory combined with out own consultation experience indicates that the whole question of entry and diagnosis in most ongoing, complex social organizations is not carefully and consciously approached. In short, social environmental realities must be an integral part of the planning for what is to be done in the client and cultural groups. Things such as fears, anxieties, histories of personal and organizational power, economic and political realities, etc., create the dynamics of the daily urban environment. This means that any change intervention will necessarily have to cope with such dynamics in order to ameliorate the conditions and environment of the target client group and cultural system.

The anomie and isolation that characterize the personal lives of little hope and despair in ghetto public housing is rooted in the absence of any real alternatives. Therefore, a principal component of project management team-building is to infuse into the community both management skill and social consciousness. The work sessions employed the use of community action designs to develop consciousness and raise awareness of alternatives. This might have taken the form of identifying existing social services: education and job, rehabilitation, or taken the form of human interaction laboratories focusing on the development of trust and pride in one's self and in one's fellow community members and community. A central premise for action in any management team and community development effort is to develop consciousness in the individuals of both the team and community . . . that one count and has real viable life affirming alternatives. This consciousness has been called in the past PAN-AFRICANISM, BLACK IS BEAUTIFUL, VIVA LA RAZA, MANHOOD, PRIDE, DIGNITY, AND BASIC HUMAN WORTH.

In closing, the authors think that it is important to discuss the impact of this training on them as consultants. The human drama and the complex interpersonal dynamics witnessed by living out the drama itself baffle description.

The fact of the consultant team's multiethnicity (Black/White) was a key factor not only in organizational entry but in their continued ongoing relationship with the project management staff. It was out of this relationship that the consultants were able to model and investigate issues of identity, stereotype, authority and power issues so much a part of the myriad of relationships existing within and between groups in urban public housing projects at all levels.

Not only did the consultants experience the pain of confronting with sometimes painful messages, but the joy of seeing efforts succeed as the project staff accepted them. The consultants also saw the subsequent emergence of the project staff as a team impacting positively on residents, as well as on higher level central office administrators. At the same time the staff was seen doing the job with effectiveness clearly shifting toward an improved state. The consultants are grateful to the Scott-Carver staff and hope that this effort does not fall on deaf ears. This consultation effort has created some feelings of pride, knowing it has some substance. The authors would like to believe that any reader of this report would turn the last page knowing that same thing.

References

Argyris, C. Interpersonal Competence and Organizational Effectiveness. Homewood, Illinois: Dorsey Press, 1962.

Beckhard, R. Organization Development Strategies and Models. Cambridge, Massachusetts: Addison-Wesley, 1969.

Blake, R. R. and Mouton, J. S. and Blansfield, M. G. The Logic of Team Training. In. I. R. Weschler and E. H. Schein (Eds.), Issues in Training. Washington, D.C.: NTL Institute for Applied Behavioral Science, 1962, pp. 77-85.

Blake, R. R., Shepard, H. A. and Mouton, J. S. Managing Intergroup Conflict in Industry. Houston: Gulf Publishing Co., 1964.

Bunker, D. R., and Knowles, E. S. Comparison of Behavioral Changes Resulting From Human Relations Training Laboratories of Different Lengths. Journal of Applied Behavioral Science, 1965, i, pp. 25-27.

Campbell, J. P., and Dunnette, M. D. Effectiveness of T-Group Experience in Managerial Training and Development. Psychological Bulletin, 1968, 70, pp. 73-104.

Chapple, E. D., and Sayles, L. R. The Measure of Management. New York: Crowell-Collier and Macmillan, Inc., 1961.

Crawford, M. P. Concepts of Training. In Gagne, R. M. (Ed.). Psychological Principles in System Development. New York: Holt, Rinehart and Winston, 162, Ch. 9.

Fleishman, E. A. Leadership Climate, Human Relations Training, and Supervisory Behavior. Personnel Psychology, 1953, 6, pp. 205-222.

Fleishman, E. A., Harris, E. H., and Brutt, H. H. Leadership and Supervision in Industry. Ohio State Business Educational Research Monograph, 1955, No. 33.

Hall, J., and Watson, W. H. The Effects of a Normative Intervention on Group Decision Making Performance. Human Relations, 1970, 23, pp. 199-317.

Hall, J., and Williams, M. S. A. A Comparison of Decision-Making Performances in Established and Ad Hoc Groups. Journal of Personality and Social Psychology, 1966, 3, pp. 214-222.

House, R. J. Group Education and Leadership Effectiveness: A Review of the Empirical Literature and a Critical Evaluation. Personnel Psychology, 1967, 20, pp. 1-32.

Katz, P., and Kahn, R. L. The Social Psychology of Organizations. New York: Wiley, 1966.

McGregor, D. The Professional Manager. New York: McGraw-Hill, 1967.

Mann, F. C. Studying and Creating Change: A Means to Understanding Social Organization. In C. M. Arensburg et. al. (Eds.) Research in Industrial Human Relations, New York: Harper, 1967.

Rubin, I. Increasing Self-Acceptance: A Means of Reducing Prejudice. Journal of Personality and Social Psychology, 1967, 5, pp. 233-238.

Schein, E., and Bennis, W. G. Personal and Organizational Change Through Group Methods: The Laboratory Approach. New York: Wiley, 1965.

Shartle, C. Executive Performance and Leadership. Englewood Cliffs, N.J.: Prentice Hall, 1956.

Shepard, H. A. Changing Interpersonal and Intergroup Relationships in Organizations. In J. G. March (Ed.) Handbook of Organizations. Chicago: Rand McNally, 1965.

Sherif, M. and Sherif, C. W. An Outline of Social Psychology. (Rev. Ed.). New York: Harper, 1956.

Sykes, S. J. M. The Effect of a Supervisory Training Course in Changing Supervisors' Perceptions and Expectations of the Role of Management. Human Relations, 1962, 15, pp. 227-243.

Wolfe, D. Training. In S. S. Stevens (Ed.) Handbook of Experimental Psychology. New York: Wiley, 1951. pp. 1267-1286.

AN OD INTERVENTION TO INSTALL
PARTICIPATIVE MANAGEMENT IN A BUREAUCRATIC ORGANIZATION*

Jack E. Taylor and Elizabeth Bertinot

Bureaucratic organizations are the backbone of most local governments. Bureaucracy and participative management have been considered antithetic terms. While an effective intervention to bring about more employee participation and commitment is difficult in most organizations, in a bureaucracy it comes close to being treasonous.

Management by Objectives is one way to provide employees an opportunity to participate in the decision making processes of their organization. Simply stated, it is a managerial method whereby superiors and subordinates identify major areas of responsibility in their work, set some standards for performance and measure results against those standards.[1]

Change Attempts Made

Few local government agencies have attempted to use the newest management methods for organizing and fulfilling their responsibility of service. Most seem to feel that bureaucracy will not yield to modern participation management practice. However, with the public's growing demands for efficiency and measurable results, combined with the increased application of the behavioral sciences, some changes are being attempted.[2]

Harris County, Texas has one of the largest county governments in the Southwest. Its criminal justice system includes district courts for felony cases and four county courts for misdemeanor offenses. The Harris County Adult Probation Department was established in 1958 to provide these courts with probation services. The adult probation department was one of the first departments of county government to institute new management methods in its work.

The change came in March, 1970 when a Criminal Justice grant went into effect setting up the Harris County Model Probation Project. Within four months a department of about 13 employees had grown to more than 60. It was at this time that the project director, Charles Shandera, decided to install a Management by Objectives system throughout the department.

No Models Available

As internal consultants and trainers it was the responsibility of the authors to design an MBO program that would fit the needs of the adult probation department. There were no existing MBO programs in use among the rehabilitation agencies that could be used as a model. Therefore the business model that was familiar to the authors was retooled to meet the needs of the probation department.

The program was installed in three stages:

Stage One: a series of meetings to teach the MBO method of goal setting and objective writing to the top administration and throughout each level of the organization.

Stage Two: a total department workshop for team building and objective writing.

Stage Three: the installation of an evaluation and reporting system, and an on-going program of updating the objectives through sessions with individual divisions and work units to revise their objectives or to write new ones. These on-going meetings would then become a feedback mechanism to the top administration indicating the concerns and motivation of the working units within the department.

Support from the Top

The effectiveness of any management program is no greater than the participation of the top administrators. The administrators in this case were open to a new management program and agreed to install MBO. Therefore, it was possible to begin the program at the top of the organization.

Only later in the program was it learned how absolutely necessary it is for the top administration to take an active role in both implementing and following through on the program. MBO, it was discovered, is not a training function. It is an administrative responsibility that must be begun and sustained through administrative direction.

The concept of MBO was introduced to the administrators through a series of training sessions. Meetings were held with the director and his assistant. In the first session, as in all the following sessions, a formal training "package" including both theory and practice was designed. The session lasted two hours. The objective of the first hour was to teach the theory of goals and objectives and provide opportunity to practice writing tentative goals and objectives. A goal was defined as an overall guiding purpose, while an objective was defined as a specific, attainable, measurable achievement which should be consistent with the overall goals. During the second hour the participants filled out a Management Responsibility Chart to help them define and negotiate their differing and overlapping responsibilities.

Three Goals Agreed Upon

The administration moved rapidly into goal and objective writing. They agreed on the following three overall goals for the department:

"(1) To reorganize the Harris County Adult Probation Department so that it can serve the court, public, and defendant more constructively (2) to strive for the upgrading of the present personnel in standards of probation work in this department and throughout the state (3) to set a model for other counties and/or judicial districts to pattern themselves after."

Under these goals they developed 24 objectives. They agreed on which of them would take primary and secondary responsibility for each of the objectives. Each took primary responsibility for about the same number of objectives.

Objectives Ranked

At the second training session the administrators met for one and one half hours and went back over the list of objectives. The objectives were rank ordered. This, in turn, led to the combining and clarifying the objectives. It was agreed that this revised list would be posted in the offices of both men.

The next part of the training session was used to assist the administrators to write their job descriptions. A special form was developed for this. The work functions were divided into routine daily work, periodic work, and work on objectives. This provided another check on crossover responsibilities.

This approach of focusing attention on both objectives and routine job functions presented a problem. It became apparent that the concept of objectives as tasks that are beyond the regular duties of the job would have to be more clearly distinguished. It was seen that these two areas of time commitment by an employee needed to be seen as distinct and yet integrated.

No Previous Definitions

Until the time of this MBO program there had been no clear definition of the department's goals and objectives. There also had been no clear and mutually agreed upon definition and division of management responsibilities between the director and assistant director.

The MBO program resulted in disciplined thinking about where the organization was going and the development of a new commitment to those goals. Further, it set the standards of teamwork, negotiated responsibilities and the use of training sessions as a way of planning and decision-making. This alone proved to be well worth the effort involved in installing an MBO program.

The next level of management in the department is the Unit Supervisor who manages a team of two or three caseworkers. These middle managers were resistant to the idea of management development training. With this in mind the sessions were shortened to one hour and began with the theory of MBO. Printed materials explaining goals and objectives was discussed. The design of the training session itself was used to illustrate objective writing. It was placed on newsprint in the form of an overall goal and specific objectives.

The Unit Supervisors were not asked to practice writing goals and objectives at this time, but merely to become familiar with the concept. This seemed to de-fuse many of their fears and hostilities. It also gave them a low-keyed introduction to what a training session was like.

Change Theory Introduced

This same approach was taken at the next level of the organization, the caseworkers and the stenos. The only difference was the introduction of change theory and how people can respond to it. It was hoped that this would give them an opportunity to look at some alternative attitudes to the approaching changes that would occur in the department as a result of the MBO program.

When every member of the organization had been trained in the theory of MBO, and after the administrators had actually written goals and objectives, the program was ready to go a step further. An overnight workshop was decided on as the most effective and efficient way to move the total department into a serious implementation of MBO. The workshop was attended by the total

63-member staff. This included the administrators, unit supervisors, caseworkers, staff personnel, and stenos.

Workshop Objectives Posted

The objectives of the workshop were clearly spelled out so that each participant would know the purpose of the day and one-half meeting. Here again the presentation of the goals and objectives of the workshop served to illustrate the format to be used in writing any goals and objectives. Part of our learning theory assumption as trainers is that the medium is the message. Therefore what we want to communicate (purpose of the workshop) takes the form of what we want them to learn (goal and objective writing). The message informing them about the purpose of the workshop looked like this:

"Goal of the MBO workshop: To teach the members of the cepartment the overall goals of the Harris County Model Probation Project, and to enlist their contributions on the accomplishment of these goals.

"Objectives of the MBO Workshop:

1. To instruct the organization's memebers in the content of the grant funding our department.
2. To set goals and objectives for each division in accordance with the overall project goals.
3. To determine responsibility for these objectives.
4. To define job descriptions in terms of routine duties, unit objectives, lines of authority, work flow, etc.
5. To institute a procedure that will aid each person to schedule his work-day, working on both duties and objectives."

The participants were also told that some of the following questions were to be discussed at the workshop:

"How did the Harris County Model Probation Project come about?"

"What are the requirements of the Criminal Justice Grant that helps fund this project?"

"What are the long range goals and objectives of the Harris County Model Probation Project?"

"How do I fit in with these?"

"What are the objectives of my Court Service Unit?"

"What are my objectives in my job?"

"How can my skills and potential be more fully used in this project?"

"What are the lines of authority in this organization?"

"What is expected of me in my job?"

Objective Writing Learned

The major result of the workshop was that the participants had learned to write objectives. This indicated that the participants could learn to plan their work around result-oriented objectives. Another equally important accomplishment was the spirit of teamwork that developed.

Ninety-two objectives were written by 11 court units with an average of about eight objectives per court unit. This indicated that much of the original dissension and resistance gave way to a task-oriented involvement. The high quality of work indicated that the participants identified with the purpose of the workshop.

An evaluation of the objectives indicated that 46 per cent of the objectives originated from the 11 unit supervisors even though they made up only 25 per cent of the total group. This, of course, means a number of things. But for the purpose of this article it seems to indicate that some measures should have been taken to ensure more participation by all members of the work units. This might have been done by structuring the exercise so that each participant would have been requested to present his objectives individually.

Another possibility is that the trainers could have intervened more often while the objectives were being written to check for full participation. Another possibility would have been to stop the exercise after a few objectives had been written and have a theory presentation on participative management.

More Involvement Needed

The data from the objectives also indicated that most of the employees' attention was focused on their own units. The evaluation indicated that 80 per cent of the objectives dealt with matters within the work unit, while only 20 per cent focused on issues outside of the units. This would indicate a need on the part of the unit supervisors to get more involvement in the total organization and its problems. It pointed up the lack of organizational loyalty and commitment within the department. It also seemed to indicate a need to make the probation court service units a more integral part of the work of the courts. The probation workers wrote few objectives which indicated any attempt to make their work a more integrated part of the court system.

The objectives written at the workshop can be classified under one of the following general headings: managing court unit personnel; improving work-flow procedures of the unit; improving the unit's relationship with the court; and supervision of the probationer. The latter area accounts for 43 per cent of the objectives. Qualitatively, it also contained the most innovative suggestions. The other categories were almost equal, with the need for improved work-flow procedures somewhat more prominent.

Enthusiasm Built

The workshop built up a great deal of enthusiasm. It was hoped that the enthusiasm could be sustained through some on-going procedure within the regular operation of the department. Therefore, following the workshop a system of reporting on objectives was installed. Each work unit was required to make a monthly report on the work accomplished on its objectives. This information was then put into a monthly department newsletter and fed back to all employees. This gave fuller visibility to what was being accomplished. It also provided a stimulus for performance because it was also distributed to the district judges who were served by these probation work units.

The department is now beginning the fourth quarter of its Management By Objectives program which was installed at the workshop. Every work unit in the project wrote objectives. Some units have accomplished almost all of the objectives that they set and are beginning to write new ones. The Misdemeanor and Personnel divisions have just completed writing new objectives.

Realistic Evaluations

The new reporting system anticipates continuing work on objectives. The report form has been altered several times to make reporting on objectives more accurate. Because of the MBO program it is now possible to evaluate work performance more realistically by measuring performance against accepted objectives.

Management By Objectives can work in a probation department just as it can work in any other organization that will install it as a total system from the top down. Where MBO is running into difficulties in this department it is generally because some aspects of the program were either not fully supported by the administration, or they were not adequately installed.

Leaders' Example Imperative

For example, the installation of a reporting system needed to be done more thoroughly through regular training sessions. It was also learned that the administrators must lead by example. They must demonstrate the usefulness of MBO by consistently using the method in their own work.

The trend in our department as in many other criminal justice agencies is now definitely toward the probation officer as a manager rather than a counselor. Management skills are more and more becoming central to his effectiveness. Therefore, it is foreseen that the MBO program is just the beginning of a much needed management development program for probation departments as well as the total criminal justice system.

References

1. Drucker, Peter F., *The Practice of Management,* New York: Harper and Brothers, 1954.

2. Terwilliger, Carl, and Stuart Adam, "Probation Department Management by Objectives," *Crime and Delinquency,* Vol. 15, Apr. 1969, No. 2.

INDEX

Academy of Management, OD
    Division, 6
Action research:
    in demotion design, 106-117
    examples of, 76-78
    one schema for, 65-76
    theoretical framework of, 63-65
Affirmative Action Act of 1972,
    200
Applications, OD:
    career development for women,
      202-204
    central role of feedback in, 42-44,
      87-102, 110-113
    confrontation design, 89-102
    crisis intervention in municipal
      agency, 161-175
    demotion design, 106-113
    and evaluation, 6, 205-218
    Flexi-Time, 130-156
    impact of "politics" on, 28
    institution building, 82-102
    interactional approach to, 19-35,
      106-129, 161-199, 235-253,
      297-312
    in job redesign, 287-296
    in local elected boards and coun-
      cils, 235-253
    and MBO, 313-320
    in military, 227-234
    multi-team building, 191-199

[Applications, OD]
    policy approach to, 130-156, 313-
      320
    precipitating incidents in, 12-14
    in public housing project, 297-312
    questions about, 15-16
    role negotiation, 78-90
    stereotypes of in industrial situa-
      tions, 12
    structural approach to, 254-276,
      282-283, 287-296
    in suburban governments, 19-35
    survey feedback design, 227-234
    task force management, 220-226
    team building, 37-46, 88-97, 297-
      312
    third-party consultation, 118-129
    underlying values of, 85-87
    variations in, 15
Authenticity as central in OD values,
    87

BART (Bay Area Rapid Transit), 82

California State Compensation Insur-
    ance Fund, 77-78
Career development for women:
    design for, 202-203
    objectives of, 202
    trainer's role in, 203-204